Fruits of Contemplation

Cross and Crown Series of Spirituality

GENERAL EDITOR

Very Reverend John L. Callahan, O.P., S.T.M.

LITERARY EDITOR

Reverend Jordan Aumann, O.P., S.T.D.

NUMBER 1

Fruits of Contemplation

BY VICTORINO OSENDE, O.P.

Translated by A Dominican Sister of the Perpetual Rosary
Milwaukee, Wisconsin

B. HERDER BOOK CO.

15 & 17 South Broadway, St. Louis 2, Mo.
AND *2/3 Doughty Mews, London, W. C. 1*

This translation was made from the second Spanish edition of
Contemplata: Momentos Místicos, published by Imprenta
Diocesana, Pamplona, Spain, 1947.

IMPRIMI POTEST

>Edward L. Hughes, O.P., S.T.Lr.
>*Provincial*

NIHIL OBSTAT

>John A. Driscoll, O.P., S.T.M.
>*Censor Librorum*

IMPRIMATUR

>✠ Henry P. Rohlman, D.D.
>*Archbishop of Dubuque*

>August 5, 1953

Library of Congress Catalog Card Number: 53-10673

COPYRIGHT 1953 BY B. HERDER BOOK CO.

Fourth Printing, 1963

*Printed in the United States of America
by Vail-Ballou Press, Inc., Binghamton, New York*

Translator's Preface &

THE present volume is a translation of the Spanish book *Contemplata* by the Reverend Victorino Osende, O.P. The word *Contemplata* is taken from the Dominican motto, *Contemplata aliis tradere* (To give to others the fruits of contemplation).

As will be apparent from the most cursory perusal of *Contemplata,* the fruits of Father Osende's contemplation, or rather, the fruits of the Holy Ghost in the author's docile and ardent spirit, are indeed worthy of rendition into every language. The fundamental message that resounds throughout the book is that souls should not be led astray by nonessentials and misapprehensions in the way of perfection and that they should focus their attention and efforts not so much on the means as on the goal of the spiritual life. It is a message that not only deserves but demands the widest possible publication. Moreover, the sublimity of the spiritual doctrine underlying this important message, the new spiritual horizons it discloses, together with the simplicity, clarity, and vigor of the language with which the author presents it, are calculated to give a new impetus to the spiritual life of souls.

It is, therefore, with the greatest pleasure that we present *Fruits of Contemplation* to the English-reading public, in the firm hope that through it the Holy Ghost will effect much good in souls.

The translator is deeply grateful to the Very Reverend Father Provincial of the Province of Spain and to the au-

thor, Reverend Victorino Osende, O.P., for the permission
and privilege of making this translation. She is also deeply
indebted to Reverend Jordan Aumann, O.P., who very
kindly read and corrected the entire manuscript and in
every way gave invaluable assistance. She extends her sincere thanks to Reverend Salvador Luís, O.P., and Reverend
Emmanuel Ubeda, O.P., for their assistance and encouragement. Finally, she expresses her gratitude to the following publishers and individuals for the courtesy of permission to use quotations from their publications: Mr. Allison
Peers, London, and The Newman Bookshop, Westminster,
Maryland, for quotations from *The Complete Works of
Saint John of the Cross;* Mr. Allison Peers and Sheed and
Ward, New York and London, for quotations from *The
Complete Works of Saint Teresa.*

May this book be a source of inspiration and encouragement to souls eager for sound, practical counsel and true
progress in the sublime science of union with God.

*Dominican Sisters of the Perpetual Rosary
Milwaukee, Wisconsin*

Foreword ✍

IN the beginning of his career, Father Victorino Osende, O.P., was on the verge of becoming a professor, or lector, as we say in the Dominican Order, when he decided that such was not his calling. The poor Indians of the Spanish Dominican missions in South America were calling him, so it seemed, as the Macedonians called St. Paul: *Transiens in Macedoniam adjuva nos.* As a result, Father Osende was sent to work among the Indians of Peru.

A close companion relates that his first care upon arriving was to construct an oratory. There in the immense solitude of a mission post, Father Osende learned to pray. There also he learned the theme so frequently repeated in this book: men complicate the spiritual life; therefore, we must return to the simplicity which is proper to the children of God. It is the echo of the wilderness, where there is no human artifice.

However, it was not in the missionary vanguard that divine Providence wanted him, for God permitted him to become ill, and his superiors had to transfer him to the rear-guard. They took him to Lima, and there Father Osende founded a periodical which he called *The Dominican Missions of Peru,* a most praiseworthy work which he directed for many years.

But the Lord had a still more important work reserved for him in the City of the Kings: the direction of souls. As spiritual director he assisted many persons, especially Dominican missionaries, on the road to sanctity and he himself learned much about the sublime science of the sanctification of souls. His first spiritual writings date from this period. In commenting on Father Osende's *Hidden Treasure,* Father Arintero exclaimed enthusiastically, "Precious pages, golden pages, for those who understand the mystical language of heavenly wisdom."

These two great spiritual writers were associated with each other on two occasions. On the first occasion, Father Arintero was a professor of natural science and Father Osende, a mere youth in the classroom. Of this first association, Father Osende retains the less pleasant memories of Father Arintero as a zealous professor who was somewhat strict with his students. The second occasion came when Father Osende was in the prime and vigor of life and Father Arintero in his deepest mystical fervor. At the beginning, this second association was in no way remarkable, but little by little the seed sown by the incomparable master bore fruits of friendship. Thenceforth master and pupil understood each other remarkably well, despite their great personal differences.

As is evident from the present work, Father Osende has a high regard for the spiritual writings of Father Arintero. But his commendation proceeds from the conviction that such is the reality of the spiritual life and not from a desire to support any particular school of spiritual doctrine. Indeed, it is only with reluctance that Father Osende accepts such limiting terms as "school" or "party." We recall an occasion when Father Arintero used the expression, "Father Osende's school of spiritual doctrine," and he promptly received a letter of reproof from Father Osende.

In writing a book, Father Osende seldom gives quotations from other authors. When a thought occurs to him, he turns it over in his mind and other thoughts are attracted to the main one. Light is given his spirit, and he hastens to put his thoughts in writing. Is it, then, entirely the fruit of contemplation or of his own experience and that of others? Is nothing in it the fruit of reading and study? It is evident from his writings that Father Osende has read much, but his reading is manifested, not as the erudition of one who has read merely to quote, but as the achievement of one who has assimilated what he has read. Experience, either his own or that of others, is also evident, but perhaps without the author even thinking about it as such. Ultimately, however, his writings are the fruit of contemplation.

The arrangement of the articles was left to the discretion of the editors and is purely arbitrary; they do not follow each other in any strict or inviolable order. The reader may open the book wherever he will, and rarely will he not find light that will clarify many problems of the spiritual life and thoughts that will delight him by reason of their substance, their profundity, their truth, and the masterly way in which they are expressed.

VERY REVEREND SABINO LOZANO, O.P., S.T.M.

Convento de San Esteban
Salamanca, Spain

Contents ৶

PART IV

The Life of Prayer

PART V

Devotion

PART VI

The Wisdom of the Tree of Life

PART VII

The Interior Life and the Apostolate

PART I

Speculative Considerations

CHAPTER 1 ✍

Mystical Evolution and Renewal

AS time goes on, the importance and transcendency of the work of Father Arintero in the field of spiritual theology are becoming more and more appreciated.[1] His teachings and writings, especially his famous work entitled *The Mystical Evolution*, have produced a veritable holy revolution, not only in the speculative, but also in the practical order of the spiritual life. Speculatively, they emphasize the importance of mystical studies which were formerly so disdained; practically, they encourage sincerely pious and serious people to accept and embrace mystical doctrine with a holy fervor and enthusiasm.

Before the publication of the books of Father Arintero and his formidable campaign in favor of mysticism, mystical matters were relegated to the remotest corners of the monasteries of contemplative nuns. Perhaps now and then a book of a mystical flavor made its appearance, but, as a general rule, this subject occupied the last place among books of piety and the spiritual life, as also in the hearts of those who professed to practice it. Mysticism was considered as something recondite and abstruse, reserved only

[1] Father John G. Arintero, O.P., a member of the Dominican Province of Spain, died in 1928 after devoting a good part of his life to teaching and writing on spiritual theology and directing souls. He has been hailed as the great champion of spiritual theology in our day and the restorer of the traditional teachings in that field. His masterpiece, *The Mystical Evolution*, has been published by B. Herder Book Co.

3

for a few privileged individuals, or it was emphatically rejected as something proper to visionaries and fools.

At best, it was regarded as something so lofty and sublime that any attempt to attain it was presumptuous. This was due to an error which had imperceptibly crept into people's conception of the interior life: the division and separation of asceticism and mysticism into two totally independent spiritual lives. This division was naturally extended to the paths of perfection, so that the ascetical or "ordinary" path and its corresponding perfection was regarded as a thing apart, having no connection whatever with the mystical or "extraordinary" path and its corresponding perfection.

In short, a dualism was established in the spiritual life and its consequences were bound to be very harmful in practice. Persons imbued with this doctrine reduced the entire spiritual life to its ascetical part. The mystical element they considered wholly extraordinary and beyond reach and, therefore, not to be considered in the direction of souls nor in the ordinary practice of the spiritual life. Consequently, those who aspired to perfection had to content themselves with ordinary or ascetical perfection, that is, the perfection which they could attain by their own efforts with the help of that grace which was also called ordinary.

This doctrine made the field of the spiritual life so narrow and barren that souls were stifled and the most promising flowers and fruits of sanctity perished. It caused many to lead a sad and painful existence because they were forced to wage a violent interior struggle between their concepts of the spiritual life and the impulses of their heart, and even to resist God, who was drawing them to Himself. They yearned and sighed for a different atmosphere, for greater light, for another mode of life in which they would be able to give free expansion to their ardent desires for divine love. Others languished away in tepidity for lack of effective encouragement or altogether abandoned the interior life and their quest after perfection, discouraged by the impossibility of attaining it by their own efforts.

During his long experience as a director of souls, Father Arintero observed and lamented these evil effects more than anyone else. Determined to remedy them, he launched his spiritual campaign, the results of which are now palpable to all, for it has done and is still doing much good for souls. Father Arintero attacked the very root of the evil: the dualism which had been introduced into the spiritual life. In opposition to it, he took as the theme of all his works the unity of the spiritual life with all that it implies: unity of way and unity of perfection; in other words, the unity of the ascetical and mystical life and the necessity of the mystical life for the full and perfect practice of the ascetical life. This has been the soul and substance of all his works and what has won for him the title of the champion of the unity of the spiritual life. From this notion of unity sprang his idea of applying the theory of evolution to all his teachings, for evolution presupposes unity, and where there is separation or discontinuity there can be no evolution.

It must be observed, however, that Father Arintero did not reject the traditional classification of ascetical and mystical life nor its correlatives, ascetical and mystical way, ordinary and extraordinary, active and passive, etc. He merely strove to clarify the meaning of these traditional terms and to give them their true value.

No one can deny that the spiritual life comprises various phases and has various modes of manifestation, as is true also of natural life. However, just as it does not occur to anyone to say that the life of a newly born infant and that of a mature man are altogether different and unrelated because of their different modes of expression or manifestation (for they are but two phases of one life), so is it absurd to consider the interior life of the ascetic and that of the mystic as two different and independent lives. The classification of the interior life into asceticism and mysticism is logical, but only so far as it expresses two stages of the one life with its distinct modes of manifestation. In this sense the differences between asceticism and mysticism are very marked; as much, indeed, as those between the infant and the mature man. Essentially, however, there are no differences; the ascetical and the mystical life are one because one is the grace or divine seed which grows and is developed in them. Moreover, their goal is the same and fundamentally their exercise is the same. Their great difference lies in their mode of operation or the role which the soul plays in them. In the ascetical phase the soul is principally active; in mysticism it is principally passive. But the mode of operation never establishes essential differences.

The same also must be affirmed of the ascetical and mystical ways, or what is called the "ordinary" and "extraordinary." They also differ as to method or mode but not substantially or essentially. In other words, these ways differ, not by reason of the grace which is communicated in them, but by reason of the mode of its communication and reception. This means simply that God can, and in fact does, communicate His graces either by ordinary or extraordinary means, that is, by the extraordinary way of visions, locutions, ecstasies, etc., or by the ordinary way of prayer and the sacraments. This does not mean, however, that the grace communicated by extraordinary methods is greater or more excellent than that communicated by ordinary channels, for in one reception of Holy Communion God can make the greatest saint. Extraordinary manifestations are indeed signs of special grace and predilection, but these same special graces of predilection can exist apart from the extraordinary manifestations. Perhaps for many souls it is far better not to receive anything extraordinary, but always to love God in an extraordinary way. In a word, on God's part, the ordinary and extraordinary ways, or asceticism and mysticism, differ only in the manner of communicating His grace and on the part of the soul they differ only in the manner of receiving it.

Finally, it is also possible to admit of an ascetical and a mystical perfection in a relative sense, according to the active or passive mode of working which is proper to those two phases of the spiritual life. But in an absolute sense no such division can be made, for perfection is the perfection of life itself, which is always one. The error, then, is not in admitting the aforesaid classifications and divisions in their true sense, for these are necessary in order to understand the spiritual life in all its phases and to instruct and direct souls. The error consists in giving them an absolute sense, in establishing a radical and essential difference where in reality there is none, and in taking as separate and independent elements those which are not so.

This is the error which Father Arintero tried with all his power to combat because it was not a purely speculative error, but one which had disastrous results in practice. It precluded mysticism and put it beyond reach, and reduced the entire spiritual life to asceticism, as opposed to mysticism. As a consequence, it confined souls to the supernatural life of the imperfect or of beginners and alienated them forever from the true perfection of the full supernatural life which is proper to mysticism. Even more, it truncated

the ascetical life itself by preventing its normal development toward mysticism.

To combat these fatal consequences of the error of dualism, Father Arintero defended and argued the necessity
of mysticism for true perfection, and even for ascetical perfection itself, that is, he taught how to practice asceticism
mystically. In other words, he propounded the true, traditional doctrine; what our Lord Jesus Christ, the apostles,
and the Fathers and saints taught.

Did our Lord establish two spiritual paths and modes of
life? Rather, did He not say, "I am the way, the truth, and
the life?" [2] What would St. Paul say if he were to see the
life hidden with Christ in God divided into two kinds and
the disciples of Christ divided into ascetics and mystics?
The same could be asked concerning the Fathers and the
saints, all of whom urged everyone alike to strive for Christian perfection, which consists in the closest possible union
with Christ and, consequently, in the most perfect charity.

There is, then, only one spiritual life, one spiritual perfection, and if we wish to divide it into two, according to
the mode and spirit which animates the two phases, then we
must affirm that the mystical life is the more perfect and
that without it no perfection is possible. For the mystical
life is the life of union with God, and unless God touch the
human heart and rid it of all its dross, man, though he work
and struggle his whole life, will never subdue his rebellious
nature or soften the hardness of his heart and strip it of all
self-love. This is the work of divine love, which fuses and
melts the human heart as fire melts steel. This is why he
who wishes to attain true perfection must practice asceticism
mystically, that is, with the spirit of a mystic, performing all
his exercises with the most pure intention of pleasing God

[2] John 14:6.

and aspiring to love Him ever more and more and to be united with Him as closely as possible. In this practice is man's greatest good and from it must come all the sanctifying efficacy of the ascetical life. Everything else is of little or no avail in the way of sanctification. He who is actuated by any other motive than that of pleasing God, regardless of what he may do or the extent to which he may go, will avail little or nothing. This is the "most excellent way" [3] of which St. Paul speaks, and which consists simply in the practice of the love of God or charity.

However, in order to follow this course it is necessary to abandon oneself to God entirely and without reserve and to have a blind faith and confidence in the designs of His infinite love. What is the cause of the sterility of the ascetical life when separated from mysticism, if not its narrowness and limitation? He who persists in that mode of life does not abandon himself whole-heartedly to God, but sets limits on the effusions of divine love. This kills or sterilizes the spiritual life, which is a life of love, for to put conditions and restrictions on love is to kill it altogether. Experience also teaches that persons who content themselves with the ascetical life never attain even to ascetical perfection, however otherwise it may appear exteriorly. Of course, to aspire to the mystical life does not imply a desire to attain the extraordinary graces which sometimes accompany it, such as raptures, visions, the gift of prophecy, etc. It is simply to aspire to the perfect love of God, which is the essence of that life.

In conclusion, whatever be the speculative and theoretical divisions and classifications which may be established in virtue of an analysis of the spiritual life according to its various phases and manifestations, on one thing it is neces-

[3] Cf. I Cor. 12:31.

sary to agree in order to avoid contradicting the doctrine of
Jesus Christ and the Church; namely, that the spiritual life
is in itself objectively one, for one is the grace which animates it and which is developed in it. Subjectively also it
is one, because the end to which it is ordained is one and
the essential means employed in its exercise and development are identical throughout. What does it matter if
crosses, trials, sufferings, and circumstances of life differ
materially, or if the means by which God communicates His
grace are also diverse? It will always be true that without
trials and crosses it is impossible to enter the kingdom of
God; that His grace, by whatever means it may come, will
never fail us; and that our intentions, aspirations, desires,
and efforts ought always to tend toward one and the same
thing: union with and the possession of God.

In working with souls it is important not to intimidate
them, not to confine them within narrow limits or suppress
their most noble aspirations, but to animate and encourage
them to rise ever higher toward God by making them aware
of the infinite riches of His love and of His desire to find
hearts disposed to receive them. The important thing,
finally, is to teach them to overcome and detach themselves
totally from self in order to receive these spiritual treasures.
They must be made to understand that one does not reach
this goal by way of high-flown notions or aspirations to extraordinary things, but through profound humility and the
annihilation of every desire that does not proceed from a
pure and holy love of God. In brief, they must be made
to realize that they will love God in exact proportion as they
die to self. What danger can there be in this? What danger
can there be in inculcating in souls the desire to be nothing
in order that God may become their all? Undoubtedly,
those who combat mysticism because of a fear of illusions

and deceptions either do not know it at all or have an erroneous understanding of it.

CHAPTER 2 ✍

Schools of Mysticism

THE first question that comes to mind in hearing about schools of mysticism is whether these are possible. Is it possible that there can be different ideas and opinions about Catholic mysticism, which in itself is truly and objectively one, as is also the doctrine of the gospel, of the apostles, and of Holy Mother the Church? In reading and hearing certain opinions on this subject one could again ask with St. Paul, "Is Christ divided?" [1]

In order to answer these questions and explain the subject properly, we must first distinguish between two general schools of mysticism: one considers the practical and the other the theoretical aspect of mysticism. Under the first category there can be many schools; as many, in fact, as there are varieties of mystical graces, temperaments, races, nations, or institutions. Thus we speak of the German, Spanish, Franciscan, Dominican, or Carmelite schools, which are distinguished in the practical order by their preference for certain means of attaining perfection. Moreover, the Spirit which animates them—which is the Holy Ghost—although one in Himself, is multiple in His effects and manifestations, as Scripture relates.

As for the schools which are differentiated from a theoreti-

[1] Cf. I Cor. 1:13.

cal standpoint, these also can be explained, although they
lack a true and objective foundation. The explanation is
found in the very nature of mysticism itself, which, since it
is ineffable, does not admit of a clear translation into human
language. Furthermore, many who treat of these profound
matters are not mystics themselves but "mysticologists,"
that is, men whose knowledge of the subject is derived
purely from external sources. If some should have first-hand
experience, such knowledge, if it is incomplete, can itself
be an occasion of error, since it leads them to think that
there is no other mystical knowledge than that which they
possess.

There is, moreover, another and higher reason for these
discrepancies and controversies. God permits them in order
that the truth may be more clearly revealed and may take
deeper root in souls. Sincere and well-intentioned souls who
earnestly seek the truth will find that, although these controversies seem at first to increase the obscurity and darkness,
the confusion eventually disappears as increasingly greater
light discloses the truth. They will then discover more and
more extensive horizons in the domain of this sublime
science.

At first it was thought that such controversies would lead
to confusion and prove prejudicial to the cause of mysticism
and to the souls who follow such paths; but in the course
of time it has been proved that this divine science benefits
by such controversies, for they lead to a more perfect clarification of its doctrines. It is true that some problems remain
to be solved, and it is possible that upon their solution others
will arise, simply because the word of God is an unfathomable abyss. With all that, however, it cannot be denied that
the study of mysticism has made remarkable progress, thanks

to the excellent works occasioned by these controversies, works which have promulgated these studies and have won for them a much more favorable position than they occupied previously.

Today it can be said that the various schools of mysticism differ mainly in the attitude taken with regard to the unity or duality of the spiritual life and the question of infused or acquired contemplation. Moreover, even these differences tend to disappear as greater light is shed upon the subject, and when the divine light will shine in all its splendor, they will disappear altogether. However, such is our human state and the limitation of our intellectual capacity and medium of expression that there will always be problems which will occasion differences among theologians, especially when they endeavor to probe and expound what St. Paul calls the profound things of God.[2]

This, we repeat, is inevitable and even necessary for the progress of mystical theology. It will not prove prejudicial if in practice one follows the criterion and direction which our Holy Mother the Church teaches and which all the saints and truly spiritual souls have followed. For it would indeed be a great evil and a deplorable error to carry into practice certain preconceived theories which would cause souls to stray from the way of perfection or detain them in their flight to sanctity. It is therefore extremely necessary that there be but one criterion and one standard of spiritual direction, just as the doctrine of Christ and His Church is one and the end to which it is ordained is one: our santification and eternal beatitude. Consequently, in order to avoid hindering the work of God in souls, whatever be the school we follow or the theories we defend on this subject (within

[2] Cf. I Cor. 2:10.

true orthodoxy, of course), in practice we should always be guided by the following norms of doctrine and spiritual direction:

1) Everyone who devotes himself to the spiritual life should do so with the absolute certainty that for him there is but one way; namely, that which God has marked out for him and by which God wishes to lead him. His ideal and goal should also be one: to attain the perfect love of God, for this embraces all perfection and sanctity. In other words, his one and only aspiration should be the perfect observance of the commandment of charity, without thinking of anything else.

It follows that it would be a grave error for anyone to start or proceed in the spiritual life with the idea of following either the mystical or ascetical way, for by thus determining his own course, he would be preferring his own will and judgment to God's and would be placing himself outside the order of divine providence. No one can foretell the designs of God or the way by which He wishes to lead souls; hence our most earnest desire should be to follow wherever He may lead. If we proceed otherwise, we go completely astray. For if we propose to follow only the ascetical way, we tie the hands of God so that He cannot give us His mystical graces. If, on the other hand, we propose to follow the mystical way, since this is not entirely within our power, we run the risk of becoming the toy of every imagination and fantasy and of every absurdity.

However, in saying that we should follow but one path, we refer to the formal element of the spiritual life and not to the material element, which may vary greatly according to the state of one's soul, God's decree, and the circumstances of one's life. All these things must be taken into account if we are to pursue that one way which contains all others, which is to be faithful to divine grace and to follow Christ wherever He may lead us. This norm or rule is of primary importance and because of their failure to observe it, many retarded souls languish and fall away from the spiritual life. The harm is further augmented by those who insist on leading souls always in the same way and obliging them to proceed always in the same manner, as if no other way were possible. The fact that God has for some time led a soul in such-and-such a way does not justify such a procedure, for God can and does change the path of souls and adapts them all to their sanctification.

2) What we have said regarding the ways of the spiritual life applies also to the manner of praying. No one should practice prayer according to an exclusive and preconceived formula, but according to the gift of prayer God has bestowed upon him, whether the prayer be affective, discursive, meditative, or contemplative. To attempt to do otherwise is to usurp the function of the Holy Ghost. They err gravely, therefore, who endeavor to make their prayer conform to what they imagine or desire rather than to what God intends. We should go to prayer with the utmost submission and humility and, like a beggar before a rich and powerful lord, calmly await whatever God wishes to give us. The only thing we must do is dispose ourselves to receive His grace and perform those acts which we know the Lord asks of us as conditions for receiving that grace. In other words, we should do whatever we can by using our faculties, yet in such wise that when the Lord wishes to work in our souls without our help, we shall not impede Him by our over-anxiety and activity, thinking that otherwise we are not praying. The most perfect prayer is that which the Holy Ghost effects in our souls when they are in a passive state.

3) As long as our Lord does not raise us to this passive or

mystical prayer we should observe all the prescribed means for good "ordinary" prayer, but without attempting by our own efforts alone to raise ourselves to a more exalted form of prayer.

4) There is no method or procedure for attaining the prayer of contemplation. In endeavoring to do so, we run the risk of falling into the error of Quietism, or other similar extremes. Truly supernatural contemplation is not acquired; God bestows it upon whomever He wishes and whenever He wishes. However, we may be sure that, as regards the mystical element of prayer, God will bestow it upon us if we practice ordinary prayer with all due perfection. Simply by praying the *Our Father* with the greatest affection and reverence, souls may be (and sometimes are) raised by God to true contemplation. St. Teresa herself affirms this, speaking from her own experience and that of her daughters.

To love God with all our strength, with all our soul, and with all our heart; to abandon ourselves to Him without limit or reserve in order that He alone may reign within us and be our only Lord and Master; this is what constitutes true mysticism. This is the end to which asceticism is ordained; this should be our aim and our most ardent aspiration in prayer; it should be the goal of our entire life. In order to gain it, we must follow wherever God leads and not try to go the way we wish. It is the only sure method.

CHAPTER 3 ✍

The Ordinary Mystical Life

WE here designate the mystical life of which we propose to treat as "ordinary," not in the sense that it is very common (for unfortunately it is not as common as it should be), but in the sense that it lacks extraordinary phenomena such as visions, raptures, revelations, etc., which sometimes accompany a holy life. To many persons this will seem contradictory, for they cannot conceive of the mystical life without such phenomena. For them there is no other mystical life than that which St. Teresa describes in *The Interior Castle*, or something similar, and the more amazing the supernatural manifestations the more mystical it seems to them.

This error is due in great part to man's natural interest in the miraculous, which has influenced authors of the lives of the saints and other holy souls to present them to us in their most extraordinary aspect, disregarding that which seemed common and ordinary. Hence the impression that sanctity is identical with extraordinary supernatural phenomena. Fortunately, this misconception is disappearing and it is now commonly understood that the mystical life does not consist in such phenomena and can exist without them; furthermore, the ordinary mystical life is characteristic of the majority of souls who attain this degree of spirituality.

Consequently, if the spiritual life of an individual is devoid of extraordinary phenomena, we should not on that account conclude that the individual also lacks that element which is fundamental to the mystical life and which is, at

the same time, the most extraordinary phenomenon imaginable, although it is not perceptible to the senses and may
take place without the soul itself being aware of it. This
great phenomenon essential to all mystical life is the transformation of the soul in God. It takes place gradually, as
the soul progresses in the mystical life, and it reaches its
culmination in the substantial and permanent union with
God.

In order to understand this it is necessary to bear in mind
that the mystical life, like our natural life, has two principal
phases: that of growth and that of stability and perfection.
Both phases are the effect of the action of the divine life
in the soul. In the first phase it tends principally to remove
obstacles and impart vigor and strength for growth and
development; in the second, it fully manifests its vital activity by means of an unimpeded supernatural energy. This
action of the divine life in souls gives rise to the various
dispositions of the soul and the diverse stages through which
it must pass before reaching the state of permanent union.
In the first stages the divine action is ordained principally
to the purification of the soul, thus disposing it for the ultimate phase, union with God, for nothing defiled can enter
the kingdom of heaven. Hence follow all the sufferings
and "dark nights" which the soul must endure before it can
reach the happy state of total transformation in God. However, although the soul cannot be perfectly united to God
as long as it is not completely purified, it is undeniable that
each purification brings the soul closer to Him, and as it
more closely approaches Him, it is more and more transformed in Him.

The ordinary mystical life, then, consists in the entire
process of purification and sanctification which the Holy
Ghost effects in the soul until it attains union and trans-

formation in God. This process generally starts with passive purifications and arid, infused contemplation, the signs of which are described by St. John of the Cross,[1] and terminates when the life of the soul is totally absorbed by the divine life. Here the mystical life begins in all its vigor and plenitude; for, although this life can become still more intensified within its own species, it cannot pass on to any higher and distinct state.

St. John of the Cross says in the prologue to *The Living Flame of Love:* "For although in the stanzas which we expounded above we spoke of the most perfect degree of perfection to which a man may attain in this life, which is transformation in God, nevertheless these stanzas treat of a love which is even more complete and perfect within this same state of transformation. For, although it is true that both these stanzas and those speak of a state of transformation beyond which, as such, a soul cannot pass, yet none the less, with time and practice, as I say, the soul may become more completely perfected and grounded in love."

It is here also that the two paths, the ordinary and extra-ordinary, meet, for the union and transformation which they cause in the soul are essentially the same and produce

[1] Although theoretically it may not be difficult to identify the beginning of the mystical and contemplative life, in actual practice it is, for generally its beginning is almost imperceptible to the soul itself. God introduces the soul into it so gradually that the exact time of its beginning cannot be precisely determined. Moreover, the Holy Ghost is not subject to rule, and with each soul He proceeds so differently that there are no two whose spiritual life follows the same pattern. Thus, even the trials and purifications differ in different souls, although they all have the same sanctifying effect; and the latter is more profound as the former are more intense. Finally, it can be said that the soul enters the mystical life when it begins to suffer divine things (*pati divina*). The soul feels as if afflicted with a strange malady that makes all sensible things distasteful and it suffers an insatiable hunger for God which gives it no rest and which it cannot yet satisfy.

the same effects. The terms "ordinary" and "extraordinary,"
therefore, when applied to the mystical life, refer to the way
or mode of that life, but never to the life itself; for, although
the latter may sometimes be accompanied by certain extraordinary supernatural manifestations, this is not usually the
case, nor do these manifestations belong to the very essence
of the mystical life. This is exemplified in the lives of the
saints, for the extraordinary phenomena which they experienced generally took place in the early stages and completely
disappeared later on. If any remained they were generally
intended for the benefit of others or for the accomplishment
of their mission in the Church, such as revelations, prophe-
cies, or miracles. God bestows these graces principally for
the good of His mystical body, and sometimes He grants
them even to sinners.

Such manifestations, therefore, are not essential to the
mystical life, nor are they in any sense infallible signs of
greater sanctity. For although such singular favors, which
God bestows upon some souls for their own benefit, are most
assuredly signs of divine predilection, they may also be
granted, as the saints tell us, because of the soul's greater
need and weakness. This is the way in which gifted souls
should consider such favors. St. John of the Cross says in
The Dark Night of the Soul that because of the weakness
and corruption of our sensible nature such communications
cannot be as powerful and intense nor as spiritual as is required for union with God. "Hence arise the raptures and
trances and dislocations of the bones which always happen
when the communications are not purely spiritual—that is,
are not given to the spirit alone, as are those of the perfect
who are purified by the second night of the spirit, and in
whom these raptures and torments of the body no longer
exist, since they are enjoying liberty of spirit, and their

senses are now neither clouded nor transported." [2] St. Teresa also was surprised to find that toward the end of her
life all raptures and other extraordinary favors which she
had repeatedly experienced ceased.

From what has been said, it is evident that basically there
is only one mystical way and life, and that the division into
ordinary and extraordinary is not founded on its intimate
nature, but on its sensible manifestations or the different
ways in which the Holy Ghost works in souls. Fundamentally the two are identical, for both have the same cause
and nature and produce the same effects. In other words,
the mystical life is nothing other than human nature's participation in the divine life, causing thereby a supernatural
transformation which is more profound as the possession of
that divine life is the more perfect.

Extraordinary phenomena, we repeat, do not constitute
the mystical life nor are they infallible signs of sanctity,
because the proper and necessary effect of this life is not
ecstasies, visions, and such like, but a transformation, a renovation of the spirit and heart of a man which completely
changes the orientation of his thoughts, affections, faculties,
and energies. It is an elevation of his nature which takes
him out of the dark and dismal regions of sin and places him
in the divine realm of sanctity. It is, in a word, the transformation into that new creature, the new Adam of whom
St. Paul speaks [3] and to whom the divine Savior referred
when He said that we must be born again.[4] This life, which
is beyond all the powers of nature and which God alone can
effect, is the true mystical life; not so, those phenomena
which are admired by those who have no clear idea of what
the supernatural life is nor of its proper effects in the soul.

[2] *The Dark Night of the Soul,* Bk. II, chap. 1.
[3] Eph. 4:24.   [4] John 3:5.

Such phenomena can be, and frequently are, confused with other phenomena of the natural order or of diabolical origin, especially by the worldly and those who have not the spirit or training to discern such things.

We do not mean to disparage in any way the veneration and esteem rightly due to extraordinary gifts of prayer and graces *gratis datae*. They are, as St. Paul teaches,[5] precious charisms which God bestows upon some souls for their own benefit and for the benefit of the entire Church. Fortunate are the souls who receive them and correspond with them! The only thing that we wish to emphasize is that they are not the only and exclusive means which lead to union with God, and we should not value their sensible manifestations more than their sanctifying effect on the soul. Sanctifying grace may just as readily be accompanied by and produce its effects through the ordinary graces and obscure or negative contemplation as through the extraordinary gifts of prayer and positive contemplation.

If rationalists and other opponents of mysticism who confuse it with extraordinary manifestations would understand this, they would cease to oppose it, for they would then see that what they are opposing is merely its external manifestations. Neither would spiritual directors labor so hard in studying and discerning the nature and origin of extraordinary manifestations, for these are better known from the effects they produce than from the nature of the manifestations themselves. For whatever is not conducive to virtue and sanctity and does not tend to good is false, however sublime it may appear.

It is therefore very important to have a clear idea of what the mystical life is, especially for spiritual directors and interior souls. Otherwise the former will be blind leaders

[5] Cf. I Cor. 14:3, 4.

of the blind and the latter will err in thinking that the extraordinary way is the only way. They will then endeavor to follow it or else they will close the door to union with God rather than pass through it, because they will see nothing extraordinary in their lives save hardships and misery. On the other hand, if they know that the normal or ordinary characteristics of progress toward the mystical life are not sweetness and ecstasies, but trials and crosses which are sometimes so severe that the master of mysticism, St. John of the Cross, compares them to hell itself,[6] then they will not lose heart, but will be greatly encouraged to pass through the terrible desert which leads to the promised land.

Let souls, therefore, leave extraordinary favors to whomsoever God gives them. And let those who receive such favors correspond with them by endeavoring to attain great holiness of life, for more will be exacted from him to whom more is given. But those who seem to receive nothing of the kind should neither seek nor envy them. Rather, they should content themselves with what is theirs, for as long as they come to love God ardently and unite themselves closely to Him, what does anything else matter? Only one thing is necessary: to love God as He should be loved.

[6] *The Dark Night of the Soul*, Bk. II, chap. 6.

CHAPTER 4 🖋

Fervent Aspirations to Sanctity

IT seems strange that even among "spiritual people," as St. Teresa would say, there should be disagreements and doubts concerning such an obvious and self-evident truth as the worthiness and necessity of earnest desires for sanctity. Nevertheless, such is the case, and all because of their failure to understand one another, as St. Teresa would also say. For it is to be supposed that basically they all agree and, therefore, they all have the same objectives and intentions. All affirm that it is necessary to have great aspirations and to aim high in the way of perfection and that the supreme ideal and goal of all our desires and efforts should be the perfect observance of the first commandment of God, that is, to love Him as He wishes to be loved. The difference is that some maintain that the ordinary graces of the ascetical life are sufficient for this and that we should not seek the extraordinary graces of the mystical life. Others, on the contrary, affirm that without these mystical graces it is impossible to love God perfectly, and therefore they should be desired and asked for.

Of these two opinions, the latter is undoubtedly the correct one. The ordinary graces of the ascetical life, however efficacious they may be, never take the soul beyond the scope of the ascetical life. That is to say, they never take it beyond that active mode of operation in which it is the principal agent of its own acts, although assisted by grace, and since the soul is the agent, its operations necessarily suffer the limitations proper to the subject which performs them. On the other hand, as the mystical graces gradually bring the soul into a state of passivity, they make it a faithful instrument of the Holy Ghost to the point where the soul is no longer the principal agent of its own actions but a kind of instrumental agent, in accordance with its nature. Then its operations are more properly works of God than of the soul itself and, therefore, they are no longer limited but are perfect to a very high degree. That is why it is said that our works are perfect when God performs them in us.

Since it is evident that without the mystical graces it is impossible to attain true supernatural perfection, it follows that we should both desire and ask for them with all the fervor of our soul, just as we ask for the realization of all our other desires and aspirations. If those who maintain that mystical graces should not be sought, could be convinced of this truth, doubtless they also would ask for them, if their desire for perfection is as sincere and ardent as it should be. For although they may reasonably have a certain fear and trepidation in this matter, I nevertheless believe that, under the pretext of humility and not desiring great things, there is concealed the fear of a life which is completely disposed for all the sacrifices which God may exact of them because such a life would be too rigorous and perfect. Or perhaps there is the fear of being considered shy and timorous individuals (for such is the popular opinion concerning mystics) and, prompted by that strange tendency of man to descend to the common-place, they wish to put on airs of nonchalance and broad-mindedness. However, this is not generally the case among sincerely spiritual people, and if they do not dare to desire and ask for these graces, it is because they have an erroneous concept of them.

The very word "contemplation" astounds some souls because they know only of ecstatic contemplation, or something similar. They conceive of contemplation only in the etymological sense; that is, an act of the understanding absorbed in the contemplation of a truth whose dazzling grandeur enraptures the soul. This may be one form of the contemplative act or one of the aspects of contemplation, but it does not constitute its essence. Contemplation is nothing other than the effect of the action by which the Holy Ghost, with the cooperation of the soul itself, purifies and sanctifies it and communicates His divine life to it. This action is so profound and secret that often the soul itself is unaware of it and perceives it only as a most painful and devastating experience which overwhelms it almost to the point of death. This is what the mystics call arid and obscure contemplation; it is the most common form and possibly has been experienced by those very souls who are frightened by the word "contemplation." It is, to a greater or less degree, the daily bread of those who have entered or are entering the mystical way.

The other kind of contemplation, which is distinct and delightful to the soul, is much more rare and is not, as is the former, indispensable for the mystical life, nor is it in itself more efficacious for the attainment of that life. On the contrary, the more intimate and profound the operations of the Holy Ghost, the more they are concealed from the soul, lest it hinder them by its own activity.

The misconception concerning the nature of contemplation extends to the other mystical phenomena which at times accompany it, such as the suspension of the senses and faculties, raptures, revelations, etc. It is generally believed that mystical graces consist in such things and cease to exist when not accompanied by these phenomena. However, the latter are merely accidental and not the substantial element of the mystical graces. The substantial element is their sanctifying efficacy, which God can communicate, and in fact usually does communicate, without any sensible manifestations.

It follows, therefore, that not to desire contemplation or the mystical graces, taken in their true sense, is equivalent to not desiring that the Holy Ghost consummate in us His work of purification and sanctification; or, to put it more clearly, it is equivalent to rejecting the full possession of the gifts of the Holy Ghost. This is the danger of the doctrine of the "double way" if an attempt is made to apply it to the guidance of souls who aspire to perfection and are still in the first stages of the spiritual life. With such a doctrine they will surely never go beyond the "ordinary" life, nor will they come to love God as the saints loved Him.

On the other hand, if souls are taught to ask, not for the extraordinary, but for the ordinary elements of the mystical life, that is, the substance and reality of these graces which give it its sanctifying efficacy; if they are taught to ask fervently and perseveringly for the perfect possession of the Holy Ghost and all His gifts and fruits, then we shall see His marvelous effects of perfection and sanctification. Then also we shall realize the blindness and folly of putting fetters and setting limits on the work of the Holy Ghost in souls.

Ardent desires and aspirations for sanctity, then, should be fomented and encouraged. After all, how do we know that God does not call us to greater things simply because we have not experienced them? Did the saints, perchance, begin their spiritual life at the heights? What danger can there be in desiring to ascend with them to the summits they attained? These fervent desires are inspired by the Holy

Ghost Himself, who pleads for us with unspeakable groanings.[1] They should not, therefore, be stifled, but strengthened and followed, taking care not to deflect them from their
true goal. Further, such desires must be true and sincere,
and not merely wishful thinking.

Those souls who say they cannot meditate and therefore
believe themselves incapable of contemplation should bear
this in mind; for, quite contrary to what they think, when
this incapacity is not due to indolence, or some other cul-
pable cause, it is a disposition for contemplation. Then the
soul is not apt to hinder the action of the Holy Ghost by its
own excessive activity. Furthermore, in its prayer the soul
is especially occupied with asking for and desiring the Holy
Ghost and invoking Him with greater earnestness. There
is no better prayer than that which rises from the depths of
our humility and misery and from the desire to receive the
Holy Ghost and be santified by Him, putting ourselves in
His hands entirely and without reserve, so that He may do
with us whatever He wishes and that we may be consumed
by the fire of His love.

If we proceed in this way, there is no danger of being deceived. Deception consists in believing that we possess the
divine gifts when we do not, or in thinking that we can
acquire them by our own industry and effort; but to desire
and ask for them with all our heart is not in itself a source
of self-deception. On the contrary, it is the best means of
freeing ourselves from all error and deception, for it is these
gifts that "sanctify us in truth." [2] This is precisely one of
the signs of a right spirit: the ardent desire to know that
one is not being deceived and to be sanctified in truth.
Therefore, good souls are always fearful and uncertain,
regardless of how great the graces and gifts they have re-

---

[1] Rom. 8:26.   [2] John 17:17.

ceived, unless our Lord has given them the most singular gift of being absolutely certain that their communications are genuine.

Another sign of the right spirit and that these desires come from the Holy Ghost is their sanctifying action in the soul. In the first place, the soul's intentions and desires are purified so that its love for God is most pure and disinterested, intent solely upon His glory and good pleasure. Moreover, the more intense the soul's desires for sanctity become, the greater its longings for purification, and the more the soul is purified, the more does it yearn for still greater purity of heart. Its greatest concern and solicitude is to beg God to bestow upon it that "perfect spirit," [3] that disposition and those characteristics which are most pleasing to Him. Its constant prayer can briefly be stated thus: "Make me what Thou dost want me to be, O Lord, so that I may please Thee in all things. I ask nothing more for myself, for I do not know what is best for me. All I ask is that Thy will be accomplished in me and that Thou be glorified in me and in all things." The greatest yearning of these souls, the desire that inflames and consumes them, is the desire to glorify God and to please Him in all things. What they want and what they base all their happiness upon is God's interests, not their own. So we see the importance of these lofty desires and the great role they play in the work of our sanctification.

Let us not, then, suppress the ardent desires for sanctity in souls. On the contrary, let us endeavor to foment them by every means possible, being careful only that they be real and sincere. Let us not be concerned whether what we ask for is ordinary or extraordinary, nor about classifications of gifts and graces, nor about doctrinal theories. These are

[3] Ps. 50:14.

all right in the schools, but not in our prayers before God, who far exceeds our petty and miserable thoughts. Let us be guided in prayer by faith and the impulses of our heart and let us constantly and ardently ask for a boundless love of God and the gifts of His Holy Spirit, for He himself has promised them to us and seeks only to find a heart upon which to lavish them. Nor let us forget that saying of the saints: The more God wants to give of Himself, the more does He cause Himself to be desired, and the more we desire Him the more does He give Himself to us, because the hope of heaven attains as much as it hopes for.

CHAPTER 5 ✍

The Shortest Way

AFTER enumerating the various graces and gifts which God imparts to souls according to the various states and ministries within the Church, and after exhorting us to esteem them highly and strive to obtain them as means of our sanctification and union with God, St. Paul writes these words which souls eager for sanctification should never forget: "And I show you yet a more excellent way." [1] Should we surmise from this that, according to the Apostle, there are different paths leading to God? No. Substantially, the path is one. However, there are different ways of pursuing it; some go slowly, others run, and others fly. Moreover, even among those who fly, there are differences; rapid is the

[1] Cf. I Cor. 12:31.

dove in its flight, more rapid is the arrow, but the most rapid of all is the ray of light.

Do you wish to know which is the most excellent and the shortest way to union with God? Listen to the words of the same Apostle: "Follow after charity." [2] In order to engrave it more deeply in our hearts, he adds: "If I speak with the tongues of men and of angels and have not charity, I am become as sounding brass or a tinkling cymbal. And if I should have prophecy, and should know all mysteries, and all knowledge, and if I should have all faith, so that I could remove mountains, and have not charity, I am nothing. And if I should distribute all my goods to feed the poor, and if I should deliver my body to be burned, and have not charity, it profiteth me nothing." [3]

Thus, according to St. Paul, neither the most sublime gifts nor the most heroic virtues nor the most extraordinary penances are of any value without charity. "Charity is the bond of perfection," [4] it is the life and soul of everything. In the spiritual order its various degrees mark the degrees of union with God.

But someone will say, "Certainly charity is everything; it is sanctity itself, but how shall we acquire it?" Charity is acquired by the practice of charity itself. Mark well that I am not referring here to exterior works of charity toward one's neighbor, which, according to the opinion of many, constitute charity. Well do the above-quoted words teach us that charity is something quite distinct from all exterior works. Charity is simply the love of God; or, in other words, inasmuch as God and love are one and the same thing, it is God Himself living within our souls. It is personal and infinite Love loving Himself within our hearts.

[2] Cf. I Cor. 14:1.   [3] Cf. I Cor. 13:1–3.
[4] Col. 3:14.

To exercise ourselves in charity, therefore, is to give
way to God in our hearts. It is to detach ourselves from
everything and to make ourselves an absolute vacuum in
order that God may fill us with Himself. As the great mystic,
Tauler, says, perfection does not consist in doing great
things, but in letting God "be magnified, that is, made great
within us." [5] And in order to let God be magnified within
us, all we have to do is give Him much space, to expand
infinitely our capacity to receive Him. This we cannot do
of ourselves, but neither will God do it unless we desire
it ardently and ask for it day and night.

God is an infinite treasure and He wants souls rightly
to esteem His value, to desire Him above all things and to
plead for Him with great yearnings. God likes to make himself desired and, as the Angel of Lisieux used to say, the
more He wants to give of Himself, the more does He cause
Himself to be desired.[6]

This most ardent desire for God is also what makes the
soul fly and even shoot forth with the speed of a light-ray
toward that supreme Center which so irresistibly attracts
it to Himself. In its flight to God, the soul is divested of all
that is earthly and mortal in its nature, and mundane things
are definitely cast aside. In the holy exercise of charity one
arrives more quickly at the summit of perfection and sanctity because in one simple act all the virtues are exercised
and all vices attacked at their very root; for the root of all
vices is pride or self-love and the root and soul of all the
virtues is charity. And how could a soul whom God has
touched and thereby reduced to nothing become proud?

[5] *Institutions,* chap. 14.
[6] Cf. "Act of Oblation" in the autobiography of St. Therese of
Lisieux.

The soul must die in order to be united to God, and he who is dead is justified and purified of all sin; it is no longer possible for pride and self-love to reign in him.

That is the reason why St. Paul enumerates as manifestations of charity the practice of all the virtues (patience, benignity, humility, mortification, detachment, etc.) and the absence of all the vices (pride, envy, etc.).[7] Charity or the love of God, if it is real, must of necessity produce all these effects in the soul. If the effects are otherwise, then it is a pure illusion. Wherefore, if we dedicate ourselves preferably and above all things, with all the earnestness of our souls, to the acquisition of the love of God, we shall quickly and in a more simple and excellent way attain our perfection.

All this means that there are two methods of procedure in the attainment of perfection: one which proceeds from within and another from without. The one which proceeds from within is that which we have described: to strive above all things to have charity. In this exercise, as we have seen, the soul fixes its entire attention upon God and all its efforts are aimed at delighting and pleasing Him and doing His will in all things. In a word, it strives to love Him as He should be loved. As this is the soul's one and only objective, it forgets about self and is not concerned about anything except the sole object to which it aspires with all the energy of its being, which is the love of God or union with God. That is why however grievous and painful the trials God may send or however difficult the circumstances of its life, the soul's attitude in this regard is one of total indifference. It matters not whether it be in light or in darkness, in consolation or aridity; everything which may affect the soul per-

[7] Cf. I Cor. 13:4–7.

sonally is a matter of indifference to it. Its only occupation and concern is to love God, which it feels to be the only thing necessary.

This, as we have said, is the shortest way to spiritual perfection because it goes straight to its object. Moreover, inasmuch as it simplifies all the acts of the soul, synthesizing them into one act, it intensifies the action of the soul and thus infinitely increases its efficacy. Above all, this is the shortest and most excellent way because, since God Himself is love, love is also His weakness and vulnerable point and hence, by means of our love of Him we can best subdue and conquer Him. Lastly, with the love of God we also attain every imaginable perfection. This is the path proper to great hearts and courageous souls who would be ashamed to bargain with God but rather abandon themselves to Him totally and without reserve. It is also the path of advanced souls who have already endured many great trials and sufferings, for these things tend to enlarge the heart supernaturally if they are borne in a supernatural manner.

The second method consists in the eminent practice of all the other virtues and exercises of piety. This method is proper to beginners and also to the proficient, and possibly no soul has ever been totally exempt from it. In order that no one may misunderstand, it is important to observe that these two methods of procedure are never entirely separated in practice, as we conceive of them in theory. What happens is that one or the other method predominates, according to the state of the soul. Thus, those who proceed according to the first method, although all their desire and affection is centered in God, do not forget themselves so completely as not to be particularly and habitually careful to do everything well. Likewise, those who proceed according to the second method, if they are well guided, will be careful to purify their intentions, endeavoring solely to please God in all they do. The second method leads to the first, and eventually both lead to the same goal, union with God.

Let no one think, however, that inasmuch as both methods eventually arrive at the same goal, it is useless to point out the differences between the two. A knowledge of the distinctions is important both for beginners and for the advanced. It helps the latter dispel all doubts and anxieties regarding the genuineness and security of the method they follow. They see that their present method differs from those generally taught and from that which they themselves at one time followed. As a result, they cannot help but experience doubts and fears upon seeing that they no longer proceed as before, although deep in their heart they experience a divine assurance which God imparts to them. Furthermore, this knowledge will serve to make them more faithful and grateful to God, for they will see how gratuitously He has communicated to them so great a grace as that of loving Him perfectly.

This knowledge is of even greater importance for beginners and for those who are yet progressing in the spiritual life, for thus their desires are aroused, their zeal is given wings, and they are taught to fly to God. Of special importance is this knowledge to many souls whom God is already strongly drawing to Himself, and who feel within themselves these vehement desires to unite themselves to Him, but as yet do not dare to comply for fear of going astray and becoming victims of illusions. Such souls will learn that an ardent, sincere, and profound desire to love God as He should be loved can admit of no deception, if, at the same time, it is accompanied by a desire, equally ardent and profound, to die to self and to all things. In other things there can be an infinite number of deceptions and illusions (as, for instance, in believing that the most sublime sanctity consists in having other kinds of communications from God), but in the desire not to be anything in anything whatever, to seek poverty and nudity of spirit, to desire to die in order that God may live within us, there can be no illusion.

In conclusion, we wish to add that these two methods of procedure correspond to the two kinds of prayer to which all prayer can be reduced: meditation and contemplation. In meditation it is principally the soul that acts; in contemplation it is principally God who acts in the soul. In the former, the soul exercises all its faculties in the consideration of holy things and makes all the acts which that consideration awakens and evokes within it. In the latter, the principal act of the soul is simply that of surrendering itself totally into the hands of God and remaining quietly and calmly in His presence in order that He may infuse into it the divine gifts and mold it into His divine image. This prayer is most beneficial and its exercise is easy, pleasant, and simple, for it requires but one act which consists in abiding with God, loving Him, and rejoicing supernaturally in Him. It is that general, loving attentiveness to God without reflections or considerations in which, according to St. John of the Cross,[8] the fundamental act of contemplation consists.

However, this kind of prayer is only for those souls who, after having exercised themselves in meditation, feel a veritable impotence or an invincible reluctance to practice it any further and experience at the same time an irresistible attraction for that other prayer of peace and love. Those who have attained this kind of prayer must be advised that

[8] *The Ascent of Mt. Carmel*, Bk. II, chap. 13.

when they feel impelled to make distinct acts of love and praise or of the other virtues, they should make them, and also any consideration or reflection to which God sometimes moves the soul. For the contemplative act is not usually permanent and it produces those acts and affections which spontaneously arise from the heart; therefore it would be imprudent to suppress them. We must remember that the best kind of prayer for each one is that from which his soul derives the greatest benefit.

Likewise, when God draws one from meditation to contemplation, that is, to the quietude of that exercise of love, he must yield to its attraction and not resist the action of the Holy Ghost. For although it may seem to him that in this exercise he is accomplishing less, he derives infinitely greater benefit. As we have already said many times, the fruit of prayer does not depend so much on what we ourselves do, as on what God does within us and if God is to work in the soul, one must remain quietly in His hands and not hinder the divine action.

One should not resist this action under the pretext of humility, protesting that contemplation is something too elevated, for there is hardly anyone who exercises himself habitually in meditation who does not from time to time experience more or less well-defined moments of contemplation. These moments will ordinarily become more and more frequent and lasting and also more intense and profound as one exercises himself in it. For contemplation, in a certain sense, is nothing more than a condensation, so to speak, of all the acts of meditation into one. In one single act of ardent love is synthesized all the spiritual life and if one should make this act perfectly, he would already be a saint.

We shall close these lines by indicating what is ordinarily meant by "the pathways of God." We have already said that substantially there is only one way, but accidentally there are many, although they all come under the two kinds of spiritual paths which we have attempted to outline. The popular saying, "God leads souls by many paths," gives us to understand that there are many paths leading to God. In this sense, the various vocations, states, and exercises; the various trials of the spiritual life or the attractions which souls experience for this or that devotion or mystery or pious practice; whatever God uses to draw us unto Himself; all constitute different paths. Thus, we say that some follow the path of penance, others, that of charity toward one's neighbor, of solitude, of persecution, of interior afflictions, temptations, and trials. Some are more moved to weep for their sins, others to meditate on the Passion of Christ, others on the last things, etc.

To be sure, in actual practice, these different paths are never totally separated, but all partake somewhat of each other. What happens is that some of the aforementioned elements will predominate and become the outstanding characteristics in the spiritual life of the soul. Yet, whatever be the path by which God takes us, the life and soul of every one of them is charity and all are ordained to the development and perfection of this virtue. That is why the best way of abbreviating all the spiritual paths consists in increasing charity by every means possible, especially by performing all our actions with the most pure intention of pleasing God, that is, by performing them with great zeal and with the sole desire of glorifying God and of praising His holy name.

This does not require much knowledge nor a great variety of interior acts. One act, repeated with all the fervor of our soul, would be sufficient. We have seen how some have sanctified themselves by frequently and earnestly repeating the phrase, "All for love of Thee, O Lord"; others, "May

Thy holy will be done in all things"; others, "Oh, Thou who didst create me, have mercy on me."

The paths by which God leads souls are many, but they all tend to the same end. It is important for us to conform ourselves to our particular path and embrace it with all our heart, for that is the will of God for us. To seek God by that means should be the sole end and object of all our ardent desires and aspirations. We should be indifferent to everything except God, who is our last end and our beatitude.

PART II

Christel, the Life of the Soul

❧

CHAPTER 6 ⚡

The Sanctification of Human Nature

IN our opinion there are two fundamental errors concerning the justification of man: that of Judaism, which upholds justification by works alone; and that of Protestantism, which affirms justification by faith alone, without works. Under the first, we can include all the errors which tend to exaggerate the value of works, such as Pelagianism and its kindred doctrines; under the second, all those which tend to minimize man's activity, such as Quietism and, in general, all false mysticism. These two extreme errors seem to be opposed to each other but fundamentally they are not, for both agree on the concept of a purely external justification, leaving man intact in his being and in his nature.

The Jew believed that he was justified by the exact observance of the works of the law, even if interiorly he remained in his sin. Christ condemned this justification, calling its adherents "whitened sepulchers." [1] He then taught the true concept, declaring that all the evil or the good in man proceeds from the heart as its source [2] and, consequently, all justification that does not produce an interior change and reformation of the human heart is false and detestable. St. Paul also preached very earnestly against this error, proving by the Scriptures that man is not justified by the works of the law, but by faith and by the grace of Christ. [3]

The Protestants then used this statement as their point of departure in order to establish their doctrine of justifica-

[1] Matt. 23:27.   [2] Matt. 15:18.   [3] Rom. 3:24, 28.

43

tion by faith without works, citing those texts of the Apostle which seemed favorable to their thesis. However, St. Paul never taught that faith alone was sufficient to justify us, nor is the Protestant faith the faith of which St. Paul speaks. The Apostle preaches a faith that works all justice and perfection and transforms us into new creatures. From worldly men it changes us into celestial men; from sons of Adam it changes us into sons of God; and ultimately it transforms us into Christ, so that we can say with the Apostle, "I live now not I, but Christ liveth in me." [4]

Protestant faith cannot do this, for it is nothing more than a mental act or an auto-suggestion, produced by the continuous and monotonous repetition of biblical texts which they interpret according to the meaning they want them to have. That is why all their doctrine and preaching can be reduced to the incessant repetition of the word "believe, believe," with or without reason, as if they were trying to hypnotize their followers.

From such a definition of faith arises their concept of justification, which, according to them, is nothing other than an imputation, so to speak, of the merits of Christ to man. This clearly demonstrates that their concept of justification is purely external and communicates nothing personal to man, for to impute is to attribute to someone that which he does not have. That is why they never tire of repeating that Christ is our substitute, but we know that to substitute is nothing more than to put one person or thing in the place of another, without modifying or changing that other. Basically, then, the Jewish and Protestant notions of justification are the same, because they leave man intact in his interior being and cover his malice with the mantle

[4] Gal. 2:20.

of a purely external justice which makes of him a veritable whitened sepulcher.

Apart from these gross errors which destroy all religion, there is also some confusion on this point even among persons who profess the true faith. Although they believe that justification must necessarily produce a moral change in man, they do not realize that this change touches his very nature. In other words, they consider the change as nothing more than a change of conduct. These also have failed to penetrate the profound meaning of justification, for they have not understood that justification, in its most elevated sense, is the same as sanctification.

We believe that merely by substituting the word "sanctification" for "justification" we can clearly distinguish between the Catholic and the non-Catholic teaching. Sanctification effects sanctity (or perfect justice), and sanctity is life; hence, far from being something exterior, it is the most intimate and profound element in a man. That sanctification should cause a profound transformation in human nature, whereby it is made capable of receiving the divine life, and that the latter should come to be in a certain sense more natural and vital to the soul than its own life, is a doctrine which theologians have proved at length. But even without demonstrations, it would be sufficient to have the *sensus Christi*,[5] or mind of Christ, to understand it thus.

This doctrine is confirmed by experience. It is manifested in all those who have been born of God and in whom lives the Word, full of grace and truth. These souls experience the transformation which sanctity effects in them in as real and indubitable a manner as they experience the change from infancy to youth or from youth to old age. In the first

[5] Cf. I Cor. 2:16.

place, they are aware of a change of orientation in all the
faculties and energies of their human nature. If the soul
was formerly the enemy of grace and resisted its impulses,
after its sanctification it not only ceases to be an enemy
of grace but is its most faithful friend and servant. If at one
time human nature tended toward the earth as toward its
center, dragging man after it and converting him into a toy
and slave of his appetites and passions, now it is impelled
toward heaven, toward things eternal and divine, and in that
supernatural region it lives as in its native element and gives
full play to its supernaturalized activities and energies. If
at one time human nature sought its own pleasure and satisfaction, now it knows no other happiness than to love and
glorify Him who made it for Himself. If formerly everything
was an obstacle and a burden and it found sin in everything,
and everything caused it harm because of its evil disposition,
now, purified from sin and cured of its wounds and infirmi-
ties, scarcely anything can harm it, and everything serves
as a motive to unite itself more closely to God. Now human
nature is able to employ itself in every kind of work, live
in any condition whatever, suffer all annoyances and contradictions.

All this is nothing more than a sweet exercise of divine
love, because of the soul's perfect union with the divine
will. Saving the divine commandments and prohibitions,
which have now become interior norms of action, the soul
can rejoice and take pleasure in every creature that God has
made to be loved by man, and this becomes a chord in the
divine canticle of gratitude and praise which the soul incessantly sings to the Author of so many marvels of power,
goodness, and wisdom. Finally, the change of orientation
and of life is so profound and radical that the soul wonders
how it could ever have thought or felt or acted otherwise.

It wonders how it could have found satisfaction outside of God, or valued and shown interest in things so vile and despicable as are the things of this world, or could have disregarded and even abhorred the immense felicity which it now enjoys and which is found only in God.

The soul feels so happy and contented in this new state that it knows not what to offer to God. Even the most heroic acts of virtue seem like nothing because of the disdain it experiences for their contrary objects and the infinite excellence of the love with which these virtuous acts are performed. It feels that everything it does or suffers for the sake of love is another immense benefit and gift of love itself, for to him who loves there is no greater happiness than to manifest that love, nor is there anything so gratifying and delightful as to see that the beloved asks for the testimonies of love, for in so doing he shows his desire to be loved.

These are not exaggerations or exaltations of the mystical sentiment. We need only read the lives of the saints to confirm this, especially those saints whose interior life is well known, such as St. Francis of Assisi, St. Francis de Sales, St. Catherine of Siena, or St. Teresa of Avila. There we shall see with what naturalness the saints conduct themselves in the supernatural order; we shall see how their sanctity, far from being an obstacle in their natural life, makes them divinely natural and simple. Conversely, their natural life is not an obstacle to them in the supernatural order but is rather a help and a medium of manifesting in a more remarkable way the intensity of their supernatural life. In the saints we observe all the operations of our nature: how like other men they love, fear, hope, rejoice, become sad, indignant, diffident, contrary, or affable. The only difference is that in them all these acts have their source and their end in God and are, therefore, just and rightly ordered.

This is observed also to a greater or lesser degree (according to their measure of sanctification) in all souls that experience His purifying and sanctifying action. Such souls will understand very well (and all the better as they approach nearer the state described) what St. John of the Cross says in his *Spiritual Canticle* when he comments on the verse: "My soul has employed itself. And all my possessions in his service."

We quote this verse because it expresses precisely what we are trying to point out. It is a palpable demonstration of the fact that justification and sanctification (or justice and sanctity) are not something exterior, nor merely a change of moral conduct. Rather, they are something intimate and profound, something which reform, transform, elevate, and perfect our very nature and from which proceeds all external perfection.

Commenting upon the above verse, St. John of the Cross says:

By all her possessions she here understands all that pertains to the sensual part of the soul. In this sensual part is included the body with all its senses and faculties, both interior and exterior, and all ability of the nature, namely: the four passions, the natural desires, and the other possessions of the soul, all of which things, she says, are now employed in the service of her Beloved, even as is the rational and spiritual part of the soul whereof we have just spoken in the last line. For the body now works according to God; the inward and outward senses are directed towards Him as to all their operations; and all the four passions of the soul she likewise keeps bound to God, because she neither has enjoyment save from God, neither has hope in aught save in God, nor fears any save only God, neither does she grieve save according to God; and likewise all her desires and cares are directed to God wholly.

And all these possessions are now employed in God and directed toward God in such manner that all the parts thereof which we have described tend, in their first movements, without the soul's being conscious of it, to work in God and through God. For the understanding, the will and the memory go straightway to God; and the affections, the senses, the desires and appetites, hope, enjoyment and the rest of the soul's possessions are inclined to God from the first moment, even though, as I say, the soul may not realize that it is working for God.

Another effect of sanctification, and a natural consequence of the one mentioned above, is the liberation from the law of sin, from that law referred to by St. Paul when he wrote: "But I see another law in my members, fighting against the law of my mind, and captivating me in the law of sin that is in my members. Unhappy man that I am, who shall deliver me from the body of this death? The grace of God by Jesus Christ our Lord." [6]

From what has been said we see that grace alone, which effects our sanctification, can deliver us from the terrible law of the slavery of sin. There are many more effects of sanctification and all are most admirable, but we shall not pause to describe them. It would be impossible and, moreover, they have already been described a thousand times better in the *Spiritual Canticle* of St. John of the Cross and his corresponding commentaries. We have merely tried to point out the principal effect of sanctification or the principal aspect of supernatural perfection, for we believe that it is the least known. But it is perhaps fitting that it should be so, for it will serve to encourage souls who aspire to perfection and who are striving to overcome the resistance of nature. Thus they will realize that supernatural perfection does not consist solely in a change of conduct, but that

[6] Rom. 7:23-25.

perfection is life, and that this life transforms our nature
in such wise that it makes it most sweet and amiable, whereas
without it, it is bitter and abhorrent.

CHAPTER 7 🖋

Transformation in Christ

THE phrase "development of the Christian life" refers to
the entire growth of the spiritual life from its beginning
to its plenitude and perfection. We make this clarification
because the general concept of the Christian life is not quite
correct and sometimes it is even completely erroneous, due
to the distinctions and divisions which have been introduced
into the supernatural life of the soul.

Among other classifications that are inexact we have the
"simple Christian life," the "pious, spiritual life," and the
"religious life." The first is considered inferior to the others
and it comprises the ordinary life of the average Christian
faithful. It comprises the observance of the commandments
of God and of the Church and of the duties of one's state
in life, together with the prayers and religious practices
indispensable for salvation. The "pious or spiritual life"
is still more perfect, for it is the life of those who dedicate
themselves to ascetical exercises, prayer, and the interior
life. The "religious life" is the life of those who, in addition
to the above, promise to follow Christ according to the
evangelical counsels.

It is apparent, however, that none of the modes of life
described is specifically characterized by what is essential to

the supernatural life: union with God by means of union with Christ. This is what constitutes the essence of the supernatural life and is the basis of the plenitude and perfection, not only of the Christian life, but also of the spiritual and religious life, which are substantially one and differ only accidentally. In reality there is no other supernatural life than the Christian life. All the distinctions between it and the other modes of life are extrinsic and refer only to a means of better attaining its perfect development. Therefore, nothing is more erroneous than to consider the Christian life as the lowest grade of the supernatural life, for if taken in its true and theological sense, it contains within itself all perfection and sanctity. To believe otherwise is to fail totally to understand what constitutes the essence of the Christian life.

The Christian life is in reality nothing other than the life of Christ in us; in other words, Christ living within us. *Christianus alter Christus.* The Christian is another Christ by reason of a participation in Christ's own life. The Christian life, then, is not simply the observance of a moral code, even though it be the Christian code. It does not consist in this or that mode of life, be it secular or religious. It does not consist even in the practice of the means or perfection or exercises of the ascetical and mystical life. All these are dispositions and means which may be indispensable for the *development* of the Christian life, but they are not the life itself.

The Christian life consists in our real and vital union with Christ by means of divine grace. Through this intimate union we participate in His life in such a way that it becomes the very life of our soul. That is what St. Paul affirms forcefully and without distinctions.[1] The Christian life, then, is

---

[1] Col. 3:4: "Cum Christus apparuerit, vita vestra."

the life of Christ in us. But what is this life and how is it recognized?

Life in general, the philosophers tell us, is movement from within; but this is merely a notional concept rather than a true definition. We cannot define life itself, but we experience it and we know it by its manifestations. It is the source of all movement in our interior and exterior faculties. It is the fountain and root of all our thoughts, affections, desires, hopes, fears, sorrows, and joys; of all our internal and external acts, and of all our spiritual and corporal works.

This is precisely what the Christian life effects in man and this is how it may be recognized when it has reached its plenitude. The life of Christ has so replaced man's own life that he feels in the innermost depths of his being that he has undergone so radical a transformation that it is no longer he who lives but Christ lives in him. For that reason he never tires of repeating with St. Paul, "I live, now not I; but Christ liveth in me," [2] and "For to me, to live is Christ." [3] As a matter of fact, his union with Christ is more intimate to him than is his very heart.

There is nothing in this world that can give us an adequate idea of this union; only the words "spouse" and "friend" can give us a faint notion of the reality. It is that consummate union of which the gospel tells us,[4] in which Christ is no longer thought of as another person, but as the life of our life. Then is verified the statement, "the Christian is another Christ," for in the spiritual order and as a member of the mystical body, he is nothing other than an extension of Christ Himself. It is then also that the Christian life attains its plenitude and perfection and produces true sanctity of soul with all its proper effects.

[2] Gal. 2:20.   [3] Phil. 1:21.   [4] John 17:21.

Christ fills all things and our heart is impelled by the same love that moves His heart; indeed, it seems then that His Sacred Heart beats within our heart and arouses in it the same affections and sentiments which move Him. The Christian is no longer of this world, nor does he have any concern or interest other than the glory of God and the extension of His Kingdom. All his happiness is founded on the knowledge that God is infinitely happy, that He will be so eternally, and that He has within Himself all grandeur and all perfection in an infinite degree. He lives totally oblivious of self and is intent solely on loving and glorifying God in all things that He disposes or permits, be they favorable or adverse, sweet or bitter, for he no longer loves God for other alien motives, nor even because He is good to him, but only because He is who He is and is worthy of infinite love, adoration, and glory.

The perfect Christian has the same sentiments toward God that Christ had, and it is Christ who communicates these sentiments to him as He communicates to him His very life. It is this life that imparts to him all that pertains to Christ: His divinity, His humanity, His sufferings, His merits, and His sanctity. Yet he offers all this to God as his own by virtue of his status as another Christ, which is conferred upon him through his incorporation and union with Christ. Likewise, this life communicates to him the same sentiments and affections of charity that Jesus Christ has toward men: His mercy, compassion, patience, humility, meekness, and, above all, zeal for his salvation and sanctification.

He can now say that his meat is to do the will of his heavenly Father, working, suffering, and sanctifying himself for the salvation of the world. In brief, this life communicates to him the very charity of Christ, which "surpasseth all knowledge," [5] for it communicates to him His very Spirit, the Holy Ghost, who fills him with celestial lights to penetrate all things, even the "deep things of God." [6] The truths of faith are so vivid to him and so full of light, that they no longer seem to come from without but to emanate from his very heart. In a way, that is what happens, for although the truths of faith may have come to him from without, by hearing, his profound understanding comes from within, from the Spirit of Christ that abides within him.

Who was it, if not the Holy Spirit, who taught St. Paul that divine theology concerning redemption, salvation, sanctification, and the other truths of our holy religion? And this was possible because the heart of Paul was the heart of Christ. The same thing occurs to a greater or less degree in all souls who have attained the plenitude of the Christian life, which is the transformation in Christ.

All this is a verification of what we affirmed in the beginning; namely, that the Christian life is nothing other than Christ living in souls. This is the only true life and in it is all perfection and sanctity. It follows from this that the various "lives" which are usually enumerated are not such in the strict sense of the term, but rather they are states of life or systems and methods of life, ordained to a more sure attainment of the plenitude of the Christian life. There is no doubt that some are better adapted to attain this end than others, such as the religious state, but this is on condition that it be practiced with the true spirit. Otherwise it may well happen, and frequently does, that a simple and faithful layman will attain greater perfection and sanctity than a religious, because he practices his religion with more fervor and greater union with Christ.

[5] Eph. 3:19.   [6] Cf. I Cor. 2:10.

All these so-called "lives," though they differ externally, have one and the same internal procedure for attaining the desired end, which is the plenitude of the Christian life. This procedure or development is marked by three phases of the supernatural life: incorporation, configuration, and transformation in Christ.

By the first, as the name implies, we are incorporated with Christ as members of His mystical body. We are, as He tells us in His gospel, grafted on Him as the branch on the vine. This incorporation is effected by the grace of baptism and, if lost, is restored by that of penance, whereby our sins are forgiven and the gates of heaven are opened to us. We are reconciled with God and made His children by adoption and heirs to His eternal Kingdom. From dry branches, fit only for the fire and incapable of producing any fruit, we are changed into living branches which partake of the sap of the vine and produce fruits of eternal life. Lastly, through our incorporation with Christ we receive in germ all the graces and gifts of the Holy Ghost, which are to be developed in the course of our life by means of our configuration with Him until they reach their plenitude in the transformation.

Configuration with Christ is effected in us by the imitation of His life and example, and especially by our likeness to Him in His sufferings, His passion and death. As the Apostle says, we are "configured with his death." [7] Only by dying with Christ can we rise again with Him to a new life in the transformation. Configuration, then, embraces the entire process of purification in the interior life in order to unite us with Christ. Here principally belong all the exercises of the ascetical and mystical life which are ordained to the imitation of Christ and the attainment of the graces

[7] Phil. 3:10.

necessary for our sanctification. Here man exercises himself in the renunciation and negation of self by taking up his cross in order to follow Christ.

However, this would not suffice if God did not come to man's assistance by sending sufferings and crosses which, of himself, man would never resolve to undertake. Nor could he bear them without a special grace. This is especially manifest when God purifies a soul by means of those "dark nights" which strip and cleanse it of all worldly dross and uproot every vestige of sin. The entire process leads to the transformation which we have already described and which is the last stage and consummation of the Christian life.

It should be noted, however, that these three stages must not be radically separated, for they are but three aspects of the Christian life and are differentiated according to the element that predominates in each one. Apart from that, they are always united to a greater or less degree. Thus transformation begins as but a seed in the stage of incorporation, and the latter becomes more and more intense in that of the configuration and is perfected in transformation. Likewise, in the stage of configuration the soul is gradually transformed until it attains the perfection proper to that stage and goes on to that of transformation where its configuration is perfected.

Thus we see that the supreme goal and ultimate perfection of the Christian life is our transformation in Christ. But what must we do on our part in order to attain it? Simply that which is necessary for the development of all life: we must exercise ourselves in it, that is, we must live the life of Christ. We must think with Christ, feel with Christ, love with Christ, act like Christ, and live always with Christ and for Him. We must substitute His interests for ours, His outlook for ours. In our exercises of piety and of the interior life we must have no intention or desire other than our transformation in Him. We should never do anything save in union with Him, appropriating all that is His and substituting it for all that is our own.

This is the way, the only way, to acquire full perfection and sanctity. Therefore they are gravely in error and misled who, accepting the various divisions of the spiritual life, pursue another path and seek another life other than the Christian life. Neither St. Paul nor the other apostles nor the Fathers ever knew of any other life or any other way. And if today many souls are languishing in their spiritual life, it is because they do not have a clear idea of what it is; neither is there anyone to tell them. They are offered other ways of life and another kind of spirituality which is not the true one, or at least it is not exact nor complete. How could souls do otherwise than languish and become tepid when they lack fellowship and union with Christ? Why should they not become surfeited and weary of a spiritual life from which they derive no other nourishment than vague, meaningless formulas?

On the other hand, how different it would be if this intimate union with Christ were proposed to them; if they but knew the treasures and infinite delights of that life and how sweet is the spiritual life of union with Christ when He reigns supremely in our heart! If they but knew what treasures of grace, of light, of ineffable joy that life contains! What happiness it is to see oneself free from all the misery of one's own heart, and to feel the love and grandeur and sanctity of the Heart of Christ! Indeed, he who bears Christ in his heart enjoys the blessedness of heaven while still living on earth.

CHAPTER 8

The Mind of Christ

THE *sensus Christi* [1] of which St. Paul speaks signifies something similar to the ordinary expression that a person has a sense or aptitude for a thing; for example, a sense of justice, a sense of harmony, an artistic sense, or a natural aptitude. According to this usage, the word "sense" refers to a kind of instinctive faculty whereby we judge and properly appreciate the value of a thing in relation to the purpose or end to which it is ordained. So the *sensus Christi,* or mind of Christ, signifies a kind of supernatural faculty by which, as if by instinct, we judge and discern those things which are or are not in conformity with the spirit of Christ. That seems to us to be the essential meaning of the expression of St. Paul. For our present purpose, however, we are not so interested in knowing what the *sensus Christi* is in itself, as what it comprises and how it is manifested in souls. Then in due course we shall consider how it is acquired and perfected, and how it is obscured and lost altogether.

As to the first point, the mind of Christ is revealed with the greatest clarity in His life and gospel, especially in the eight beatitudes, which summarize it completely. From the standpoint of the beatitudes it could be said that the mind of Christ is a contradiction to human reason deprived of divine light. What greater paradox can there be than to call blessed those who mourn, those who weep, those who suffer persecution, the meek, the humble, and the poor in spirit? All this is absurd and incomprehensible to a human

---

[1] *Nos autem sensum Christi habemus* (I Cor. 2:16).

reason which lacks faith. But once the mind is illumined by divine faith, this doctrine is no longer absurd, but it is the most beautiful and sublime truth that the human mind and heart can conceive. For the beatitudes proclaim in a most lofty manner the meaning of the goodness, beauty, and spiritual grandeur of man and the significance of human perfection as the incarnation of the divine.

Accordingly, the *sensus Christi* is humility, meekness, patience, detachment, generosity, and total abnegation. In a word, it is infinite charity, of which the eight beatitudes are but a reflection. It is not our present purpose to develop this point, but we recommend that anyone who would know perfectly and possess the mind of Christ should meditate profoundly on His teachings and example and try to reproduce them in his own life.

As to the effects or manifestations of the mind of Christ in the souls of those who possess it, the first is that it communicates to them the gift of discerning truth from error in the matters of faith and religion. This divine sense preserves from error those humble and simple souls who love Christ but have not had sufficient instruction or learning to defend themselves against the innumerable sophisms and errors with which the spirit of evil covers the venom of his deceptions and lies. It is the great rampart against which all the arrows of falsehood are shattered; it is the indestructible defense of our holy religion.

It is not the discourses or arguments of the learned that have prevented and are preventing our holy religion from being totally destroyed by the attacks of its enemies, but it is this divine sense which abides in the souls in whom Christ dwells. Such souls so keenly feel the goodness and truth of their holy religion that all the arguments of men and of demons cannot make them vacillate for one moment, and they would readily die a thousand times rather than deny their faith. They have the awareness and invincible conviction that everything that goes against the Spirit of Christ and their holy religion is false and diabolical. This is sufficient to make them reject everything that opposes or departs from either one, though it be disguised with all the adornments of eloquence and have all the appearances of a shining truth newly discovered.

It must be thus, for just as it is impossible for wisdom to abide in a body given over to sin, so is it impossible for error to abide in a soul in whom Christ dwells, for He is eternal truth and wisdom. It was this mind of Christ that guided and instructed the early Fathers of the Church, enabling them to discern falsehood from truth among the many heresies and errors they had to combat at a time when the truths of the faith had not been so thoroughly studied nor so clearly defined as they are today. We may also say that it was this same mind of Christ that gave St. Thomas Aquinas a prodigious faculty for choosing, selecting, and defending the purest Catholic doctrine.

It will perhaps be said that all this pertains more to the gift of understanding, whose specific function it is to give us light in order that we may penetrate the meaning of the truths of faith. But it is one thing to understand the truths of faith and another to know which truths pertain to faith. However, we shall not dwell on these distinctions, for we do not think it inaccurate to admit that the *sensus Christi* is but an extension or participation in the gift of understanding. Since it is a gift of the Holy Ghost, it is also a gift of the Spirit of Christ, for the two are one and the same Spirit.

Closely related to this is the second function or manifestation of the mind of Christ, which is to distinguish the false from the true, the good from the bad, and the useless from the beneficial in matters of devotion and piety. In this matter also there are frequently found many errors and deceptions, as a result of the intrusion of a worldly or even a diabolical spirit which appears under the guise of the divine. Souls who possess the mind of Christ can very readily discover these deceptions. They can separate the gold from the dross and can tell which devotions and pious exercises are most profitable for them and have the greatest sanctifying efficacy.

Generally, these souls are very simple in this regard, as in everything else, and have but few pious practices of their own choice. Rather, they concentrate all their activity and devotion on the official exercises of the Church, especially on the divine liturgy, which to them is a most fruitful source of lights and graces and magnificently expands their interior life. It is true that under certain conditions they prefer quiet and solitude rather than exterior acts of worship, but such states are transitory. Their main objective is to rid the soul of all excess attachment to the sensible order and prepare it for a more spiritual appreciation of those things which are more directly ordained to His glory, such as the external acts of worship which so admirably express the interior state of adoration and homage to the Lord.

The mind of Christ is manifested in a still more admirable manner in the higher stages of perfection and sanctity. Superior lights are required here in order to perceive the height, the breadth, the length, and the depth of the "charity of Christ which surpasseth all knowledge." [2] No one is capable of explaining this subject properly and only the *sensus Christi* can lead us into those depths and enable us to discover the immensity of their grandeur. Thus, as the soul

[2] Eph. 3:19.

progresses in perfection, it is ever discovering new and wider horizons of sanctity without ever finding a terminus in the supernatural world.

The mind of Christ communicates to these souls an impulse or supernatural instinct which inclines and impels them to examine all things carefully in order to discover their value and importance and the good or evil effect they may have on the spiritual life, the glory of God, and the good of souls. This is true even in regard to worldly affairs, whether they are social and political or whether they pertain to the family or the individual. Persons who possess the *sensus Christi* and must occupy themselves with affairs of this kind can readily detect the good or evil and the beneficial or dangerous elements in them. They seem to sense where the venom of evil is concealed and where good is to be found.

However, it is in matters pertaining to perfection and sanctity that this divine instinct shines forth more resplendently. Sanctity is that precious pearl of which the gospel speaks and which is hidden in the earth of our hearts, beneath the thousand folds and layers of our self-love. In order to uncover it, it is necessary to penetrate through all those layers to the depths where it is hidden. This is what the *sensus Christi* effects in souls: it makes them go straight to their object, which is God, without allowing anything to deter them, though it have all the appearances of the divine. Such souls seek God and in God they seek nothing but Himself.

These souls can readily distinguish between true and false mysticism, for they are truly humble and poor in spirit. Their life is simplified and reduced to the most perfect unity because it is directed to that one thing necessary about which our divine Savior spoke: the love of God. That is their one and only desire and their only glory. They desire to die to all things, completely to detach themselves from them, so that in the same measure the love of God may reign in their hearts. That is why, unless it have the seal of the Spirit of Christ, which is humility, charity, detachment, mortification, and the renunciation of self-love, they reject and renounce all grandeur, though it appear in supernatural array and present itself with all the appearances of the divine.

That is why also these souls are the last to consider themselves mystics; nor are such distinctions among Christians pleasing to them, for they seem to introduce an element of division among the children of God. For them there is no such thing as mystics and non-mystics, but only good and simple souls who renounce and despise all things in order to love and serve God and live only for Him who is their all, or souls who have other views and intentions, other objectives and ambitions, which are not in accord with this supreme end. In fine, they possess the sense of true mysticism, for they know the voice of their Shepherd, who is Christ, and they cannot confuse it with any other. The tone of His sweet voice cannot possibly be mistaken by those who truly know it.

Souls who do not possess the mind of Christ or possess it but imperfectly, do not recognize His voice and they confuse it with the voice of mercenary shepherds or with the promptings of their own self-love which interferes in all things, even the most spiritual. Frequently they confuse the means with the end and they regard as sanctity something which is but a means to its attainment. Thus, they believe that they will be saints when they have carried out to the letter their idea of the spiritual life or practiced all the rules and norms that are prescribed for the attainment of perfection. If they are religious, they believe they will become saints simply by fulfilling faithfully the observances of the regular life. All this is certainly very good and holy when it is done for the purpose and in the spirit with which the rule was established, which is none other than to make us living copies of the life and Spirit of Christ.

However, if it is not done in this manner, and if the sanctity of our state and the satisfaction of believing ourselves good and perfect because we observe certain rules make us more proud, less charitable, less submissive, more stubborn in our views and opinions, and more conceited; if our heart and spirit are so far from those of Christ that we do not at all resemble Him in our sentiments, views, words, or actions; then of what use are all the religious observances and all the pious practices except to make us more responsible before God for the abuse of His grace? That is why there is nothing more pathetic or lamentable than the state of so many pious persons and even religious who, in spite of their many devotional exercises and practices, manifest no other sentiment in their words and actions than that of the children of this world. Wherefore, these persons should watch with the greatest care lest the *sensus Christi* be perverted or extinguished within them, for that would be their greatest misfortune. Without that sense, what meaning has the religious life, or what merit can their practices and exercises have, however mortifying and painful they may be? He who has lost the *sensus Christi* has lost everything.

But is it possible for a religious to lose this sense in spite of his many spiritual readings, instructions, and meditations? It is not only possible but probable, if he does not take due precaution to preserve and increase it. No one should trust in himself alone, but should be ever mindful of the force that constantly urges us to follow our own inclinations, seconded by the spirit of the world and of hell.

Everything in the world conspires against the mind of Christ. We hear nothing but words and doctrines that contradict it and we so frequently see examples that destroy it. Those who allow themselves to be guided by it are taken for fools and lunatics, while those who judge everything according to worldly prudence are considered wise. To such people, humility, charity, meekness, obedience, and the other Christian virtues are a mere hypocrisy which covers and disguises a subtle egotism. At most, they indicate the shrinking, cowardly spirit which is characteristic of a lowly and contemptible temperament.

Thus, the idea is inculcated that no one ever acts through lofty motives or practices virtue or sacrifices himself for anyone else. All without exception seek only their own profit and welfare as the ultimate end of life. So the heart of the children of men is filled with malice and their sense perverted, so that they all stray and "become unprofitable. . . . There is none that doth good, no not one," [3] as the Prophet said. Such universal defection is a disastrous example, especially when it reaches even to the sanctuary and some of those who by profession and ministry are obliged to fight and oppose this current, allow themselves to be carried away by it and become contaminated by the evil influence of a worldly spirit.

He who would remain firm as a rock in the midst of the waves and storms of this raging sea must be very attentive and wary of its assaults and firmly grounded in the example and teachings of Christ in order to withstand all attacks. There is no more terrible or tenacious battle than that which a man must sustain in order not to become contaminated by the malice of other men. And the fervent prayer of one who wishes to remain faithful to God's law is that

[3] Ps. 13:3.

He will not permit human malice to corrupt his sense and estrange him from the mind of Christ. He who wishes to preserve and develop this sense should, above all, live in union with Christ and be constantly mindful of His doctrine and example, using them as a standard of judgment for everything he sees and hears and especially his own thoughts and sentiments, in order to determine whether they are thoroughly conformable to those of Christ. This should be the touchstone of our whole spiritual life. By it we may always know whether we are drawing nearer or departing from Christ.

Above all, we should live in union with Christ by means of an intimate and constant communication with Him through the Eucharist. In saying "through the Eucharist," we do not refer solely to the reception of Holy Communion, but to an interior devotion to Jesus tabernacled within our heart. That is to say, our union with Christ should not be something purely mental or imaginary, but something that is real, vital, and personal; something that is flesh of our flesh, blood of our blood, and life of our life. Has He not said that he who eats His flesh and drinks His blood abides in Him and He in him? [4] Wherefore, our incorporation as members of His mystical body must be real and vital, even to the point where we can say it is no longer we who live, but He lives in us. We shall know what this is like when we shall have the same way of feeling, thinking, and acting that He had.

Finally, we should live in union with Christ and with Him crucified, bearing all our crosses and sufferings in union with Him and for love of Him. Nothing can so refine and purify the *sensus Christi* within the soul as suffering. It is a fact proved by the experience of the saints that from

[4] John 6:57.

the cross always comes light. The souls who suffer most generously are also the most illumined.

CHAPTER 9 🖎

The New Law

THE New Law is so called not only because it succeeded the ancient law of Moses, but also because its very nature and properties distinguish it from the latter. St. Paul calls the ancient law a law of precepts [1] because of the countless commands it contains. He calls it a law of fear and slavery because it was enforced by threats and penalties which reduced man to a kind of servitude. He also calls it a law of sin and death [2] because sin was the reason for its existence and it presupposed man as deprived of grace. Moreover, it was the occasion of sin and death, for although it imposed great obligations, it did not of itself justify man nor give the grace to fulfill those obligations. The ritual of this law of the Jewish people was totally abrogated by the coming of our divine Savior, and its morality was substituted by an incomparably more perfect one, which is the New Law or the law of grace.

The New Law is called the law of grace not only because it is itself an immense grace and was gratuitously given to us by Christ, but also because it is a law which emanates from the very nature of grace. Contrary to the ancient law, it does not come from without; neither is it imposed by violence or limited to precepts and the imposition of obliga-

[1] Rom. 7:10.   [2] Rom. 8:2.

tions. It is a living law, rooted in the inmost depths of the soul and is, at the same time, the fulfillment of every duty and obligation. For grace is a participation in the divine nature and, therefore, its law derives from the law of God, the law by which God governs Himself, a law which emanates from His very nature which is all goodness and love, justice and mercy. That is why the law of grace is perfectly adapted to the soul which possesses grace, for by grace it participates in the divine nature and this participation transforms it into a new creature which demands a new law to conform with its new being. Thus the New Law becomes, as it were, its natural law.

From this also arise all the other characteristics which distinguish the New from the Old Law. In the first place, the New Law is a law of perfect liberty, as St. James calls it,[3] for it is fulfilled not only without violence, but with the greatest spontaneity. Violence would serve only to arrest its impulse. This is all the more true as the impulse is more powerful, and it is as powerful as man's desire for happiness. In the fulfillment of this law man finds the perfect satisfaction of his most noble desires, which are to love, to perfect himself, and to enjoy peace, liberty, and all the benefits of God.

For this reason it is also called the law of love, for its fulfillment consists in love. Love produces all the works of this law and makes us cherish all that is commanded. This is so because grace effects man's transformation in God, who is love, and He it is who produces in man all the works of the New Law.

Finally, it is the law of the spirit of life, as St. Paul teaches,[4] for it gives us life in Christ and delivers us from the law of sin and death. Hence the Apostle said, "the law of the spirit

---

[3] James 1:25.   [4] Rom. 8:2.

of life, in Christ Jesus, hath delivered me from the law of sin and of death." [5]

Such is the New Law of grace and such are its principal characteristics. However, that this law may produce all its effects, it is necessary that grace act in the soul without any obstacles. That is, it is necessary that grace effect in the soul that transformation in God which will convert it into a new creature in all its perfection. This new creature is born, grows, and develops as all other creatures until it reaches its perfection, and this growth is proportionate to the measure in which grace takes possession of the soul.

Many Christians, even in the state of grace, do not enjoy the law of perfect liberty because they are still children in Christ. In spirit they seem to live under the ancient law rather than the new, for grace is in such an incipient state within them that it scarcely gives any signs of life. It is smothered and suppressed, as it were, by many worldly appetites and desires, by many worldly ambitions and preoccupations. Its action is impeded by so many obstacles that its effect is hardly noticeable in the soul.

This is also the reason why there are so few who serve God according to the spirit of the New Law, through love, and enjoy the full liberty of the sons of God. The majority serve Him only through fear and aspire only to escape eternal punishment and be saved. They do not wish to renounce their worldly aspirations nor to mortify by the Spirit the deeds of the flesh.[6] Thus they place obstacles in the way of grace, impeding its development and its work of perfecting the soul's transformation in God. In spirit they are more Jews than Christians and the excellency and consolation of the New Law they know only from hearsay.

Moreover, not only ordinary Christians who have scarcely

[5] *Ibid.* [6] Rom. 8:13.

any notion of the spiritual life and are content to avoid grave sin in order not to be condemned, but also many who profess virtue and practice the spiritual life, live more according to the spirit of the ancient law than the new. The latter, perhaps, endeavor to attain their perfection, but they desire to be justified by their own works, as if they believed that justification were of their own making, as the Jews did. Accordingly, in their practice of virtue they look more to the perfection of the virtues or the justice of external works, rather than to the perfection which comes from the grace of Christ. The reason for this is their erroneous idea of perfection and the role which our works play in justification.

Perfection does not consist in many works, but in an increasingly intimate and intense union with Christ. This is what all souls desiring spiritual perfection should strive for and desire: to endeavor by every possible means to intensify their union with Christ. If they lose sight of this, they run the risk of intensifying a Jewish and mercenary spirit and even spiritual pride, believing themselves justified simply because of their exact external observance of the law.

Do not be deceived. There is no other perfection or sanctity than Christ living in the soul. To attain this, external works are indeed good and necessary, but only when they are done under the motion of the Holy Ghost who truly makes us resemble Christ and initiates us into the holy mysteries of His life and death. When souls shall have attained this perfect union with Him, their own heart and spirit will move them to do what the law commands. Then they will also know from experience the happiness and consolation of the New Law of love and, like the Prophet, they will see the end of all perfection.[7] They will comprehend what is the breadth and the depth of the law of the Lord.[8]

[7] Ps. 118:96.   [8] Eph. 3:17, 18.

They will know what true liberty of spirit is, when, by the grace of Christ, they see themselves freed from the slavery of their passions and from the earthly bonds that had prevented them from flying to God and finding Him everywhere. Then they will see and love God in all things, without being subject to the conditions or vicissitudes of life nor to particular spiritual methods or exercises. Neither will anything whatsoever be able to separate them from the charity of Christ.[9] Finally, they will observe the precept of love perfectly, for their very being and life will be an act of the love of God.

CHAPTER 10 ✍

Mary, Model of Fidelity to Grace

THERE is a general tendency to attribute all of Mary's greatness principally to her divine maternity and the other privileges and excellencies with which God adorned her from the first moment of her existence, disregarding or at least attributing little importance to her personal merits, in which her own proper greatness consists.

We say "her own proper greatness," although it is to be understood that all is a gift from God, for the graces and privileges that a soul may receive are not so much the result of the soul's personal merit as of the pure goodness of God. Yet, to make them its own, it is necessary that the soul in some way merit them through its cooperation with divine

[9] Rom. 8:35–39.

grace. It is not enough that God give; we must receive and to some extent make our own that which He gives us.

A newly baptized child has potentially all the graces and gifts of a saint, but he will become a saint and possess these gifts and graces in their plenitude only by means of personal cooperation throughout the course of his life. He possesses the divine seed which must develop and grow until it attains the fullness of the life it contains within itself. In order to assimilate and make the divine gifts his own, therefore, man must cooperate with the action of God; in other words, he must be faithful to grace and second its impulse in order to be capable of enjoying the divine life in its plenitude.

How does one accomplish this? By self-denial and detachment from all that is not of God. A great spiritual master (Tauler) has well said: Perfection does not consist in doing great things, but in allowing God to be great within us. That is, it consists in making room for God, in giving Him the greatest possible space in our heart. This is done precisely by fostering the action of grace without offering any resistance (for grace itself inclines and impels us to it), letting ourselves be led by this supernatural movement and cooperating with it as much as we can. The divine action in the soul always tends to this, as do also all the means of sanctification, especially the trials and sufferings endured by the soul for this purpose. Nothing so enlarges the heart and increases its capacity to love God as does suffering.

It is not enough that a heart be divested of all if that "all" is of little worth. It must be a total and complete despoliation of all the goods which we esteem highly and whose surrender will wound us in the innermost depths of our soul and tear at the very roots of our heart. That is why in the purification of souls God inspires profound and ardent affections and afterwards exacts their renunciation. Moreover, the more intensely and profoundly He wishes to purify a soul and the higher the degree of sanctity to which He wishes to elevate it, the more occasion does He give it for self-renunciation and suffering.

Thus, He first exacts the renunciation of the love of the base pleasures of this world, then the love of life and health, then the more elevated love of parents, relatives, friends, and perhaps even of country. Afterwards comes the renunciation of moral goods such as the love of renown and the desire to be respected and loved; then the spiritual values in their endless gradation. To this end God sends sicknesses, humiliations, temptations, desolations, fears, and, in short, the whole series of interior sufferings which St. John of the Cross calls the "dark night of the soul." He does this in order to give the soul a realization of the vanity of all temporal things and to inspire it to practice mortification and penance. However, it is not necessary that a soul undergo each of these sufferings in particular; all do not need the same purgation because all do not have to be purged of the same defects, vices, and attachments. But what is necessary for all, however innocent they may be, is the martyrdom of love. The Blessed Virgin herself, though pure and immaculate, had to suffer this martyrdom, and with a greater intensity than all the saints together.

Divine love is a celestial fire that begins as a mere spark and gradually increases until it becomes a blazing fire which consumes and reduces to ashes all other loves. It is this fire of divine love that effects the soul's purification. So the most holy Virgin's growth in sanctity can be explained. She was already holy from the first moment of her immaculate conception, but not with such intensity and profundity as after Calvary. Together with the growth of the great gifts she received, there was also brought to perfection in her the divine seed of the immense graces deposited in her at the moment of her immaculate conception. During the course of her holy life, her heart and soul were infinitely expanded through her correspondence with grace and the docility and love with which she embraced the innumerable sacrifices and martyrdoms which God asked of her. Wherefore, if we wish to measure to some extent the sanctity of Mary, we must appreciate as much as possible the intensity of her martyrdom, of her self-denial, and of her detachment. Let us consider the pure, holy, and divinely beautiful affections she had to sacrifice and the excellencies and supernatural privileges from which her heart was totally detached.

With regard to the first, that is, the sacrifice of her love, Calvary tells it to all who meditate attentively upon it. We shall call attention only to the fact that, if ever a creature had the right to surrender herself wholly and without restraint to the impulses and effusions of love, it was Mary, for hers was the most pure, the most holy, and the most divine love there could possibly be in heaven or on earth, and its object was God Himself. Painful as it may be to renounce a love when we do not have a high esteem for its lawfulness and purity, it will never be even remotely as painful as the renunciation of a love, the purity, holiness, and beauty of which produce an infinite regard for the object loved. A sublime form of love is produced when the mind and heart agree on its excellence, but if that mind and heart are elevated by divine grace and elevated to the degree that Mary's were, then, clearly, all possibility of calculation and appreciation is lost and we can but remain rapt in admiration.

However, the martyrdom of the Blessed Virgin is not the most neglected or forgotten devotion of pious souls. They frequently make it the subject of their meditations and more or less feel and understand the terrible sufferings of the Mother of the Redeemer. If some do not feel them more keenly it may be due to their erroneous conception of sanctity, for not a few imagine that sanctity kills or rejects human sentiments and makes the saint little less than absolutely impassive. They do not realize that in purifying the sensitivity of human feelings, sanctity also refines it. The saint is not insensible to love or contempt or any of the other lawful sentiments of our human nature, but neither is he a slave to them. Christ Himself, the model and exemplar of all perfection and sanctity, felt the ingratitude, the contempt, and, above all, the hatred of the Jews with all the poignancy of which human nature perfected by grace is capable. How could He possibly have done otherwise, He who was all love? Let us conclude, then, that His Blessed Mother, far from suffering less because of her incomparable sanctity, suffered much more because of the very perfection that her sanctity communicated to her immaculate nature. While her highly perfected nature made her apt for the greatest possible joy, it also made her capable of the greatest possible suffering.

However this is not the least known, least studied, or least meditated aspect of the interior life of Mary. There is another aspect which, although closely connected with and, in fact, reducible to the first one, presents itself to our minds as a quite distinct feature of her sacrifice, total immolation, and complete holocaust. This aspect, more profound and important than the first, consists in the Blessed Virgin's complete interior detachment and renunciation of all the graces and privileges which she had received from God, including her divine maternity, a privilege she loved above all else because it made her the mother of such an amiable Son.

Here we must pause to observe that in saying that we must detach ourselves from everything in the supernatural order, even from the highest supernatural goods, God alone excepted, we do not mean that we should despise or ignore such gifts. On the contrary, no one appreciates or esteems them more highly than the holy soul. We are commanded to renounce them, as all the saints did, only so far as they can become objects of attachment or of human covetousness. For however excellent and lofty a thing may be, if sought without God, it loses all value. Wherefore, in order really to possess a thing, we must first renounce it whole-heartedly and maintain an habitual state of detachment in its regard, for in the supernatural order it is not possible to possess anything except through detachment. This truth is verified even in the natural order, for to possess a thing is to be its proprietor or master, and he alone is master of a thing and can truly enjoy it who is detached from it. If he is attached to it he is not its master but its slave.

To return to our subject, we repeat (however strange and even scandalous it may seem to some) that the Blessed Virgin renounced her divine maternity and by so doing she practiced renunciation in the most heroic degree conceivable, for the very reason that a greater good or a more exalted dignity for a mere creature is inconceivable. That she renounced that sublime dignity before it was conferred upon her is an indisputable fact. We all know that the condition she stipulated in becoming the Mother of the Messias was that her virginal purity should remain inviolate. As a matter of fact, she had already renounced that dignity at the very moment she vowed perpetual virginity.

However, this renunciation proved much less costly than that which she was to make later, for she could not at that time experience the ineffable delights which would be hers as the Mother of the Savior; neither could she feel the close bonds of love which would unite her to her Son. This first renunciation, then, referred principally to the immense glory which that high dignity held for her, a glory for which through so many centuries every daughter of Israel had yearned, and which was so deeply impressed upon their race and spirit that it could not but appear to them as the most glorious thing of all time. To be the Mother of the Messias, the Mother of the Savior of Israel! Oh, what immense glory for a daughter of Sion! And what sanctity was Mary's to be able to renounce all that glory!

However, as we have said, this was not the most painful phase of that renunciation, nor was that phase possible until Mary's heart had tasted all the delights of her Son's love. How did Mary practice that renunciation? Let us begin by declaring that the first soul that Jesus sanctified was that of His Mother. And, incidentally, when we speak of the purification or sanctification of Mary we do not regard these actions as a purification from sin, but as an ever increasing elevation and capacity for divine things. Jesus desired that just as His Mother was co-redemptrix, she should also be the first and most perfect model of sanctity. That is the way it had to be. His love for His Mother was greater than His love for all other creatures together. Hence it was fitting that He should raise her to the highest possible sanctity, for in sanctity is the greatest good, the greatest perfection, and the greatest happiness of any creature. And because He loved her so much, He had to make her suffer, although it caused Him unspeakable torment, for that is how true love is demonstrated. We may say, therefore, that Mary practiced this renunciation because Jesus required it of her. When we say that she practiced it, we wish it to be understood that it was only the interior act of detachment and not the external reality.

In order to give proper emphasis to this fact and to penetrate more deeply into the grandeur and sublimity of her renunciation, let us state it thus: the Mother of the Savior in some way renounced her Son and the love He had for her. The hand trembles as it writes this sentence, for it was an immense and terrible sacrifice for Mary. But that is how it was. That is the sword of the Spirit of God which penetrates the most profound and mysterious depths of the spirit.

However, for our own consolation, we must remember that God does not kill save to give a new, more elevated, and more divine life. Wherefore, if Mary in some way renounced her natural maternity, it was to be elevated to the spiritual maternity of Jesus—that maternity about which our Savior spoke when He said: "Who is my mother, and who are my brethren? . . . Whosoever shall do the will of my Father, that is in heaven, he is my brother, and sister, and mother." [1] Moreover, by that renunciation she merited the title and reality of spiritual Mother of all men. Therefore we see that Jesus Christ, in addressing her from the cross as "Woman" rather than "Mother" (thus alluding to this mysterious renunciation), proclaimed her at the same time Mother of all men in the person of the Beloved Disciple. Thus also was her spiritual fecundity for the children of men proclaimed and consecrated. For, in giving us Jesus and Mary as the models of the supernatural life, God manifested in them all the mysteries of that life to the highest degree, and one of those mysteries is the union of souls.

When God unites two souls in the bonds of His love, He endows them with the gift of spiritual fecundity for the good

[1] Matt. 12:48–50.

of other souls, as is repeatedly seen throughout the history of the Church. But that gift is not fully bestowed upon them save in exchange for a spiritual renunciation whereby the love itself becomes more intense, more pure, more profound, more beneficial, and more fruitful.

Accordingly, the Blessed Virgin practiced this renunciation and Jesus exercised her in it gradually, as He does all souls. This fact stands out clearly in the gospel story. At the age of twelve, Jesus already began to exercise His Mother in detachment and to show her the degree of perfection to which He intended to elevate her. Undoubtedly, up to that time she had innocently enjoyed all the tender endearments and affection of the Child Jesus. That is why on finding Him in the temple, after three days of untold agony, her heart could not suppress that most tender complaint: "Son, why hast thou done so to us?" [2] Jesus, however, instead of undoing Himself in fervent protestations of love, as we would expect Him to do in order to console His Mother, answers her with those seemingly stern but profoundly divine words: "How is it that you sought Me? Did you not know that I must be about My Father's business?" [3] By these words He meant to tell her: "Mother dear, remember that I am more than man, I am God, and to Me the bonds of flesh and blood mean nothing if they are not purified and sanctified by divine love. I have come to sanctify the world and to sanctify thee first, raising thee to a degree of perfection which, although thou hast a faint glimmer of it, thou does not as yet know it in all its clarity and splendor."

That is how Mary understood the words of Jesus, for they were accompanied by a most luminous and mysterious light which she, the most humble and docile of creatures, received into her heart with infinite gratitude, making them the sub-

[2] Luke 2:48. [3] Luke 2:49.

ject of her profound meditations. Thus Jesus prepared Mary
for the successively profound detachments which were yet
to come and which she would have to practice to the end of
her life. It should be noted that the few times the Blessed
Virgin appears in the gospel after this passage, it is to teach
us the lesson of detachment.

Such was the case at the wedding of Cana where her divine
Son, although He obeyed her and at her suggestion performed His first public miracle, manifesting that no one
recognized the rights of His Mother as much as He, answered
her in a way that seems calculated to exercise her in detachment. The most pointed of these incidents, however, is
related in the passage where Jesus was preaching the kingdom of God to the multitude and received the message that
His Mother and relatives wished to speak to Him. He answered by saying that His mother and brothers were those
who did the will of His Father. He did not intend to deny
His Mother, but to convey the idea that His love for her was
not founded so much on natural bonds, however close, but
on spiritual ones. It was as if He had said that He loved
her more as a saint than simply as a mother.

Finally, Jesus gave His Mother an occasion to practice
a detachment that was complete and definitive when on
Calvary's height He uttered the words: "Woman, behold
thy son." [4] Oh God, what an awful ending! Not even in that
dreadful hour did Mary have the consolation of hearing
a word of affection from those divine lips!

However, we must not think that Jesus was cruel to His
Mother; that would be blasphemy. It is true that to our
human nature divine love at times seems lovingly cruel and
inexorable. God never exempts the soul He loves from the
suffering necessary for sanctification. The soul may groan

[4] John 19:26.

and weep, but nothing will assuage its pain. But God will console it in a mysterious manner by turning its suffering into the most rapturous delight.

That is what happened to Mary. She understood Jesus and she knew the purpose of that apparent severity. She knew He loved her with a love that the world cannot even begin to understand and she suffered only because she saw that Jesus felt obliged to treat her thus in order to complete His mission on earth. Mary realized that love is in exile in this world and it cannot find here its full satisfaction. On the other hand, if we consider the matter well, we shall see that in treating His Mother thus, Jesus was doing her the greatest possible honor. For He treats souls according to their need: the weak with consolations and raptures; the strong with sufferings and trials.

All this teaches us the necessity of detachment from all things both for our sanctity and for our happiness. That is the only way of possessing all things. "In order to arrive at possessing everything, desire to possess nothing," [5] says St. John of the Cross. This is the "hundred-fold" which Christ promised His followers even in this world. His kingdom begins here on earth for those who love Him. Wherefore, if we wish to be as happy as possible in this life and to enjoy all things in God, let us endeavor first of all to renounce all and to detach ourselves from everything for love of Him.

[5] *Ascent of Mount Carmel,* Bk. I, chap. 13.

CHAPTER 11 🖎

How to Hear Mass

IT is not our intention to teach here a new practice or method of hearing Mass. Enough has already been written on that subject and there are many devotional books which contain the most appropriate exercises and prayers and which teach the manner, spirit, and intention with which Mass should be heard. What is not taught, or at least is not sufficiently stressed, is the essential and fundamental disposition with which we should attend the celebration of such a sovereign mystery and the importance of this great and sacred act of worship in our holy religion. Many of the faithful assist at Mass as mere spectators and not as actual participants in the Holy Sacrifice. They have no other disposition than that which is ordinarily understood by the expression "to hear Mass"; that is, to be present at a sacred act and to fulfill a Christian obligation and thus obtain the graces and benefits for which such acts are offered. But they are far from penetrating the deep sense and significance of this act and the disposition which it requires.

To understand this and to acquire the right disposition and attitude of spirit, it is necessary that those who assist at Mass know the role they play in it, which is not that of simple spectators or hearers, nor even of cooperators, but of veritable co-celebrants of the Holy Sacrifice. This does not mean that they can fulfill the functions proper to the priest, but that in union with him they form one spiritual body and all at the same time celebrate, sacrifice, and offer to God the Sacred Victim on our altars.

That is what St. Paul teaches when he says: "For we, being many, are one bread, one body, all that partake of one bread." [1] St. Peter calls the Christian people "a kingly priesthood," [2] meaning the collective power, so to speak, with which all the faithful offer this Holy Sacrifice and the special participation which each one has in it. In this sense we can say that they all share in the priestly dignity and ministry, and the only thing that distinguishes the priest from the rest of the faithful is his personal and exclusive faculty of consecrating, of fulfilling the functions peculiar to his ministry, and of representing the Christian people before God. However, they should all exercise these functions in intimate union of spirit, as if each one were himself offering the Mass personally.

What happens here is something similar (though much more real and effective) to what happens when a group of people gather to render homage, to present a gift, or to make a petition to a person of importance. In this case one person speaks, presents the gift, or pleads in the name of the entire group, although it is understood that they all speak and act with him as if each were doing so individually, and that is the way the person addressed understands it.

Such also should be the intention and spirit with which one assists at Mass. We have already said, and we repeat once more for emphasis, that we should assist at Mass not with the intention and disposition of merely hearing it, but of celebrating it. That is why Louis of Granada used to assert that we should not say, "We are going to hear Mass," but "We are going to celebrate Mass." In this way we would be reminded of the proper disposition for assisting at Mass.

From all that has been said, we conclude that the best way of hearing Mass is to do so with the same dispositions

[1] Cf. I Cor. 10:17.　　　　[2] Cf. I Peter 2:9.

and intentions which the priest should have, excepting those which are proper to his special ministry. As for the rest, each one should endeavor to have the same purity of heart and conscience and the same affections and intentions which he would want to have if he himself were offering the Holy Sacrifice and in this spirit make all the acts of thanksgiving, adoration, reparation, satisfaction, and petition.

In order to know what these intentions, affections, and acts should be, it is necessary to understand as thoroughly as possible what the Holy Sacrifice of the Mass is and the purpose for which it was instituted by our Lord Jesus Christ. We shall make a few observations on this subject, leaving the rest to the meditation and prayer of the reader; for these things are not learned from books nor from human teachers, but in the school of the Holy Spirit, which is prayer and meditation on the divine mysteries.

The Holy Sacrifice of the Mass is the same sacrifice as that of Calvary, renewed in an unbloody manner on our altars. We use the word "renewed" and not "repeated," because the Sacrifice of Calvary is not repeated; it is eternal, as is the priesthood of Christ, who "entered once into the Holies, having obtained eternal redemption." [3] That is why at that moment all other sacrifices ceased and the veil of the temple was rent. Thenceforth there would be only one sacrifice, which would last forever and would be renewed throughout the face of the earth in the eyes of the whole world. The Sacrifice of the Mass is, therefore, the renewal of the Sacrifice of Calvary, which is actualized each time that it is renewed. We say "actualized" because, although man's redemption was consummated on the Cross, it was yet necessary that its effects be applied to each and every man.

[3] Heb. 9:12.

Man must be personally associated in this divine work and take part in his own redemption.

This is what takes place in the Holy Sacrifice of the Mass, wherein man himself offers the sacrifice of his redemption, and this is the purpose for which it was instituted by Jesus Christ in the Cenacle. To make man, so to speak, the author of his own redemption by his participation in such a divine work is one of the most marvelous inventions of the love and wisdom of God. To this end, Jesus Christ gave Himself to man completely and put in his hands the infinite treasures of His graces and merits. "For us men and for our salvation He descended from heaven." [4] "And he delivered himself up for us." [5]

Jesus Christ is all ours and He has put in our hands all the treasures of the redemption. He is our High Priest, our Altar, and the most pure Victim whom we offer to the infinite majesty of God in reparation for our sins, in satisfaction for all our debts, in thanksgiving for His benefits, and, above all, to render Him a tribute worthy of God's honor and glory.

Jesus Christ is all ours: ours are His body and soul and divinity, His justice and sanctity, His life, passion, and death, and all His merits; ours are His thoughts and affections, His most holy intentions and dispositions, and His ardent love for His Heavenly Father. Yes, Jesus Christ is all ours, and, lest we should doubt it, He gives Himself to us in Holy Communion in order thus to become flesh of our flesh, blood of our blood, and our very life.

If we but knew the gift of God! [6] Then we would indeed know how to hear Holy Mass well, offering Christ as our own and all things in Him, with Him, and through Him;

[4] Nicene Creed.   [5] Eph. 5:2.   [6] John 4:10.

substituting His intentions, His dispositions, His merits, and all His thoughts and desires for ours. What can we poor, miserable creatures offer to God that is worthy of His infinite majesty and sanctity? But in Jesus Christ we have all things and He is all ours. We have every right to offer Him to our Heavenly Father, and in union with Him we can offer ourselves and all that we are, all that we do, all that we suffer. In this way we cooperate with and complete the work of our redemption, as St. Paul says.[7] Thus our very life becomes a sort of perpetual Mass in which we consummate and offer to God our own sacrifice, becoming victims pleasing to His divine eyes. United with Christ we form one mystical body; we become new Christs, brothers of our Savior, and adopted sons of the Heavenly Father to whom Christ is most pleasing.

Thus we shall ultimately attain the true perfection of the Christian life, which consists in substituting the life of Christ for our own by means of this intimate union. Then all our interests, desires, and intentions, all our solicitude and the whole interior movement of our life will be those of Christ, so that we shall be able to exclaim with St. Paul, "For me, to live is Christ." [8] In this way our redemption is fully consummated, liberating us from the slavery of sin and the devil and from the tyranny of self-love to transport us to the divine region of purity and sanctity, of truth and life and holy liberty, which is God. Wherefore, as long as we cannot truthfully say "For me to live is Christ," we have not yet reached the perfection of the Christian life, nor have we fully reaped all the fruits that we should from hearing Holy Mass well.

[7] Col. 1:24.   [8] Phil. 1:21.

PART III

The New Man

PART III

The New Man

CHAPTER 12 ✍

Why There Are So Few Saints

THERE are few saints, few who arrive at the perfection of the love of God, because there are few who give themselves sincerely and completely to God. Fewer still are those who, after having made this consecration, this total offering of self, steadfastly hold to it for the required length of time until it will pass from a mere intention to an actual reality. This is effected through God's acceptance of the offering, which He takes for Himself in such a way that it can never be recovered. Then does a man attain the state of sanctity, for he is no longer his own; his soul is not in his own hands, but in the hands of God, who is eternal stability.

One rightly infers from this that sanctity comprises two indispensable acts: total abandonment of one's self to God and God's acceptance. However, for the abandonment of self, it is not enough to make a half-hearted and feeble act by which we offer ourselves to God and expect Him to do the rest and give us sanctity without any effort on our part. It must be an efficacious and sincere act which springs from the inmost depths of our heart and is a true expression of our desire and will.

For this reason, once a person makes the act of total abandonment to God, it is usually necessary that he frequently renew it more or less implicitly in all his actions. Thus, although not actually expressed, every action of the soul totally consecrated to God bespeaks this sentiment: "All for Thy sake, Lord, all for Thee." In this way, every work and act, besides being a reiteration of our intention and a profession and protestation that we are persevering in our original purpose, perfects more and more our act of abandonment until it is as intense and true as possible, which is what the Lord demands for its acceptance.

That is why it is so necessary in the interior life to renew these acts, so that, repeating them many times and each time with greater vehemence, we may some day make one that is really true and perfect. The day that we do this we shall have arrived at true sanctity. Then it will hardly be necessary to repeat any act, for in such a state the will is stabilized and is itself, so to speak, a continuous act of consecration and union with God. Then love so rules and dominates us that love itself does all things. We shall not need particular acts in order to manifest it, because it will constantly manifest itself. To tell God that we love him it will suffice to say that we exist, for love will be the substance of our whole life.

Until this happens, however, we need to manifest our love for God, and the way to do it is by means of our interior and exterior acts, intensifying the efficacy of the former by fervent repetition and performing the latter with the greatest possible perfection and ardor. We should remember that what is worth much costs much, and since God is worth everything, it is necessary for man to give everything for Him: all that he is and all that he does.

At this point we meet with a conflict. Some souls seem to have the best intention and will and yet their actions are far from corresponding with their will and intentions. Should we conclude from this that they are false and deceiving? They may or may not be so. It is necessary to understand each case well in order to correct the one and not to confuse the other. It is not very difficult to verify whether a soul seeks God sincerely or seeks itself in God (or its idea of God, for if it truly sought itself in God it would be acting very wisely). The soul that seeks God alone and not self seeks the love of God in its greatest possible perfection. It seeks to please God and forget self. Since it seeks nothing for itself, such a soul does not expect God to treat it with favors and it even ignores its own perfection so far as it may be a source of complacency. He who truly loves forgets everything else and thinks only of loving.

It may happen that these souls do not perform their external actions with all possible perfection for, after all, they are limited and deficient creatures. But in spirit they always act as perfectly as possible, or at least they tend so to act if they have not as yet attained the state of perfection. We say that they tend to that when they are animated by the right spirit because the dispositions of the soul also undergo a somewhat long process of perfection. Therefore we must not be too quick to condemn their spirit or intention if in the beginning there is a mixture of spiritual or worldly self-interest in their actions and intentions. It is necessary, however, always to strive for total detachment and perfect love.

No one, no matter how imperfect he may be, should renounce the perfect love of God. Even if he deems his interior disposition to be of the worst sort and his actions still more so, he may still become a great saint, a great lover of God, if his humility equals his malice and he continually begs God to save and sanctify him, while he abandons himself to God and maintains this abandonment until God accepts it. Then he may be sure, by Christ Crucified, that God will do His part.

It is not our sins or miseries or natural defects that hinder us from becoming saints, even great saints, but our ill-will and bad disposition of heart. We are not saints because actually we do not wish to be. We know that in order to be saints we must renounce everything, give up everything, and before anything else, we must renounce ourselves. And that is what we do not want to do. We would perhaps be willing enough if we had to give to God merely external things, but to give ourselves, to give our soul, our life, our heart with all its desires, attachments, and yearnings, to renounce absolutely all self-seeking in everything, that is very difficult for us and few resolve to do it. The reason why the majority do not resolve to do it is not so much the impossibility of realizing it, for they know that with the grace of God all things are possible, but because they fear that God may take them at their word and that it will be realized. In short, they are despicable, petty creatures, ill-willed souls.

However, it is necessary to understand the facts correctly in order not to confuse natural resistance with ill-will. It is possible to be of good will and yet feel the greatest rebellion against the idea of belonging wholly to God. A person's good will and sincerity are demonstrated in the firmness with which he maintains his resolution in spite of the combats and resistances he may experience. The latter do not constitute the intention nor are they a manifestation of one's true dispositions. Feelings of rebellion against sanctity are often not only independent of, but even contrary to our will. Therefore, they need not be an obstacle to sanctity; they may even help greatly in its attainment, if the will fights to overcome them. They will then serve to strengthen and intensify the will and that is equivalent to an intensification of sanctity itself.

It must be noted that the goodness and sanctity of man reside basically in the will and in the struggle for sanctity a man always retains power over his will—his intense, absolute, and sincere desire to be good. That is why, first and above all, God asks of man his heart, his will, his absolute and sincere desire. But often a man's actions and even his interior natural dispositions are not in his power fully to control. God sees this and does not demand it of him. However, He does demand that when He shall grant a soul this power, he should be grateful and correspond with divine grace to the fullest extent of his capacity. In conclusion, what God asks of man is his good will, the sincere desire to sanctify himself and to love God with all his heart. In return, man should preserve this desire at any cost, confidently trusting that God will grant him its fruition.

Nothing should separate us from God, for He is the one thing necessary. What matter the numerous falls through human frailty or the arduous battles and conflicts we may experience? What matter if we do not even feel the desire to be good and holy or experience no attraction for God? Of far greater importance than sentiment or feeling is the sincere will which is manifested by our constancy and perseverance in the midst of spiritual dryness and bitterness. It does not matter if by nature we should be inclined to the worst evil and should experience difficulty only in doing good, for what we lack we can ask for and it will be given us.

If we lack good will, let us ask for it; if we have no desire for God or for things spiritual, let us ask for it; if we are blind and torpid in regard to things spiritual, let us beg God to awaken, illumine, and vivify us. He who infused life and intelligence into the dust of the earth can also illumine that intelligence and give new life to the heart. All our failure and disappointment in the way of sanctity are due to the fact that we do not desire it enough. From the very fact that God gives all to him who asks, and sanctity more readily than anything else, it follows that if there are few saints it is because few really want to be such.

I know that in reading this, the eternal rejoinder that saints are extraordinary beings and that in order to be one it is necessary to do extraordinary things, will occur to the mind of more than one reader. It is unfortunately true: saints *are* extraordinary beings, for there are very few. The blindness and foolishness of men have made a rarity of what ought to be the most common. It is also true that in order to be a saint one must do extraordinary things or, rather, the one extraordinary thing, which is to give oneself totally to God. How sad that this should have become extraordinary! Sadder by far than that the love of children for their parents should become extraordinary! But if anyone believes that in order to become a saint one must do those things which are considered extraordinary in the lives of the canonized saints, such as their unusual penances, raptures, visions, and so forth, then he is in error. The essence of sanctity consists in charity or the love of God. In order to attain this, no other mortification or penances or pious exercises are necessary than are needed to do the will of God and to keep ourselves united to Him.

Who has urged you to imitate the canonized saints in their penances and pious practices? The only thing that is asked of you is to equal or even surpass them, if possible, in the ardent love of God. As for the rest, leave it to God, who traces out each one's path and mission and knows why and wherefore He inspired the saints of the altars to perform those deeds you so admire. Meanwhile, you can see the great need there is for the examples of the saints in order to confound the indifference and coldness of men toward God and their own souls.

Conform yourself to your own lot, however poor and lowly it may be. Embrace it heartily as a manifestation of the will of God, and with all the more love as it is the more lowly. Be satisfied with loving God much and leave the rest

to Him. If you are a person of good will, if you seek God
sincerely and you desire to be all His, then peace be to you.
Do not fear anything; let nothing terrify or frighten you;
do not be afraid of the sacrifices or the aridities of the spiritual life; do not fear obscurities or darkness or fluctuation,
still less any danger. If God is with you, who is against you? [1]
He will guide and conduct you across all the chasms with
greater security than over firm rock. Fear nothing and let
yourself be carried in His arms without knowing whither
or how; for "in order to arrive at that which thou knowest
not, thou must go by a way that thou knowest not." [2] Do
you wish to know more than God? Let yourself be guided
without the least resistance and ask nothing. Do you not
know that it is God who is leading you? Do not, then, do
Him the injury of distrusting or doubting Him, for that is
the greatest injury a child can inflict upon so loving a Father.

On the other hand, if you are a person of ill-will, that
is, if your will is vitiated and distorted; if you worship other
gods, other idols in your heart; if you seek yourself; if you
desire your own glory, your own ambitions and satisfactions
outside of God and do not wish to renounce them but prefer
them to the God; if you do not even dare to ask God sincerely and whole-heartedly to deliver you from such slavery
and tyranny, but on the contrary, you desire to be subject
to them because their yoke seems to you sweeter than that of
Christ; in short, if you do not wish to conquer and renounce
yourself for His love, then the peace of Christ will never be
yours and you can expect nothing but constant misery. And
if in your own wisdom you think that it is not necessary to
renounce either of the two alternatives and that you will

[1] Rom. 8:31.
[2] St. John of the Cross, *Ascent of Mount Carmel,* Bk. I, chap. 13.

be able to unite the service of Christ with that of self-love,
remember that He warned us that no man can serve two
masters.[3]

Oh precious soul, if up to now you have hesitated to
give yourself completely to God, resolve upon it once and
for all! Forget self; detach yourself from all things for the
sake of God. And if you know not how or do not have the
strength to do so, ask God to help you; ask Him constantly,
persistently, and never weary of this petition. If you make
it earnestly, I assure you that God will not be able to resist
it, so much does He love those who love Him! He desires
so greatly to be loved by souls that if He were to fail to heed
you, He would cease to be what He is: Infinite Love.

In summary, sanctity comprises the total abandonment of
self to God and God's acceptance of that abandonment. God
verifies that abandonment when He accepts it, taking possession of us through love, and it is this divine love which
truly perfects and sanctifies us. It is not enough that man
make this consecration of self only once. He must repeat it as
many times as is necessary to make it true and effective,
until God shows Himself pleased with our good will. The
abandonment of self will be all the more efficacious as it is
made with a greater spirit of detachment and self-renunciation and a greater desire for union with God. God wants
nothing from us but our heart. We need not be perfect in
order to give ourselves totally to God; rather, we should
do so in order to become perfect, even though this be the
last thing to be attained, for the last thing in execution is
the first thing in intention. The reason why there are so
few saints is because there are few generous hearts who will
give themselves totally to love, for nothing is more opposed
to love than restraint and niggardliness.

[3] Matt. 6:24.

CHAPTER 13 ✍

Why Many Souls Do Not Find God

Disciple: Tell me, Master, why is it that many souls seek God all their life long and with all sincerity, making use of every available means, and despite all this, they never possess Him fully nor attain sanctity?

Master: Presenting the question as you do and assuming that they seek God with all their heart, then I can only answer that they do not find God because they seek what they already have.

Disciple: But how can that be?

Master: The same thing happens here as when a person looks for something he already has in his possession but is unaware of it. The moment he begins to look for it, it is as if he did not have it.

Disciple: Then you think that in reality such souls already possess God?

Master: Yes. The proof of it is that they seek and desire Him with all their soul and this, as St. Augustine says, they would not do if they did not already in some measure possess what they seek. That is to say, inasmuch as they love God, they already possess Him in that very love.

However, I must admit that they do not possess Him as perfectly as they could and should, precisely because they are unaware of what they have. For if they realized what they possessed, the very appreciation of the great treasure within them and the knowledge of the goodness and benignity of God toward them would cause their love to expand unto infinity, and their thoughts and sentiments would be quite different and much more pleasing to God. In short, they would live the life of union and they would be holy and perfect in charity.

That is why I believe this to be one of the most subtle deceptions of the devil and a most deplorable and harmful error, for it hinders the greatest spiritual good: the life of union in souls already disposed for it. I call it one of the most subtle deceptions of the devil because he hides beneath a mantle of humility, pretending great esteem and respect for the things of God.

"How can I, unworthy as I am, aspire to such lofty things as union with God and sanctity?" say these unwary and blind souls. "How can I who am so miserable, so frail, so rebellious and ungrateful, and who find nothing good within me, occupy myself with the things of the saints and still less take myself for one?"

Blind souls, foolish souls! Who tells you to take yourselves for saints or occupy yourselves with the extraordinary things of the saints? What you are told is simply that God loves you and that you can and should love Him as much as possible; that God is with you and awaits only that you open wide the doors of your heart so that He can fill it to overflowing. You are told to animate your faith and confidence in Him and believe, believe firmly, not because of what you are but because of what He is.

Blind souls! What do you seek in God? Do you perchance seek figments of your imagination, great things, lofty sentiments, sublime ideas, ineffable consolations and communications? Do you perchance seek your own perfection as you have imagined it: exemption from weaknesses, frailties, fears, doubts, and even from the natural sentiments of mankind? Do you seek to be always firm, invincible, and unaffected by the turmoil and confusion of human life? What do you seek in God? If you seek His love alone, you will find it in your own love. Love Him; love Him ever more and more, and in order to do this, believe in His love for you. Believe that He loves you infinitely in spite of what you are, and all else will be added to you. But it will come, not as you imagine, but as He knows and wishes. Your part is to believe, believe firmly, blindly, for you know that God is love and love does not deceive.

Disciple: From what you have said, it seems that you reduce all the means of going to God to one alone, that of loving Him. However, love seems to be more an end than a means; consequently, there must be another means that will lead us to it.

Master: Love is both a means and an end, just as *to look* is an end when taken as a synonym of *to see,* and a means when it is done as an exercise to perfect one's vision. I do not mean, of course, that there are no subordinate means for the acquisition of love, such as those which remove obstacles and dispose us to receive it. But in reference to the souls we are now considering, we presume that they have already made use of these means and are disposed to receive the fullness of love. Therefore, I say that some of the means that they make use of usually become obstacles because they no longer serve as means. Furthermore, for these souls it is the worst and greatest of obstacles, for it upsets the entire spiritual order, for it converts the means into the end or goal.

Disciple: I should like you to explain that to me more clearly, for I do not understand how that confusion takes place nor how the means can become ends.

Master: The means in themselves never become ends, but by evaluating them and using them as ends we can convert them into such. This happens frequently in the subject matter we are now treating. At least, that is what happens in actual practice, although theoretically the values may not be confused. The fact of the matter is that many souls, by dint of hearing certain means or methods highly praised as infallible in the attainment of the love of God, and by reading that a particular person attained sanctity because he did some particular thing—because he was very poor, or did a great deal of penance, or prayed much, or hardly ate or slept, or lived in perpetual solitude, or practiced some specific pious exercise—become convinced that sanctity consists in such exterior works and that if they were to do the same or something similar, they also would become saints by the mere fact of having performed such works. Actually it is not strange that they should think so, because that is the current manner of speaking: St. X was an extraordinary saint; confirming evidence of the fact is that he scourged himself so many times, he never ate meat, and he went to confession every day. All this is equivalent to saying that the saint loved God very much because he did these or similar things.

Without in the least depreciating these means, I say, paraphrasing St. Francis de Sales: What does the love of God have to do with all that? To love is to love and nothing else; it is to live for the sake of the beloved. If you love God with all your heart and if love asks it of you, you will do all that and much more, but you will never consider that your love consists in those acts. Your love will be yourself, your heart, your spirit living in God or God living in you. Therefore, with or without such practices, you will be loving Him always and everywhere, whether you are praying or sleeping, eating or working, suffering or rejoicing. It will make no difference whether you are rich or poor, honored or despised, healthy or sick, occupied or unoccupied. To him who loves God, all things serve as means of finding Him, for he sees God everywhere and in all things. God is an infinite abyss and the soul that lives submerged in Him finds Him everywhere it turns. It is at this stage that the means may become obstacles, for the soul no longer has need of them. As St. John of the Cross says, love has now become its sole exercise,[1] and if the soul engages in other things they will only hinder it in that supreme exercise. This does not mean that the soul should not do anything, but that in all its exterior works and practices, its only exercise is that of love.

Methods, methods! How badly that word sounds to the soul united to God and who has Him in the depths of its heart! It seems that such things do nothing but estrange it from Him and put a wall between the two. God is so near! The union that prevails between the two is so ineffable that everything that denotes distance or separation becomes intolerable. That is how it should be for everyone. How strange it is that man does not see God in spite of His being so evident and that he does not find Him in spite of His being everywhere. Indeed, it seems as if he employs all his energy in raising mountains to separate him from God, and when there is no longer anything to impede his union with Him, he invents other means of remaining estranged from Him, placing so many conditions and requisites for union as to make it impossible of attainment.

Disciple: But has not Christ said, "Narrow is the gate, and strait is the way that leadeth to life"?[2]

Master: Yes, and its extreme narrowness is amply demonstrated by the few who walk in it. But it is narrow, not because it exacts many difficult works as did the ancient law, but because so few are poor in spirit, humble, de-

[1] *Spiritual Canticle.*   [2] Matt. 7:14.

tached, and seek God alone. So narrow is it, in fact, that it is necessary for man to strip himself of everything, even of his attachment to means and methods and all things that are not purely God. Ah, yes! Few are those who walk in it. But it is not the fault of the way itself nor of God, but of the man who obstinately tries to walk in it and enter the narrow gate that leads to life while he is still encumbered with innumerable obstacles of his own making. It is not by acquiring but by denying, not by building castles in the air, but by destroying them, that one travels the true way.

Remember St. Teresa's analogy of the silkworm and the cocoon. The worm forms its cocoon, shuts itself up in it, and dies in order to emerge transformed. If it were to go on forever forming the cocoon, it would only succeed in making its prison all the more inescapable. Similarly, in the spiritual life, the soul forms its cocoon, which is the edifice that it builds through works, However, if that edifice is not afterward destroyed, the soul will not be able to emerge from it renewed and transformed.

Disciple: But if our spiritual edifice has to be destroyed, it would be better not to build it at all.

Master: Regarding whatever is truly *our own,* it would be better not to build it because whatever comes from ourselves is more of a hindrance than a help. However, it is not possible to have the one without the other. God wants us to do our part, even though it be imperfect, for He will come afterwards to perfect it. For that reason we do not absolutely condemn all methods and practices. On the contrary, they are indispensable at the proper time. How can we dedicate ourselves to God if we do not, in spirit at least, separate ourselves from the world? How can we give ourselves to prayer if we do not practice mortification? How can we receive grace if, being able, we do not receive the sacraments which are the channels through which it is communicated to us?

That is why I stressed the fact that we are here considering only those souls who perhaps for years and years have been doing all that and yet have not attained the end to which such practices are ordained. And even for those souls we would not prohibit such means, but simply warn them not to treat them as ends. We would have them know the purpose of such things and what to look for in them. We would have them know that the only thing necessary is love in everything. To him who loves God all things serve as means, yet none is necessary save doing His holy will, in which true love consists. This is accomplished by doing what He wishes us to do and by suffering what He wishes us to suffer.

Lastly, I would like to convince everyone that God is not as far away as we imagine Him to be, and if He is, it is because we separate ourselves from Him. If we were simple and humble we would readily find Him, for He is closer than the very air that surrounds us and He is more intimate to us than our very heart, for He is love itself, which is the life of the heart. It seems that souls deliberately refuse to believe that God loves us in order to avoid having to correspond with so much love. O Lord, how sad it is to see Thee beg love of souls and to see them disdain Thee as if Thou wert not worthy of love. O souls, if you feel the sweet call of His love do not resist Him.

CHAPTER 14

The Grandeur of Life

DO not underestimate your life nor yourself, for that would be slighting God and you would be doing yourself the greatest possible harm. God does not do things on a small scale. In Him all things are great. He has created you according to His image and likeness and has given you the power to become His child and, as such, to become God by participation in His own divinity. You will therefore be divine if you will but act divinely.

Do not mark your misery and lowliness and say: "I am a poor mortal born for the things of earth; heaven is too high for me and I am not able to mount to it." Do not underestimate yourself this way nor underestimate the work of God. For if you are part earth, you also have a spark of divinity that makes you greater than the universe.

It is not external things that make you great, but you must magnify or make great all things. The smallest thing, the most insignificant action, will become great if you will perform it with a magnanimous spirit. Before God what is great and what is small in the material order? To Him there is but one greatness in man: greatness of heart. Just as God is equally great when He creates an ant as when He creates the universe, for in each case He operates with the same power, so also the man who acts in virtue of his interior greatness elevates all things to his own greatness.

Wherefore, do not mark the external lowliness of your life; do not mark the servility and insignificance of your occupations and believe yourself bereft of the right to true greatness, which is to become like God. Did He not spend thirty years in a carpenter's shop? He did it in order to consecrate your life. Thenceforth there would be no vile or base occupations. Everything is great, everything is holy, everything is divine if we but do it in the spirit of the children of God. What does it matter, then, if my actions and occupations are lowly, if in them I accomplish the will of God and through them I ravish His heart? For nothing pleases Him more than humility of heart!

Sing, then, O soul, sing with jubilation to your God while your hands sow the seed or carve the stone, for thus you sow seeds of eternal life and fashion your eternal crown.

CHAPTER 15

Holy Pride

ALL the passions have a good as well as a bad aspect, but by reason of regarding them always from their bad aspect, we forget the good that is in them. Pride, ambition, anger, and all aversions and affections are bad only when they are disordered, that is, when they deal with unworthy objects or when they are wrongly exercised concerning good objects. Pride is evil if it is founded on one's own worth or induces us to despise others. Ambition is evil if it impels us to strive after false honors and dignities or makes us as eager for false as for true honors. Anger is evil if it moves us to act unjustly or, though justly motivated, exceeds due limits. In short, the love of evil and aversion to good are bad because that is the source from which all sins flow.

However, these same passions are good and holy when they deal with worthy objects and are rightly exercised. Even self-love, which is the root and sum of all the passions, becomes good and holy when it is founded on just motives and deals with objects worthy of man. Righteous self-love is the father of holy pride which makes us esteem ourselves and take just pride in our exalted state as children of God. It is the father of holy ambition which make us despise all things earthly as unworthy of noble and generous hearts that only the immortal, eternal, and divine can satisfy. It is the father of holy indignation which reveals itself with indomitable energy against every action or intention beneath the dignity of a being whose soul is marked with the seal of divinity.

This is what good self-love and holy pride teach us:

Do not occupy yourself with nor attribute importance to anything but the divine, the immortal, and the eternal, for that alone is worthy of you. Do not occupy yourself with anything earthly, not even to despise it.

Do not sell your holy liberty for anything, for you are worth more than the whole world. Do not make yourself a slave of men or submit to their judgments and whims, for they are not your judges nor your God. God alone is superior to you and only He can judge you.

Conduct yourself well and do all the good that you can for everyone, for you are a child of God and you should do as He did; but never expect any recompense from man. To know that one is good is the best reward.

When that which at one time gave you pleasure becomes a source of mortification to you, then you will be perfect.

He who is a slave of his passions is a slave of every tyranny.

No one can be free if he does not liberate himself from himself.

To him who has the approbation of God, the praises and vituperations of men matter little. He who has a place among the angels is little concerned about having one among men.

He who realizes his divine greatness can easily humble himself. Contempt humiliates only the contemptible. He who is proud with a holy pride recognizes no other absolute sovereignty than that of God.

Do not attempt to enslave him whom God has made free, for it is a vain attempt. He will forever sing his sublime *Magnificat:*

I am nothing

I am miserable

I am the least of men.

But God has regarded my humility and has done great things to me.

In God I am great.

In God I am free.

In God I am divine.

No; it is vain to try to enslave him whom God has made free. His heart is free, his soul is free, and his spirit is free, for they are slaves of love and of truth.

Be, therefore, proud with a holy pride and do not taint your dignity or sell your sovereignty for all the world.

CHAPTER 16

Man's Supernatural Perfection

THE fundamental doctrine of all evangelical and apostolic teaching on the supernatural perfection of man is that it consists in a new life, a new being, which man can attain only by means of a transformation into a new man. You must "be born again," [1] said our divine Savior to Nicodemus, and then He added, "unless a man be born again of water and the Holy Ghost, he cannot enter into the kingdom of God." [2] St. Paul also in his epistles frequently insists on this idea, presenting it in different ways. According to him, it is necessary that the man of sin, the old Adam, be destroyed in us in order that the new man, or new Adam created according to God in justice and holiness, be reborn in Jesus Christ. [3] He presents this same idea with even greater force and emphasis when, in order to destroy the false idea the Jews had concerning perfection and sanctity, he says peremptorily, "In Christ Jesus neither circumcision availeth anything, nor uncircumcision, but a new creature." [4] We already know that circumcision and uncircumcision are here taken as synonyms of Judaism and paganism, or of the positive and natural law.

According to St. Paul all this of itself is of no value whatever in the spiritual order. It is as if he were to say: "If we disregard the new creature, the transformation into the new man created according to God in justice and holiness, all that we of ourselves can do, all the justice and perfec-

[1] John 3:3.   [2] John 3:5.   [3] Eph. 4:24.
[4] Gal. 6:15.

108

tion which we can attain by our own power, is of no value whatever." As a matter of fact, if the law—and more so the positive than the natural law—has any value whatever, it is in relation to its end, which is the perfection of man. Wherefore, if we disregard the latter, it has no value whatever, for of itself the law is only a means.

This reversal of values was precisely the great error of the Jews and the cause of all their other errors and misconceptions, inasmuch as it was an inversion of values which led them to give to the means the importance of the end. Perfection for them consisted in the exact observance of the smallest details of the law and of the rites and exterior exercises of worship, without concerning themselves about the interior perfection of man or the end to which such precepts and practices were ordained. Man would be perfect if he observed them, even though interiorly he should be a sepulcher of abominations.

The errors and evils to which this gave rise were amply manifested in the life of the Savior when the Jews, in order to revenge themselves, committed the most atrocious injustices and crimes, thus clearly proving how disastrous was the error from which they proceeded. The fact is that this error occasions spiritual pride, which is the worst kind of pride and a most difficult evil to cure or remedy. Thus we see the constant battle that Jesus Christ had to sustain during His life against the Pharisees. So manifest was this, in fact, that it seemed as though He had come for nothing else but to wage war against the error of these men. And we see also the implacable war—the greatest and most obstinate possible—which they waged against the preaching of the gospel. How clearly they manifested the absolute opposition of their spirit to the gospel.

Nothing more revealing or more grievous could be said

against this Jewish error. But with all that, this error has not yet disappeared, and still less the pharisaic spirit. The strangest thing of all is that in many souls it exists in conjunction with the evangelical doctrine. If we were to ask many Christians today what religion is and what its purpose is, it would not be difficult to find that pharisaic spirit in their answers. Certainly there would be very few who would know that religion has no other end than to sanctify us and to perfect us through our union with God; that the object of its ceremonies and sacraments is to infuse into us the divine sap of grace which will transform us and make new men of us. How many are there who, on receiving Holy Communion, consider the fact that they are receiving the Bread of life, the divine ferment which invades our nature and transforms it, making us other Christs? How many think about sanctifying themselves, of amending their lives, or of becoming perfect when they practice their religion? The most that the generality of Christians aspire to is to save themselves, to escape hell, to attain heaven, and to be delivered from the evils of this world or the punishments of God.

All this is commendable as the beginning of justification, but if a man does not pass beyond that, if he considers religion as a contract by which God should give him heaven in payment for his services, if he cultivates within himself the mercenary spirit of advancing his own interests, be they spiritual or otherwise, he runs the risk of losing everything and of making himself the most abominable of men. First and above all we must seek the kingdom of God and its justice and everything else will be added unto us.[5] Before all things we must seek God, purely and unselfishly, and not merely His gifts, for that is abhorrent to Him.

[5] Matt. 6:33.

But it is not only the generality of Christians who some-times fall into this error. Even persons dedicated to piety, religious themselves and those who concern themselves with the interior life, are guilty of it more frequently than one would suppose. And in their case the evil is much worse, as is always true in the corruption of the best. There are, in fact, some religious to whom the very exercise of the spiritual life has given occasion of becoming more imper-fect and perhaps more abhorrent to God, precisely because it has been for them a source of pride and self-love. Such souls become incorrigible. Because they have dedicated themselves to that life they think they know it all and they have nothing more to learn. But they have gone completely astray because instead of seeking God in their religious life they seek themselves; they feed their spiritual egotism, serv-ing God selfishly and not with the intention of loving Him sincerely. Nothing is more contrary to love than selfishness, in whatever order it may be.

However, not all the persons about whom we speak are equally reprehensible. There are sincere souls of good will who seek God earnestly and endeavor to attain true per-fection but fail to do so because they do not understand clearly in what it really consists. They have been influenced by the popular concept of perfection which makes it con-sist principally in exterior works, in the subjection of the passions, or in the practice of the moral virtues, all of which elements constitute the dispositive part of supernatural perfection.

These souls especially must be made to see that perfec-tion consists in something much higher, so that they will dilate and enlarge their heart and aspire to that divine per-fection which will fill it to overflowing. They should realize that the moral virtues and all the other meritorious acts that man can practice are merely dispositions for receiving the new life which gives true perfection. Then when they hear that a saint was very great because he did this or that extraordinary thing, they will not believe that that was the reason for his sanctity, but merely a sign of his great disposition for it or an effect of sanctity already acquired. They will realize that in itself sanctity is quite distinct from all exterior works.

We have already defined sanctity in the words of St. Paul: sanctity or supernatural perfection consists in nothing else but the new creature and it is this creature who performs works of perfection according to God. So it must be, for perfection is synonymous with the integrity of a being according to its nature. As the philosophers say, that being is perfect to which nothing is lacking or excessive.

This idea of perfection coincides perfectly with that which makes perfection depend upon the relation of a being with its end. A machine is considered perfect when it fulfills its end perfectly; for a thing is not said to be perfect except so far as it attains its proper end. And, inasmuch as God is man's supernatural end, man must receive a new, divine being, without which he will not attain his end. His perfection, therefore, will consist in this new being and if it is perfect, his works will be perfect also.

These basic concepts about perfection in general apply to man's supernatural perfection and, as we shall see, they are laden with truths of the highest significance. Man is a being elevated to the supernatural order and, in accordance with this mode of being, he can acquire supernatural perfection; that is to say, the plenitude of being in that order.

Primarily and essentially, therefore, man's perfection is in *being* and from there it extends to his actions. This is the evangelical concept of perfection. "A good tree cannot bring forth evil fruit, neither can an evil tree bring forth good fruit." [6] We insist so much on the true concept of supernatural perfection because we judge it to be of primary importance for the spiritual life. Then sincere souls who seek it will know what to strive for and what spirit should animate them in the service of God. Moreover, they will not content themselves with that perfection which goes no further than what they can conceive and comprehend and which consists in practically nothing more than the subordination of their passions to reason and the practice of the virtues according to their ability. Instead, they will aspire to something infinitely greater.

It is therefore necessary for them to know that the paths upon which they walk do not end where they imagine, but where God has determined, and that is something infinitely better, more exalted, and more wonderful than they can conceive. And if they are to serve God, they must think about and hope for things worthy of God, things which are beyond all feeling or understanding. That is why they must give wings to their aspirations and dilate their hearts unto infinity, so that they will not content themselves with small, petty things nor allow such to detain them in their flight or limit their yearnings for love and detachment. Souls should realize that the goal of their interior life is not the attainment of a perfection such as they imagine, a perfection conceived solely according to human reason, even under the principles of religion; neither is it a perfection which consists in holding the passions under control and practicing the virtues within their spiritual capacity. All this means a great deal as a disposition to perfection, but if separated from its source it has no substantial,

[6] Matt. 7:18.

supernatural value whatever. What has value before God
is the *new creature*. This new creature is formed within
them during their period of purification in the interior
life, and the day will come when it will be born in their soul
and they will comprehend all its mysteries and they will
be truly perfect, for the old man, the old Adam, will have
disappeared and will have been replaced by the new, the
godlike Adam.

As long as the *homo peccati*, the man of sin, remains and
is not destroyed within us, it is impossible to be perfect,
for everything we do will be more or less infected with the
poison of sin. This poison will find its way even into spiritual things and our works will be imperfect, distorted, for
even in them we shall seek ourselves and not God alone. We
shall be full of darkness with regard to divine things and
we shall not be able to perform perfect works as befits children of God. Who can determine the measure of sanctity
and purity that this requires? And who but the Spirit of
God can communicate them to us? It is foolishness, if not
blasphemy, to think that a mere creature can perform works
worthy of the infinite sanctity of God. He alone can perform them within us. Operation follows being and, therefore, to perform divine works we must be divinized.

The supernaturally enlightened soul should conclude
from all this that inasmuch as true perfection is beyond
anything it can imagine or conceive (for it consists in being
transformed into a new creature which performs holy and
perfect works pleasing to God), it should not be content
with attaining any preconceived perfection, but an infinitely superior one which is designed by God. It should
understand that any other perfection is nothing more than
a disposition and a means of arriving at true perfection.
To this true perfection the soul should direct its most fer-

vent longings, ardently begging God for it and abandon-
ing itself to Him whole-heartedly. Through this vehement
desire for true perfection wherein is contained sanctity
and redemption, the soul will become more solicitous about
practicing the other perfection which is within its reach,
for God has disposed that we shall not attain the one without the other.

Thus, although true perfection is not a fruit of our efforts
nor even, in a certain sense, of our merits, but of the grace
of God and an effect of His love, nevertheless it is never conferred save on those who are properly prepared and disposed and who, with the help of divine grace, have done
their part to the best of their ability.

Let us do what falls to us and hope with all confidence,
with absolute and blind confidence, that God will do His
part and effect in our souls that incomparable work of love.
He who hopes much, attains much.

CHAPTER 17 ✍

How Love Perfects Us

ST. PAUL says that charity is the bond of perfection.[1] He
does not say that it is integral perfection itself, for the
latter, as we have seen, consists specifically in the plenitude
of being. Hence, although charity and perfection are at
times used interchangeably, they nevertheless differ as cause
and effect. Charity is the cause of our perfection precisely
because it is the bond which unites us to God, who is our

[1] Col. 3:14.

last end and from whom we obtain that plenitude of supernatural being in which our perfection consists. This is why the word "bond" is so exquisitely apt when applied to charity.

The above doctrine refers to consummated perfection, however, and in order to arrive at this supreme degree we must pass through others of an inferior order which also are effects of charity. Both in the natural and supernatural order love is nothing other than a tendency of the being toward its perfection or plenitude. This tendency gives rise to two movements within man: one of expansion and one of attraction. By the first, man is impelled to diffuse his good to other beings, and by the second he tends to attract them to himself. Both movements proceed from the same source or root, the irresistible impulse of his being toward its perfection and plenitude.

So manifest is this in the natural order that some materialistic or sensualistic psychologists have attempted to place the origin of all man's vital manifestations in his instinctive tendency toward procreation. This error proceeds from the fact that these psychologists have studied life from the viewpoint of their personal sentiments and sensations which, being of such an inferior order, have caused them to reverse the truth of the matter and subordinate the superior to the inferior.

But in spite of the error of such a doctrine, it confirms what we have said, namely, that in the natural order man tends toward an expansion of himself in all the phases of natural life, as much in the domain of the senses as in those of the will and of the intellect. Moreover, to this movement of expansion corresponds that of attraction or union by which he tends to appropriate to himself whatever falls within his radius of expansion. From this proceeds all vital

movement, for even in the natural order all things are ordained to attain their perfection or the plenitude of their
being.

Similarly in the supernatural order, love is the origin and
cause of perfection because it is the principle of all supernatural movement. Like natural love, charity also has two
movements: one of expansion and another of attraction.
By the first, man tends to diffuse himself, so to speak, in
God and by the second, to attract God to himself and to
possess Him. The first of these actions is what St. Thomas
calls the love of friendship and thus charity establishes true
friendship between God and man.

However, as directed to God, the operations of love are
manifested in different ways, according as they refer to Him
as a distant or absent good or as a present good possessed
by the lover. When love is directed to God as a good which
is already possessed, it causes joy, delectation, and repose in
the Beloved, and in this it finds its perfection. Under this
aspect love is the bond of perfection. But when love is directed to God as an absent good, it tends to Him by means
of self-denial and detachment, for God is an infinite Being and in order to possess Him and unite himself to Him,
man must also become in some way infinite. To do this,
he must despoil himself of his finite characteristics. To love
God, man must die to self and make room for God. That
is why we are taught that the way to perfection is a con-
tinual denial of self for the love of God. In this way the
love of God perfects us, for it makes us die to all things in
order to possess the God whom we seek.

By way of summary we can say that charity effects our
supernatural perfection because it gives us God, who is the
plenitude of our being. We call it "supernatural" perfection in order to make it clear that this perfection is not

like natural perfection, which is the development of our
own personality and largely the result of our own efforts.
In the supernatural order it is not our own but a divine
being that is developed. This new being is communicated
to us through grace, which grows and increases in the measure that our capacity increases to receive it more perfectly.
Ultimately grace and charity transform man into that new
creature of which St. Paul speaks and which is the product
of man's union with God.

In the spiritual life, the new creature or new man is
generated through man's union with God in love. We say
that it is a union of love in order to eliminate beforehand
all other kinds of union that could be effected. It is not,
therefore, an essential or substantial or personal union in
which the natures or persons are fused, but it is a union of
divine love. Moreover, since the love is divine, the union
which it effects is the most intimate that one can conceive
short of the hypostatic union. It is much superior to the
unions which take place between created things and is so
intimate as to be totally ineffable. We cannot comprehend
it but we can describe its effects.

In this union of love man possesses God and God communicates to man His own divine life so far as it can be
shared by a creature. At the same time, man's natural being
undergoes the transformation necessary to make it capable
of participation in the divine life. Hence, to study the new
creature or new man we must consider the divine life in
itself and man's life as it is modified and transformed by
the divine. We must analyze the life of God, so far as that
is possible, in order to understand what that life will be
in man and the effects which it produces. God's life is His
very being; in itself, it is comprehensible to God alone.
However, we have some notions about Him through His

manifestations, for these reveal to us His properties or attributes which enable us to learn something of the nature of His inner life.

CHAPTER 18

The Love of God in Man

ALL the manifestations of the divine life can be comprised under the notion of God's love, for in God they are all one and the same thing. For our purposes, however, we shall consider them separately in order to understand better the nature of that life and its effects.

For a clearer understanding, we must observe that when it is said that God lives in the saint or that the saint possesses the divine life, we should not think of the creature as an inanimate subject in which God resides or lives and executes operations distinct from those of the saint. God lives in the saint because, being united to him, He animates his soul, his faculties, and his operations with His own life. God, so to speak, unfolds His vital activity in the life of the saint and the latter participates in this divine motion so far as he cooperates with God by his own vital actions. Thus God loves Himself, knows Himself, glorifies Himself, and rejoices in the soul of the saint and the latter, by participation, loves God with God's own love, knows Him with His light, rejoices in Him and glorifies Him with the same joy and glory with which God rejoices and glorifies Himself within Himself.

The most practical procedure on this subject would be

to dispel certain errors on the concept of the love of God, for it is frequently confused with human love or sensible love. Even if considered as an affection or sentiment of a most pure and lofty type, it would yet be merely human love, whereas the true love of God is of a much superior order.

Human love does not produce anything in the beloved nor is it anything more than a transitory act in the lover. Divine love, however, has very different effects and qualities, for it engenders in the soul a stability which is the terminus and product of God's love. In order to understand this it is sufficient to point out that charity is a reciprocal love between God and the creature, a true love of friendship, as St. Thomas teaches. Now, love of friendship tends to unite the friends in a close bond through the total giving of each to the other. Hence it is said that a true friend is another self. The mutual giving of self between God and the soul effects so intimate a union that God possesses the soul and the soul possesses God, not merely in an external, superficial manner which affects only external acts or manifestations, as is the case with creatures, but in the vital relationship of being to being and substance to substance. For when God loves the soul He desires for it all supernatural good, which is Himself in His inner life. And since God's love is efficacious and produces in the beloved all the good which He desires for it, the soul enjoys a participation in the very life of God and a communication of His own divine being. God's love produces a new divine being and a new divine life whereby the soul no longer lives a merely natural life but God lives in it.

Similarly, when the soul loves God supernaturally, it gives itself completely to Him. God then possesses it not merely externally, through its operations, but in its very core and substance, so to speak. The soul is, as it were, dispossessed of its own being and it receives as a recompense the divine substance and being which are then communicated to it by participation. Hence divine love is not merely an act of the soul which tends toward God, but one which enables the soul to possess God Himself in an ineffable manner. That is why some call this a substantial union; not in the sense that one substance is transformed into another or that from the union of the two a completely new substance is formed, but in the sense that God touches the very substance of the soul by possessing it through grace (for grace is received in the substance of the soul), and the soul touches the very substance of God in possessing Him through love. Charity, as St. Thomas teaches, has God Himself as its object and not His extrinsic manifestations.

Such is the essence of the love of God; such is true charity. Everything else is secondary and accidental. Moreover, charity can exist in a soul, and in fact usually does exist, without any sensible manifestations. However, it is true that by a reflexive consideration on his union and transformation through charity, the holy soul may enjoy an awareness of union and experience a sensible love. But he is well aware that these feelings are accidental and transitory and that what constitutes his love is something far beyond any natural feeling and understanding. What he will not be able to avoid experiencing, save for passing moments of spiritual darkness, is the complete transformation which love has wrought within him. This transformation is manifested chiefly by the awareness of a remarkable death to self and to all things and an ineffable life hidden in God, which he cannot explain.

It is the ecstasy of love, the ecstasy of the soul's own submersion in the divine. For this reason the saint constantly feels lost to self and submerged in God. He is lost to self because he no longer has the passions and interests which naturally serve man as guides; more precisely, they no longer rule or govern him; they do not reign within him. "Say that I am lost," [1] he exclaims with St. John of the Cross, when others wonder at seeing him forsake the ordinary human paths. And truly, he does feel lost, for he can no longer see the paths that lead to God; he is so submerged in God that he finds Him everywhere and seldom if ever emerges from that infinite abyss of divinity.

The saint, then, truly feels his love for God, but in an ineffable and supernatural way. He feels it without any feeling, for it is above all sense. He will not say that he loves, but that he is love, for he is transformed and dissolved in love. Love absorbs his whole interior life; it is his one and only spiritual exercise. Within his soul, as the mystical doctors teach and as those who have arrived at this degree of union know by experience, is reproduced the mystery of the Blessed Trinity, or rather, the intimate life of the three divine Persons. Within the soul, the Father, knowing Himself, begets the eternal Word, His only Begotten Son; then the Father and Son, loving each other in the mutual union and communication of their nature, produce the Holy Spirit, eternal and uncreated Love who is equal to them in all things. However, these most intimate and sublime operations of the soul in God cannot and should not be measured by our imagination or reason. We cannot grasp such things and in attempting to give them a concrete, definite form, we falsify them completely.

The soul knows the mysteries of the divine life by an experimental knowledge, for they are reproduced within

[1] *Spiritual Canticle.*

it. It feels that it lives in an infinite abyss which is all light and love—light inaccessible and love incomprehensible. A light of the highest wisdom comes to the soul from a profound obscurity or night and is at once both light and darkness to the soul. "The darkness thereof, and the light thereof are alike." [2] An incomprehensible love springs from an absolute emptiness or death of love.

This phenomenon gives rise to those mystical paradoxes and that strange language which so startle the worldly-minded and yet are natural and common-place to initiated souls. The reason for this is that two beings or two lives of opposite qualities are fused, so to speak, in the saint: the one finite and the other infinite. The union of the two requires that the finite lose its limited form and receive an infinite one, and since this is equivalent to a death or destruction, the saint experiences both death and life, light and darkness, love and loneliness, allness and nothingness in all his spiritual operations.

Another reason for this experience is that the object of all the operations of the spiritual faculties of man, both in the order of the true and in the order of the good, is determined by some form or species, and if this determination or specification is removed, the faculties are left absolutely empty and vacuous. But at the same time they share in the divine plenitude which resides in the soul, and hence arise those strange and seemingly contradictory feelings and sentiments.

Of course, this is only a partial explanation of the ordinary mystical phenomena. However, the mystical phenomena will never be properly explained. They will always remain the greatest mystery of the interior life, a mystery

[2] Ps. 138:12.

which we shall know clearly only in heaven, where we shall see God face to face and it will be manifested to us what we are now and what is our life hidden in Him.

CHAPTER 19 ✍

The Sanctity of the New Man

IN the same way that we have considered the love of God in the new man we should also consider his sanctity: as a participation in the sanctity of God. God's sanctity, of course, is not distinct from his nature. God is essentially holy; He is holiness itself. However, God's holiness does not signify what we commonly understand by the terms "holy" and "sanctity." We call a person holy who does not commit sin and who complies with the whole law, but God is impeccable and has no law with which to comply, for He is His own law.

Nevertheless, there is a notion of sanctity which enables us to approach the true concept of the sanctity of God. According to an accepted meaning, "holy" or "saintly" signifies the same as separated from the earth. In this sense it can be applied to God, signifying that He is infinitely elevated and removed from everything that the human mind can conceive, not only from material things and from all creation but from everything He could possibly create. Philosophically, it could be stated as God's necessary transcendence over all created or creatable beings. For that reason the holy of holies in the temple was considered so sacred a place that no man could approach it, and in heaven the seraphim prostrate themselves as they sing, "Holy, Holy, Holy," signifying that God is the mystery of mysteries, the infinitely hidden, incomprehensible, and ineffable One, before whom all creation should bow in adoration.

This same sanctity or holiness of God, as it abides in man, is what constitutes and causes man's true sanctity. The reason for this is that divine sanctity, like the other divine attributes, is man's by participation, and is the cause of man's sanctity. In the first place, man's spirit, when united to the divine, is infinitely removed from everything earthly and from every creature. He lives, as it were, in ecstasy, in the regions of the ineffable, contemplating things of which it is not given to man to speak. Mute and rapt in perpetual adoration, he becomes a veritable holy of holies and bears within himself the nameless Spirit of God. The saint lives in perpetual adoration.

From this also proceeds the notion of man's sanctity as synonymous with purity and sinlessness. Sin causes a stain in the spirit of man due to his adhesion to all that is not God. Therefore, as long as he remains united to God, he will be infinitely removed from all that could defile him and he will possess spotless purity.

Consequently, in order to attain sanctity it is first necessary to pass through a period of purification which carries the soul through all the stages of self-denial and detachment and disposes it to receive the sanctity of God. The purification begins, logically, with the lowest degrees or those which pertain to the flesh and the senses. Thus we call chastity, purity, although it is only the first degree of man's purification. In its full significance, purity is that which detaches us from all that is not God. However, if we regard it only in terms of separation and detachment, it becomes a merely negative purity. God Himself is positive and infinite purity. Actually, the two are never separated because to each degree of purification or detachment there corresponds another degree of deification, for every void which purification leaves in the soul of man is immediately filled by the divine Spirit.

For the purposes of explanation all this is considered as successive, but in reality it is not so. The selfsame communication of the divine Spirit causes the soul's purification while it destroys all pre-existing forms in order to infuse its own. It is He, therefore, who causes the sanctity of man, both as regards its disposition as well as its effects; hence He is called the sanctifying Spirit. This does not mean that sanctity is exclusively God's work in the sense that it does not require man's corresponding action. Man must contribute and use whatever God has bestowed on him; that is to say, his liberty and all the faculties under his control. Yet this is not the efficient cause of man's sanctity, but only a dispositive cause.

Here we have the reason for all the means used to attain sanctity: self-denial, recollection, silence, prayer, etc. These practices enable us to cooperate with the divine action which tends to separate us from everything and unite us to God, to make us saints. We shall become such when the soul receives as its own that Being who is infinite and is the very essence of sanctity.

To recapitulate, the divine life in man, the indwelling of God in man, or man's union with God (these and similar expressions are equivalent and differ only so far as they refer to some aspect of the union between God and man) is the cause of man's sanctity. First, it destroys in man all limited forms and disposes him to receive the Being who has no form. Secondly, it communicates to him that Being who is the very essence of sanctity because He is limitless and infinite and eminently surpasses all finite being. Thirdly, it bestows on man those dispositions which he should have toward God, and especially the spirit of adoration which is the proper attitude of the creature toward the Creator.

Such are the principal effects of the indwelling of God in man, considering God from the aspect of His sanctity. However, from these same effects proceed other qualities which complete man's sanctity. The effects enumerated above refer principally to the sanctification of man's *being;* the latter pertain more particularly to his *actions.* Fundamentally, of course, the two are identical, since a creature's actions follow in accordance with his being.

In the first place, true humility is engendered. Humility signifies an awareness and knowledge of one's own nothingness and of the allness of God. Humility is truth; better still, it is that disposition of soul which establishes man in truth.

There is a good reason why humility should be singled out as a special effect of man's participation in the sanctity of God. Man knows and realizes the infinite distance that separates him from God with regard to their respective natures, for although they are united under the bond of love, neither of them loses his proper nature. The distance is all the more evident since the Fall. Man's nature can be fully restored spiritually by reason of the divine union, but the same is not true with regard to its physical part which retains many of the penal effects of original sin, though the sin itself may have disappeared completely.

We know that God, in His infinite wisdom, leaves many of these effects in chosen souls for their greater merit and glory. St. Thomas explains that although the redemption destroys all sin in man, it does not destroy all the consequences of sin during this life and this is for man's greater good. Accordingly, true saints may experience all the miseries of human nature except that of sin, but even if they do not actually experience sin, they realize that the reason why they do not do so is because of the divine sanctity that resides within them. Left to itself, their wounded nature could lead them to commit every sin and excess imaginable.

An experimental knowledge of the infinite sanctity of God within them and of their own misery and natural corruption keeps the saints humble. Moreover, this disposition of soul, derived from that light which establishes them in truth, is the root and source of all their sanctity, inasmuch as it makes them capable of possessing God. It also makes them comply with all the demands of justice to God, to man, and to themselves. To God, because they return all glory to Him by acknowledging Him as the sole source of all good, by serving Him as He should be served, as absolute Lord and Sovereign of all, and by rendering Him true worship with all their mind, all their heart, and all their will. They also practice justice to their fellow men and themselves because he who is truly humble claims no other right for himself than that of being good and of doing good to all.

Another effect of the divine sanctity in man is the alienation from every created thing so that he rises above the inferior part of his nature and tends to separate himself from all that is temporal, to unite himself to the immortal and eternal. That is why the saints are almost constantly recollected and cannot interest themselves in the innumerable trifles which absorb the attention of other men. Although they live in the world and are occupied with mundane affairs, although their senses perceive all the movements of the exterior world, and although their passions may momentarily become agitated, none of these things can absorb or enslave them. All these things vanish into thin air, for there is nothing to sustain them or give them life. That is why the passions of the saints seem to be dead or asleep and incapable of disturbing their peace and interior harmony. They may succeed in disquieting these holy souls for a while, but they can never destroy interior peace altogether. The saints dwell in the secure refuge and protection of the Most High where evil and the scourge of sin do not touch them.

CHAPTER 20 ✍

Perfection and Goodness

ALTHOUGH perfection and goodness are basically the same thing, they differ considerably according to the popular acceptation of the terms, as may be seen by analyzing the common notions concerning the perfect man and the good man. The perfect man is the man without defect. He observes every detail of the law, fulfills his obligations to the letter, and regulates all his thoughts, feelings, words, and actions according to the dictates of an upright and inflexible conscience. According to this meaning, perfection is a quality which constitutes man's personal moral integrity; it bespeaks a state of the subject himself wherein everything is subordinated to his individual perfection. Goodness, on the other hand, implies a relationship with others. Thus the good man is understood as equivalent to the unselfish, generous, and detached man; the man who, in his exterior works, looks not so much to his own good as to that of his neighbor. His personal goodness consists in doing good to others.

In spite of these apparent distinctions, goodness does not differ from perfection, except that it is a higher grade of perfection; for in order to be truly good one must first be perfect. Goodness as commonly understood is an effect of the plenitude of good which naturally tends to diffuse itself. Wherefore, goodness presupposes a greater perfection or a more elevated kind of perfection. It could perhaps be said that perfection as defined above is the perfection of justice, while perfect goodness is the perfection of charity or love.

It is not necessary to enlarge on these concepts, for one can form a clear idea of what the terms signify by reflecting on the commonly accepted meaning of perfection and goodness. It suffices for our purposes to touch briefly on their nature and differences so that we may determine the kind of perfection that Christ teaches in the gospel and to which good souls should aspire.

We do this because it is frequently observed that many souls decline in their spiritual life or stray from the way of perfection because they do not understand clearly in what it consists. It is not unusual to find souls of good will, even generous and heroic souls, who do not attain true perfection because of their limited and inaccurate knowledge. For such souls the ideal of perfection would be never to commit any fault whatever, to fulfill to the letter all their resolutions and plans concerning the spiritual life, and to maintain such perfect control over their passions and all internal movements that not even the slightest contrary thought or feeling would ever be able to disturb their peace.

Without a doubt, this kind of perfection is very good and

holy, but it is not the highest perfection. Moreover, God is not wont to confer a perfection of this kind, absolutely devoid of all defect and weakness, because it can readily become the occasion of pride and self-complacency, since it subordinates everything to the individual. But even if He should grant it, that would not mean that the person had attained the perfection which Christ teaches us in the gospel, the perfection of goodness which He proposed to His disciples when He said: "Unless your justice abound more than that of the Scribes and Pharisees, you shall not enter into the kingdom of heaven. If you love them that love you, what reward shall you have? do not also the publicans do this? But I say to you: Love your enemies, do good to them that hate you: and pray for them that persecute and calumniate you. And if a man will contend with you in judgment and take away your coat, let go your cloak also unto him. If one strike you on your right cheek, turn to him also the other." [1]

This is the code of goodness and the sublime norm of perfection to which Christ invites us and He gives us as a model His own Father, "who maketh his sun rise upon the good, and bad, and raineth upon the just and the unjust." [2] From what has been said it is evident that the perfection which Christ teaches and demands of us is the perfection of goodness to which we have already referred. Furthermore, this perfection does not exclude that other perfection which consists in maintaining perfect emotional equilibrium, but it presupposes it and raises it to a superior level. For in order to practice perfection to such a sublime degree, it is first necessary to die to self and all the interests of self-love and to possess the virtues, especially humility and charity, in all their fullness.

[1] Matt. 5:20–46, *passim.*   [2] Matt. 5:45.

But how are these virtues acquired? Generally they are acquired in a way contrary to what man imagines. Man thinks that such virtues, and all perfection and sanctity, must be the fruit of his own efforts and industry. Hence, when he begins the work of his spiritual perfection he concentrates all his efforts on the attainment of a kind of impeccability in which, according to his way of thinking, the highest perfection consists. However absolute impeccability is never attained and the perfection which God grants is not the fruit of man's efforts, but of divine grace. Everything depends on divine grace, although it is true that the latter is granted only to him who is properly disposed for it.

It is sometimes necessary that a man spend all his efforts in the work of his perfection before he realizes his incapacity to attain it by himself. Then he learns to ask and hope for it from God. So it is that true humility is born of the failure of human efforts to attain perfection, and from the knowledge and awareness of one's own misery are born mercy and compassion. A man is then imbued with the spirit of humility and meekness; he can no longer condemn anyone, but he shows compassion and pardon. His heart overflows with compassion for others because he realizes how much compassion God exercises in his behalf. He learns to distrust self and to trust in God and realizes from his own experience that all good comes from God, even the least good thought.

Finally, he learns the great secret of the interior life: how to transform one's defects and imperfections into goodness and perfection. It is a divine celestial alchemy whereby the clay of human misery is converted into the gold of charity. The poorer one sees himself to be, the more is he inclined to humble himself before God and to hope for all things from that infinite goodness who delights to communicate Himself to the weak and lowly. Hence, the more profoundly a man realizes his nothingness and misery, the more is he filled with the goodness and charity of God. The divine goodness which fills the human heart to overflowing is what makes man truly good and perfect, as the heavenly Father is good and perfect.

From all this we deduce a very practical and profitable conclusion for souls who aspire to perfection and one which is highly recommended by the masters of the spiritual life; namely, not to become discouraged on account of failures and falls along the way of perfection, but to reap still greater profit and perfection from them. Without a doubt, if souls knew the high designs which God has in permitting those failures or falls that so humiliate and torture them, they would never yield to discouragement; they would even consider themselves fortunate to engage in a conflict so pleasing to God. As a philosopher once said, "Man's struggle for the sake of justice is a spectacle worthy of God." Moreover, when failures and difficulties are accepted with humility of heart, they make man truly good; that is, they engender in the human heart true love of God and neighbor, that divine charity which is the bond of perfection.

CHAPTER 21 🖎

Unity and Diversity of Spirits

THE word "spirit," as applied to the supernatural order, is generally understood in two ways: to signify a personal being, such as God, the angels, or the devil, or to signify their action or influence on the soul of man. In the second sense we speak of a diabolical spirit, a spirit of peace, or a spirit of contradiction. Treating of the unity and diversity of spirits, we use the word in its second meaning. Furthermore, we refer only to the good spirit and the various effects which its action produces in the spirit of man.

The unity and diversity of spirits is the first phenomenon that one observes when studying the various manifestations of the spiritual life in souls. For proof of this it is sufficient to read the lives of the saints. We shall not find any two the same. Each one manifests a different aspect of sanctity; each one presents a spiritual portrait which does not resemble any other. One can truthfully say that just as in the physical order there are not two men whose features are identical, so in the supernatural order there are no two souls whose spiritual characteristics are the same in every way. Rather, the differences are at times so marked that if one did not bear in mind the identity of the interior spirit that animates them, he would believe that they were informed and moved by truly distinct spirits. What greater difference can there be than that which exists between the lives of the apostles and the lives of the fathers of the desert? What greater diversity of spiritual characteristics than those displayed by St. Bruno and St. Francis de Sales, St.

Joan of Arc and St. Therese, St. Stephen of Hungary and St. Francis of Assisi?

Moreover, these diverse manifestations of the one spirit are observed not only in different saints but also in one and the same saint, as much in his exterior as in his interior life. Thus we see that St. Bernard, enchanted with the delights of the cloister and the tranquillity of the monastic cell, went forth into the world to preach the crusades and recruit armies for the conquest of the Holy Land. We see that St. Teresa of Avila, no less enamored of the retirement of the cloister and a confirmed enemy of worldly affairs, was entangled in all the details of reforms and foundations, even to the point of being involved in controversies and lawsuits which she so much abhorred and in the affairs of her relatives from whom she had so often fled.

A diversity of manifestations can also be observed in the interior life of the saints as they passed through various stages or phases in the course of their sanctification. In all of them a progressive change or transformation can be observed in their manner of perceiving and experiencing the things of God and in their mode of operation in the supernatural order. "When I was a child," writes St. Paul, "I spoke as a child, I understood as a child, I thought as a child. But when I became a man, I put away the things of a child." [1] The characteristic note of this transformation is a tendency to ever greater unity and simplicity in all the external manifestations of their interior life. Thus, in the first stages holy souls are intent upon finding ways and means of perfection and upon practicing numerous exercises ordained to that end. Gradually, however, they tend to simplify all this until eventually they are intent solely upon the accomplishment of God's will, doing and suffer-

[1] Cf. I Cor. 13:11.

ing whatever He disposes or whatever their obligations or
state of life impose upon them. As St. Paul puts it, they observe what is the good pleasure of God in order to accomplish it perfectly.

Their interior acts are even more unified and simplified
until at last everything is reduced to love. If in the beginning their prayer consisted in many affections and considerations, eventually it is all reduced to an act of love.
Indeed, their entire life is thus simplified, for it all becomes a perpetual prayer. This, of course, is fully realized
only in the last stage of the interior life, which corresponds
to the mystical or passive stage. Here the unity of spirit
is finally achieved, for the soul now possesses the spirit of
wisdom which, being one, contains all else. This is necessarily so because it is the Holy Ghost, the Spirit of wisdom,
who informs and animates all mystical souls.

It follows, then, that the unity of spirit depends upon
the Holy Ghost, whose sole purpose of action is to dispose
souls to receive Him and to communicate Himself to them
in the measure that they are so disposed until He takes
full possession of them. The object of this action is to draw
souls to God, who is unity itself, and for that reason it is
said that the spiritual life is the way of unity.

The diversity of spirits, on the other hand, depends upon
both God and man. It depends upon God because He dis-
tributes His gifts according to His good pleasure and in
conformity with the degree of perfection to which He destines each soul for the greater variety and beauty of the
supernatural order. As St. Paul says, "There are diversities
of graces, but the same Spirit," [2] that is, the Holy Ghost
gives to each according to His good pleasure. Since God
can be shared and imitated by His creatures in an infinite

[2] Cf. I Cor. 12:4.

variety of ways, and since sanctity is nothing more than the supernatural participation and imitation of God, who is the essence of sanctity, it follows that God will be manifested in each saint in a different manner, saving, of course, the fundamental unity which is common to all. Thus, the image of God and the manifestation of His attributes are more perfectly realized in all the saints together, though some of the divine attributes, as we understand them, may seem contradictory to one another. So also, the number and variety of the mountain streams manifest the plenitude of the source from which they flow.

The diversity of spirits depends upon man so far as he responds to the divine action according to his dispositions and capacity and according to his manner of receiving it. Wherefore, the diversity of temperaments and characters, the various dispositions and natural aptitudes and talents, the diverse states of life, ministries, employments, and occupations: all these have a bearing upon the diversity of spirits. The philosopher would state this truth in the following axiom: "Whatever is received is received according to the condition of the recipient." In the spiritual life that which is received is the divine Spirit and the recipient is the spirit of man. However, it is not our intention to indicate the various reasons and causes of the unity and diversity of spirits (which, at any rate, are discerned easily enough), but simply to call attention to the fact of the matter and to deduce certain conclusions which apply to the practice of the interior life.

What are these practical conclusions? In the first place, the doctrine on the diversity of spirits should teach us to interpret rightly and evaluate justly the various teachings which are proposed on spiritual matters. Frequently we discover doctrines even among the canonized saints which,

if not downright contradictory, seem difficult to reconcile and leave us perplexed as to their application. Some authors, for instance, will recommend penance, others patience; some the particular examen, others union with the will of God; some advise discursive prayer, others contemplative prayer; some recommend the practice of this or that virtue as most excellent, others propose a particular devotion or pious practice as most important and efficacious. Each one will try to convince us that his method, practice, or exercise is the most excellent and the shortest and easiest way to perfection.

What are we to think of all this? Does it mean that such doctrines are false or that their authors deceive us? Not at all. These doctrines are true in themselves and if there is any falsity in them, it is in the exclusiveness and exaggeration with which they sometimes are presented. Neither are the authors trying to deceive us; but as the popular saying goes, "Everyone speaks of the fair as he fared in it." Every man reflects his own spirit in his works. "Out of the abundance of the heart the mouth speaketh." [3]

Therefore, these doctrines should not be rejected *en masse*. We should accept them as good and true in general. However, their application in each particular case requires selection and discernment. At a banquet or feast we do not partake of every dish but only of those which are agreeable to us; so also it would be imprudent to burden ourselves with every spiritual practice and method that is suggested, without considering whether or not it is in conformity with our particular vocation or with the actual state of our soul.

We should not, therefore, be misled or puzzled when we read or hear about saints who held a certain axiom as the

[3] Luke 6:45.

norm of life, who practiced some special spiritual exercise, or taught spiritual doctrines that are not in perfect accord with those of other saints or masters of the spiritual life. Much of what the saints said and did they did, not as saints, but as aspirants to sanctity. They also, generally speaking, had to pass through a long *via crucis,* that is, a lengthy process of purification to arrive eventually at transformation in God. During that process they received spiritual lights which gradually deepened and enlightened their understanding. Indeed, even after their transformation they continued to advance in wisdom and understanding.

It is absurd, therefore, to look upon the saints as if they had always been saints or as if they had always been such in the same degree. In order to evaluate their words and deeds correctly it is necessary, with them as with everyone else, to consider the degree of the interior life to which they had attained or their spiritual state at the time.

Another consequence of this doctrine is that in the direction of souls one should never impose on them preconceived methods or systems of the spiritual life, but those which are in accordance with the spirit which God has given them (after verifying that the spirit is truly from God and is conformable to the doctrine of the Church). To attempt to do otherwise and to impose one's own ideas of perfection or methods of attaining it, without consideration for the particular path by which God is leading the soul, is to supplant God and to become one of the blind guides referred to by the Savior.[4]

The good director of souls should take care only that the spirit of God be developed in the soul. In order to do this, he should observe what ascetical exercises are appropriate in view of the dangers and difficulties that obstruct that

4 Luke 6:39.

development and what kind of prayer and devotional exercises most attract and benefit the soul. In other words, good direction consists in cooperating with the action of God in the sanctification of souls; bad direction is to anticipate or nullify it. The good director should first of all probe the soul until he knows it intimately and discovers the talents God has given it and the return He demands from them. The principal thing which the good director should seek to discover in the manifestations of the spiritual life of an individual soul is whether the spirit of God abides there, for however great the diversity of spirits, each and every one must be informed by the one and the same Holy Spirit. If the spirit manifested by an individual is truly from God, all the operations of the soul will be marked with the seal of humility, simplicity, detachment, death to self, and a vehement desire for union with God.

Finally, a knowledge of the unity and diversity of spirits is an efficacious means of putting an end to many disagreements and controversies in the field of spiritual theology, most of which are born of an excessive individualism and the desire to impose one's own ideas as the supreme norm of perfection or to establish as an absolute truth what is merely relative. This is what happens when people unduly praise and recommend the merits of their own state or profession, their spiritual methods and practices, their prayers and devotions, giving one to understand that without such things perfection is hardly conceivable or at least very difficult to attain. Even more guilty of this error are those who, under the pretext of zeal, censure and condemn actions which in themselves are not wrong, but only in the judgment of those who condemn them. St. Paul becomes very indignant toward such people and he reprimands them in the persons of the early Christians who created arguments and discord over the question of eating meat that had been offered to idols. Substantially he says: Who are you that you judge others? Who has authorized you to judge over us? Why is my liberty judged by another man's conscience? We are all children of the same Father and serve the same Lord, and whether we eat or fast, sleep or watch, live or die, we do all through Him and for Him, for we are always His.[5]

Wherefore, let us allow each one to go his own way and to act in accordance with his own conscience, as long as all conform to the unity of spirit and serve the same Lord as He wishes to be served. Let us abide by that precious rule St. Paul gives us in his Epistle to the Ephesians: "I therefore . . . beseech you that you walk worthy of the vocation in which you are called, with all humility and mildness, with patience, supporting one another in charity, careful to keep the unity of the spirit in the bond of peace." [6]

CHAPTER 22 🖌

Spiritual Childhood

THE doctrine of St. Therese of Lisieux concerning the way of spiritual childhood is not a new doctrine, but her manner of presenting it is new. For many souls an introduction to her life and teaching is exhilarating news, a spiritual surprise that is most gratifying, or a kind of gospel that they had never heard before. She has a special appeal for souls

[5] Cf. I Cor. 10:29, 31.   [6] Eph. 4:1–3.

that aspire to the love of God above all things and yet find nothing within themselves which would make them worthy of such great good. There is nothing extraordinary in their interior or exterior life save that supreme yearning that God has implanted in their heart. Yet, all that they have previously heard and read has given them the idea that in order to attain union with God one must be rather extraordinary, and when they see how poor they are and how far removed from all that, even perhaps groaning under the weight of their misery, they think it impossible that they will ever attain the perfection of charity or intimate union with God.

Consequently, when they are told and are finally convinced that the kingdom of heaven is for the poor and humble and that they also can love God as the great saints did, they experience an ineffable consolation and their heart swells with joy. It seems to them that they are hearing the canticle of the angels at the stable of Bethlehem: "Glory to God in the highest: and on earth peace to men of good will." [1] Indeed, it was precisely for such souls that this divine canticle was sung. The extraordinary joy with which they receive the doctrine on spiritual childhood is ample demonstration of their good will. The fact is that their will is already directed to God and tends to Him with all vehemence, even though their works are not as lofty as their desires. This, however, serves to keep them humble and makes them appeal to God with greater ardor and put all their confidence in Him.

That is the secret of the irresistible delight which souls derive from the life and doctrine of St. Therese. As far as we know, no one has ever presented the evangelical doctrine of poverty of spirit and spiritual childhood in so clear

[1] Luke 2:14.

and attractive a manner as she. These two concepts may seem to be fundamentally the same, but in reality spiritual childhood is a consequence or effect of poverty of spirit. He who has nothing and is conscious of his weakness and poverty necessarily turns to God with the sentiments of a helpless child turning to his generous father from whom he expects all things.

No, the doctrine of St. Therese is not new, but she has presented it in such a way that many souls feel as if they were hearing the gospel for the first time. Indeed, this doctrine is so benign and favorable that some souls can hardly bring themselves to believe it. How strange that the bountiful goodness of God should seem incredible to men and that they should be more severe and demand greater perfection than God Himself does for meriting His love. The fact of the matter is that men do not understand the nature of God nor what He expects of his creatures in order to please Him and ravish His heart.

Men think that God looks for great things, as if there were anything great outside of Himself. They do not seem to realize that He already has greatness in abundance and that He now seeks littleness and falls in love with it. God so loves the humility and littleness of His creatures that it could almost be said that He became one of them in order not to be deprived of this ineffable delight. However, for a creature to be truly lovable and pleasing to Him, it must be content to be what it is. It must embrace its littleness and delight in it and even esteem it above all things for the love of God, for He loves the poverty and littleness of souls who are such in their own estimation.

This is poverty of spirit: not to want anything that is not God, neither graces nor honors nor virtue nor perfection nor gifts nor anything that is not God Himself. The poor in spirit place no value whatever on ecstasies, visions, revelations, or any of the other great gifts we read about in the lives of the saints, save so far as they are means to union with God. They value only the love of God and if they can attain it by means of humiliations, they will love these above every worldly good. However much they may detest their faults, the poor in spirit are not scandalized at themselves, for they know themselves so well that nothing surprises them. They may see that they are deficient in goodness, weak in holy desires, and full of inclinations that are unworthy of a holy soul. Nevertheless, they resign themselves to all this for the love of God and thereby derive the great benefit of true self-knowledge and humility of heart.

Oh, if we could open the eyes of those souls who do not yet understand in what their true perfection and happiness consists! The only real happiness, one which has no name in human language, is to be loved by God. To this happiness all souls should aspire. Their only endeavor should be to learn how they can become pleasing to God; how, so to speak, they can ravish His heart. This is the only thing that matters.

Actually, God is vanquished, subjugated, and conquered by humility. It is impossible for Him to resist the enchantments of humility; if He did not love it, He would cease to be infinite goodness and love. But God is the essence of goodness and therefore He is essentially communicative and diffusive, so that where there is an emptiness He must immediately fill it with Himself. A vacuum cannot exist in the atmosphere because as soon as it is produced, the surrounding air immediately rushes into it. So also in the spiritual order, whenever a void is produced God immediately fills it. Thus it is a fundamental principle of the spiritual life that God increases in us as we decrease; in other words, the more we empty ourselves of self, the more we shall be filled with God. The emptiness or void is made within us by humility or self-contempt for the love for God.

Such is the significance of St. Therese's doctrine for little souls, for the poor and humble, for those who neither want nor seek anything outside of God. It is as if someone were to say to them: "Rejoice! You have so good a God that He asks only love of His creatures. He does not ask for great things nor does He love us for what we are, but because of what He is. He desires that we know Him and that we know ourselves. All He asks of us is humility, poverty of spirit, death to self, and detachment from all things for love of Him."

How incomprehensible are the goodness and love of God! He falls in love with souls that are most oppressed with sufferings and afflictions. According to a revelation made to a holy soul, He especially favors those who offer Him their miseries and afflictions as their only title to His love. And although these souls may suffer their miseries in spite of themselves and detest them vehemently, they nevertheless acquire a kind of love for their afflictions, for they realize that because of their miseries they are loved by God. The reason is that such things help to keep souls humble and thus attract to them the tenderness of God's infinite love.

In imitation of Mary, these souls can now intone their *Magnificat,* which is the overflowing of a heart divinely enraptured with the incomprehensible goodness and mercy of a God who loves the humble and does great things to them, while He disdains the proud in their own conceits. "My soul doth magnify the Lord: and my spirit hath rejoiced in God my Savior. Because he hath regarded the humility of his handmaid: for behold from henceforth all generations shall call me blessed." [2]

Fortunate indeed is the soul who understands the value of humility in capturing the heart of God and for love of Him, loves it above all else. For such a soul the kingdom of heaven has already begun in this world; for the kingdom of God is within us but we ourselves are naught but misery and nothingness. Wherefore, in order to find God we must first discover our misery and feel it in all its intensity. He is truly miserable who does not realize his misery.

[2] Luke 1:46–48.

PART IV

The Life of Prayer

CHAPTER 23 ✒

Prayer and Perfection

NOTHING is so encouraging to us in the cultivation of a life of prayer as the knowledge that prayer in a wide sense of the term is a synthesis of perfection and that its use eventually becomes most natural and pleasant to the heart of man. A life of prayer simplifies and unifies the practices of perfection and transforms them into acts of love. It puts the heart of man in contact with the heart of God and in its highest grade it is completely identified with perfection, so that together they constitute the state of sanctity.

The life of prayer simplifies and unifies the exercises of perfection. St. Augustine said that he who prays well, lives well. That is indeed true, for the life of prayer requires the exercise of all the virtues, both theological and moral. Who doubts that faith, hope, and charity have their most intense exercise in prayer? And who does not perceive that in order to devote oneself to a life of prayer one must practice mortification in all its forms? The passions and external senses as well as the internal faculties—imagination, memory, understanding, and will—must be held under control so that they will not disturb the peace of the soul and cause distractions in prayer.

A life of prayer presupposes the presence of God and constant recollection in order to direct to Him all our thoughts, words, and actions, as well as our trials and sacrifices. And as we offer them to God, we must endeavor to keep them free from any sin or imperfection that may displease Him.

Hence the life of prayer is inseparable from the practice of perfection. More properly, the life of prayer itself constitutes the sum total of that practice, for he who practices perfection in the spirit of prayer converts his entire life into a prayer. This is a very important truth and should be called to mind frequently by those small, timid souls who are disheartened and discouraged by the multiplicity of means that are proposed or demanded for the attainment of perfection. Let them forget these things and resolve solely to pursue the life of prayer, removing all the obstacles and difficulties which oppose it and directing all that they do to the attainment of that one goal: sanctification of self and the love of God. There is nothing else that they shall have to do.

The life of prayer facilitates the practice of perfection because it turns it into an exercise of the love of God. To practice the virtues only with a view to their immediate objects is always painful and difficult and it costs fallen nature a great deal. However, to practice them out of love and with the purpose of attaining the possession of God, we shall not say that it removes entirely the intrinsic difficulty, but it does give us the strength and courage to overcome all obstacles and it so sweetens the sacrifices that we come to regard them as the greatest joy. Love conquers all things and can accomplish all things. "For love is strong as death." [1] When done for the love of God, the struggle for perfection becomes easy and delightful; without it, everything becomes difficult or impossible.

Above all, the life of prayer facilitates the practice of perfection because it puts us in constant communication with God, the source of all perfection and sanctity. Here is the great secret of all grace and sanctity. Apart from this,

[1] Cant. 8:6.

one works and wearies himself to no avail because human powers cannot produce divine effects, of which man's sanctification is one. On the other hand, how easily God can do that which is impossible to man! Simply by touching the heart for an instant, briefer than a ray of lightning, He dissolves and annihilates it like a ray of heat melting soft wax. Then he renews and transforms it in such a way that it no longer knows itself nor thinks about or remembers itself. Though living, it dies of love for Him who has mortally wounded it.

It is this divine ray that removes the barriers and walls that separate the human heart from the divine. Henceforth there are no more conflicts, resistances, fears, or difficulties; no more walking in the dark or in the shadow of death. Now everything is light and peace, joy and happiness, similar to the joy and happiness of the blessed on the day of their eternal nuptials. Here all the difficulties of prayer come to an end, for the soul has now found Him whom it sought with so many sighs and yearnings. Now all that remains is to rejoice in the presence of the Beloved who abides in the depths of its being. The soul now practices constant prayer, and in such wise that it cannot conceive how one could live without prayer or how any occupation or labor could interrupt it.

Now all places and times, all offices and occupations serve to unite the soul more closely to God. Nothing and no one can distract it from that interior occupation which fills it completely, for it is the fullness of God. For that reason the soul can be occupied in any employment whatever without danger of dissipation or lukewarmness or of losing the spirit of prayer, for its very spirit is like a divine transformer which converts everything into prayer and love. Ah, if all those who discharge the offices and duties of human life had this plenitude of the interior life, how much fruit they would produce in souls and in the world, and how much sanctity and merit they would attain for themselves!

At this point the life of prayer and the life of perfection or sanctity become one. For sanctity is love, love in its most perfect degree, that of mystical union with God in the spiritual marriage. And this is exactly what the life of prayer is in its highest grade. We shall not insist on this because it is evident, but we would like to insist unto exhaustion, nay even unto death, and we would like to have all the authority of the saints, and we would wish also that our word had all the efficacy of the word of God, in order to convince souls that all their good lies in prayer as it is here explained; that the life of prayer is the royal road that leads directly to God. Let them not weary themselves in looking for other roads, for they will only go astray and kill themselves with useless efforts. The life of prayer is the key to the entire spiritual life and the secret of all perfection. In its plenitude, the life of prayer is perfection and sanctity itself. For sanctity is love, and to pray is to love, and to love is to abandon oneself totally to love. Moreover, for him who has already completely abandoned himself and all things, to love is to die of love for the Beloved.

CHAPTER 24 🔏

Difficulties in Prayer

DIFFICULTIES in prayer arise from two fundamental causes: the lack of the proper disposition or the use of an improper method. The first is usually experienced by beginners or those who are not practiced in prayer; the second, by those who are already habituated and properly disposed for prayer but practice it as if they were not so disposed. The former have difficulty in recollecting their senses, restraining their imagination and memory, and concentrating their attention, understanding, and will on the object of their prayer. Since their heart is not yet completely orientated toward God, it inclines toward the earth, drawing all the senses and powers with it. To overcome this difficulty they will have to use the means prescribed for this end, such as spiritual reading, vocal prayer, and meditation, and they will have to put into practice the rules for learning the practice of this divine art.

As a general rule, all this is indispensable for beginners, for they do not yet know how to pray or commune with God or remain recollected. Like infants, they must be taught how to speak and even be told what to say. Otherwise they will not know how to do anything and if they attempt prayer, it will be with such great effort as to exhaust them.

This is the greatest difficulty of beginners. However, sometimes they are also confronted by the second, that is, by the desire to pray in a manner which does not suit them. The fact that they read or hear of the benefits of a certain method of prayer greatly contributes to this difficulty, for they immediately want to put it into practice without considering their abilities and spiritual dispositions or whether it is in conformity with the actual state of their soul or the gift of prayer which they have received from God.

These souls ought to bear in mind that everyone should pray according to the particular gift of prayer which God has given him. In order to do this they must first know what it is. This they will know from experience, for one's gift of prayer is that which one finds the easiest and most beneficial. All persons cannot meditate or exercise all their faculties in prayer, but they must not on that account think that they are absolutely incapable of prayer, for all can love, adore, give thanks to God, ask pardon for their sins, and make as many petitions and acts of piety as their needs require. Prayer is in reality the simplest thing in the world. Our mere presence before God—if we keep in mind who we are, who God is, and why we are there—is already a prayer.

As for those who are already habituated and well disposed for prayer, their difficulty arises from the attempt to pray as if they were not already well practiced. They pray in the manner of beginners and according to the rules by which they first learned that art. This is as absurd as if a finished musician never wanted to play any selections other than those which he first learned; or as if a person, after arriving at the destination where he is to perform several tasks, should want to traverse the distance anew before each task. For such souls there is no other difficulty than that which they themselves create by resisting the impulses of their heart which tends to unite itself to God. By not fighting against obstacles, they resist the action of the Holy

Ghost who prays within them with unspeakable groanings.

Souls who are already proficient in prayer do not need all the preparations and precautions prescribed for beginners, nor does the maxim of Holy Scripture, "Before prayer prepare thy soul" [1] apply to them. They have already fulfilled it because they are habitually so prepared. To make a perfect prayer it is sufficient for these souls to place themselves in the presence of God and remain in it, for in this simple act are contained all the other acts prescribed for this end. For souls who are adept at prayer or who already possess the gift of constant prayer, it is hardly necessary to renew the presence of God. It is sufficient for them to remember that He is within them, that He abides in their heart, and that He Himself teaches them to pray and tells them what to ask and what to do. He inspires all the acts and affections of love, adoration, reverence, praise, and joy that cannot be expressed in human language. Such souls have nothing more to do in prayer than to allow themselves to be led by the divine impulse, to give free rein and full expansion to the affections of their heart, and to allow the divine Spirit to work in them without restrictions or impediments of any kind.

But it may be asked: "Could there not be danger of illusion in this, so that a soul may take human inspirations as divine?" For souls who are truly in the state of perfect prayer there is no such danger, unless they wilfully blind themselves and refuse to see what is before their eyes. For these souls have more than ample light to distinguish between what comes from God and what comes from human nature, what leads to God and what separates them from Him. However, for greater security and because the Holy

[1] Ecclus. 18:23.

Ghost Himself who abides within them so inclines them, they should, whenever possible, seek the approval of a person competent in these matters.

The danger, however, is not in this, but in believing ourselves to be in a state of prayer in which we are not. In order to find out the degree of one's prayer there is no better rule than that of the divine Savior: by its fruit you shall know it.[2] One who is in the state of perfect prayer is in the state of sanctity and it will be manifested in his spiritual disposition and in his comportment with respect to God, his neighbor, and himself. Manifestly, sanctity and self-love are diametrically opposed and absolutely incompatible and sanctity without humility and charity is the greatest of illusions.

Let the Christian, therefore, observe whether his prayer proceeds from a profound self-annihilation which makes him hateful and despicable in his own eyes; whether it proceeds from an absolute detachment and total death to all selfish interests and, at the same time, from a divine plenitude of love which fills the soul all the more as the abyss of its nothingness is greater. Let him also observe whether all this manifests itself in patience, charity, humility, joy, peace, and the other fruits of the Holy Ghost. By these fruits he will know with certitude whether or not his prayer is true, whether it is a reality or a delusion. If the soul perceives these fruits within itself in a greater or less degree, then it can let itself be carried away by the impulses which prayer produces or tends to produce. There can never be any deception in this, for the devil may be able to counterfeit other effects of sanctity, but he can never produce the fruits of the Holy Ghost.

[2] Matt. 7:16.

CHAPTER 25

Constant Prayer

SOULS that have not attained the state of constant prayer find it difficult to understand how such prayer is possible, for there are so many obstacles which impede its exercise and so many occupations and cares in life which seem totally incompatible with the attention which this kind of prayer demands. Moreover, it seems to them all the more inexplicable as such cares and occupations are greater, as were those of many saints and perfect souls to whom this kind of prayer is attributed in a special manner. How is it possible that many saints whose lives were examples of the most amazing activity, who successfully carried out great enterprises for the good of the Church and of souls and fulfilled difficult and tedious charges and offices, could at the same time practice constant prayer, with their minds and hearts always recollected in God and divine things? Did God miraculously enable them to divide their attention and fix it on many things at the same time? No. This is neither naturally possible nor does God ordinarily work miracles in order to bring it to pass. The only miracle in this matter is that incessant and constant prayer becomes as spontaneous and natural to the saints and holy souls as breathing.

In order to understand this we must observe that prayer can be of two kinds: prayer of the mind and prayer of the heart or of the spirit. As St. Paul says: "I will pray with the spirit, I will pray also with the understanding: I will sing with the spirit, I will sing also with the understanding." [1] Both, of course, can be practiced at the same time. Prayer of the mind is reflective and conscious and requires all our attention and care and the actual exercise of our faculties. Such prayer cannot be continuous in this life except by a miracle of God who is not wont to perform such miracles. The continuity of this kind of prayer would make sleep impossible, and even Jesus Himself had to sleep.

The prayer of the heart or of the spirit (which we shall call "unconscious" prayer because it is done without reflection and without our attention's being actually fixed on it) can and should be continuous throughout one's life. The reason for this distinction is that, although we cannot fix our mind on two things at the same time nor continue to think always, we can love always. Moreover, prayer, at least unconscious prayer, is nothing more than an act of love; better still, it is love in action. Wherefore, he who loves is always loving, whether awake or asleep, occupied or unoccupied; moreover, he is always praying, for when directed to God, to love is to pray and to pray is to love.

What does it matter if our mind and senses are occupied with a thousand different things? Our heart is elsewhere, fixed on God, so that everything we do and think, we do through Him, in Him and for Him, and our entire life becomes a constant act of love of Him. Who does not see that this is possible, and very possible? Do we not see that, even in the natural order, when the heart is dominated by a great love, no matter what the person does, his entire soul and life are on what he loves and not on what he does, though he may apply to his work all his mind and attention? If natural love does this, how much more should divine love which is the Holy Spirit Himself abiding in our

[1] Cf. I Cor. 14:15.

hearts and praying in us with unspeakable groanings [2] and communicating to us the very love with which God loves Himself?

Souls who aspire to constant prayers should not doubt that it exists. It is something so real and effective that he who possesses it is as clearly aware of it as he is of his own existence, and he finds it so easy to practice that no occupation or distraction can interrupt it, not even sleep. When he awakes he perceives that his heart has not been separated from God nor ceased for one moment to beat for Him, nor has God ceased to abide in him in the most intimate union of love.

Notwithstanding what has been said, we must admit that although only unconscious prayer can be continuous in a strict sense, conscious prayer can also be designated as such, so far as the former causes the latter to be as continuous as is possible.

He who practices unconscious prayer in all its plenitude, that is, he who has attained the state of constant prayer, finds that his mind is almost constantly recollected in God and divine things, for his spirit draws him irresistibly toward the divine and eternal and his heart is drawn to where his treasure lies. Hence St. John of the Cross says: "To him that is pure, all things, whether high or low, . . . all the operations of the senses and faculties are directed to divine contemplation. Such a man . . . finds in all things a knowledge of God which is joyful and pleasant, chaste, pure, spiritual, glad and loving." [3] Since this kind of prayer is most beneficial and most delightful and desirable for the soul that seeks the fountain of living waters which is found

[2] Rom. 8:26.
[3] *Ascent of Mount Carmel,* Bk. III, chap. 26.

therein, we shall briefly indicate the road that leads to it, so that those who feel an insatiable thirst for that "water springing up into life everlasting" [4] may know how to find it.

In the life of prayer the action of God and that of the soul concur and it is necessary to know their respective activities in the process of its development. As regards the divine action, the life of prayer can be divided into the same stages as the spiritual life, namely, the purgative, the illuminative, and the unitive. The first stage ordinarily has two phases: that of sweetness and consolations and that of trials, conflicts, crosses, sufferings, and desolation. The object of both is to disengage the soul from earthly affections and purify it like gold in the crucible, in order to dispose it to receive the love and Spirit of God. This second phase is ordinarily of much longer duration than the first and souls suffer pains and trials beyond description. The great master of the spiritual life, St. John of the Cross, has described them in great detail in his famous *Dark Night of the Soul.*

Toward the end of the purgative stage, which is a veritable and dreadful desert in the spiritual life, God gradually communicates greater light to the soul regarding supernatural perfection, light which at times increases the soul's torment at seeing how far it is from consummate perfection and, above all, from God. At the same time, He communicates the gift of more perfect prayer and thus irresistibly draws the soul to Himself. The soul then observes that without being aware of it, it has been praying almost constantly and cannot find repose out of God. At the same time, it seems to feel a sort of rejection or coldness on God's

[4] John 4:14.

part which hinders it from being united to Him as intimately as it would like.

Human nature also intervenes in this conflict, urging the soul to seek consolation in things other than God, since He will not give it. This is impossible, however, because God makes those consolations bitter and frustrates every effort of the soul to find them. So stubborn and hard-fought is this battle that sometimes it seems to the soul that it is suffering a divine persecution which allows it no peace. At other times, in the midst of such desolation and grief, the soul thinks that it is on the verge of death or insanity. This is a presentiment, for in truth the soul is to die mystically and will be outside itself with divine love. This occurs in the unitive stage of the life of prayer, which is the perfection of prayer.

When the soul reaches this point, a divine ray touches it and annihilates it in a mysterious manner, so that it dies of love and is raised to a new life which transforms and deifies it. This transformation places the soul in a stable and permanent passive state. It is that state of constant prayer to which we have already referred.

In the development of the life of prayer the action of the soul should correspond with that of God by cooperating with His activity in order to remove the obstacles which hinder it and by doing all in its power to make its effect as intense as possible. To do this, the soul should know what God's designs are in the various stages of prayer and also what its degree of prayer is here and now in order to use it to advantage. Moreover, it should practice the life of prayer by every means possible and persevere in it, though it may cost a thousand deaths and an entire life of martyrdom.

With respect to God's designs in the various stages of prayer, He desires to purify the soul and detach it from all things in order to unite it to Himself. Therefore the soul also should propose this end to itself in all its prayers and devotions and in everything it does or suffers in them. This also should be the goal of all its thoughts, words, actions, affections, joys, and sufferings. When God leads the soul into the desert of the spiritual life and it experiences fears and desolations, let it remember that this way leads to the promised land of peace and abundance. These sufferings and trials are so necessary and beneficial that if the soul knew their value it would consider them the greatest of divine favors. The soul, therefore, should endeavor to purify its intentions, detach itself from all things, and accept the cross that God sends. This will shorten the road that leads to Him. If God is often obliged to make us endure many trials, it is because we do not wish to surrender our own judgment and affections and because in prayer we seek His gifts rather than Himself.

We say also that each soul should know its particular gift of prayer and make use of it, for through it God will communicate the grace He wishes the soul to have. A soul will recognize its gift of prayer by the facility, pleasure, and benefit it finds in a particular method of prayer, be it mental or vocal, or by the attraction it feels for some mystery of the life of our Lord, the consideration of some eternal truth, or a particular exercise of piety or devotion. The director, or some truly spiritual person, can also help the soul in this matter. This is extremely important, for there are some souls who disdain their own gift of prayer, judging it to be inferior and insignificant. Influenced by what they read or hear, they seek other methods of prayer which seem to them more lofty and sublime. As a result, they fail to find what they seek and they go astray or lose the way altogether and never reach their goal.

In the actual practice of prayer, we should make use of all the means that raise and unite us to God. In other words, we should live the life of prayer as it is ordinarily understood. To do this, it is absolutely necessary to place oneself from the very beginning on a supernatural plane and to regard everything as ordained and disposed by God, as it truly is, for our sanctification and to accept it as coming from His divine hand. Finally, we should avail ourselves of every occasion and opportunity to preserve and foster our life of prayer.

As to perseverance in prayer, we shall remark only that this is the touchstone, so to speak, of the entire life of prayer and of its final triumph. We need not insist on something so evident and so frequently repeated, but we wish to state that, if at times we seem to relax somewhat in our fervor and even to become lukewarm, this is not necessarily opposed to perseverance. The important thing is never to abandon the path altogether, never to give up, though we may fail many, many times. The important thing is to rise and begin again with greater resolve than ever. If we do nothing more than this in our entire lifetime, we would not be deprived entirely of the fruit of prayer. For the latter does not depend so much on what we do in prayer as on what we suffer in it for the sake of obtaining the possession of God. What God desires of us is our heart, our determination to be all His, cost what it may. It captivates and delights Him to see that we spare no pain in our efforts to persevere in seeking and finding Him. It is perseverance that determines which souls will attain union, for only through perseverance do they become worthy of it. Wherefore, he who wishes to attain union with God has nothing more to do than to persevere in prayer.

CHAPTER 26

Answer to Prayer

GOD delays, or appears to delay, in answering our prayers precisely in order to oblige us to pray always. The end of prayer is prayer itself in its highest degree, which is union with God. However, in order to attain that degree of prayer it is necessary to acquire the habit of prayer, and this habit is acquired only by praying. That is why God often does not grant us or at least does not make us aware that He grants us what we ask. He wishes only that we attain our true beatitude, which is the possession of the supreme good. This should also be our supreme aspiration and any particular goods which we desire should be subordinated to this.

Those who dedicate themselves to prayer should be ever mindful of this. They may ask of God whatever they wish. They may, and in many cases should, propose to themselves the acquisition of some particular virtue or perfection. But their ultimate end should be prayer itself, or intimate conversation with God. This is the greatest of all goods. So it happens that by persevering in prayer we obtain every good we can desire, although we may not receive each and every one exactly as we expect.

God always hears our prayers and fulfills our desires, but

He does it in a way infinitely beyond our understanding. Often by denying us what we ask, He grants us what we really desire, for He knows better than we. How admirably divine wisdom is manifested in the interpretation and fulfillment of our most secret desires! We have our ideas and plans of the spiritual life and we ask God to fulfill them just as we understand them, thinking there is no other solution nor any other way in which we can be perfect and happy. But God intervenes and destroys our plans and petty notions and solves our problems in a way befitting His infinite greatness and power. Then the soul is enraptured at the contemplation of such wisdom and power and goodness, and it joyfully sounds the depths of its nothingness on seeing that God is magnified and glorified in it.

Faith, humility, and blind confidence are necessary in order to obtain the precious fruits of prayer, for we must give ourselves blindly and with holy abandonment to the mysterious operations of divine love. Nothing is so opposed to this as clinging to our own ideas, however holy they may be, and endeavoring to impose them upon God, desiring that at all costs He lead us in the way we have charted. God is absolute Lord and Master and the soul must abandon itself to Him with a submission that is also unconditional and absolute. He is also infinitely free and the soul must allow Him to work freely. There is no greater happiness than to be in such hands and there is no greater misfortune than to be in our own. That is why we must renounce our own ideas and cares, for they serve only to mislead us. We must be solicitous only about remaining united and abandoned to God. This is what He desires of us and why He has disposed all things so that we are obliged to pray, to hasten to Him, to be with Him. He wants us always to cling to Him, as an infant clings to its mother.

In relation to God, man is always an infant, for he is always receiving from God his being, his life, and all that is necessary to sustain and develop that life. That is why God does not give us once and for all everything we need. He does not wish that one meal alone should nourish us sufficiently for our entire lifetime, but that we should eat every day. So also, He desires that every day we should have recourse to Him, not to make it difficult for us, but to keep us near Him and to remind us that we are but infants who have need of our heavenly Father. We must not forget that everything in the world is subordinated to and disposed for a life of love. That is why everything is ephemeral and passes away quickly, for love itself is only passing through this world on its way home to heaven, and the very inconstancy of things makes it fly all the more rapidly toward God.

Wherefore, if God has placed us in the happy necessity of praying, of praying always, and of being always near Him, we should cooperate with His intentions and take advantage of that very necessity in order to attain our highest end. We must pray and pray always in order to give a divine orientation to our hearts. Then we shall have obtained the supreme end of prayer and its exercise will not only become easy, but we shall not be able to leave it, even if we should want to. It will become the source of all our happiness in life. The divine orientation of our heart will make us turn to God by a kind of necessity in all the events and vicissitudes of our interior and exterior life. Just as steel, when in contact with a magnet, acquires the properties of the latter, so the heart of man, when it has remained in contact with God through prayer, acquires a divine magnetism that obliges it to turn irresistibly toward Him. Then everything that happens in the world and all the turmoil of life serve only to make it dart forth with greater momentum toward the divine magnet of hearts.

CHAPTER 27 ✄

Attention in Prayer

FOR souls who cannot meditate, St. John of the Cross recommends a general loving attentiveness to God in prayer. Although this recommendation refers principally to those who have practiced meditation for some time and can do so no longer because God is leading them to contemplation, nevertheless, if rightly understood, it can also be applied to all souls who for some involuntary reason are unable to meditate. There are many such, as many or even more than those who can. They complain that they do not know how or are not able to pray and because of this they grieve much and suffer great interior trials. They are even tempted to abandon prayer altogether, thinking that God will not grant them that grace.

The reason for this is that such souls, influenced by what they have read or heard or what they see in others, imagine that apart from vocal prayer there is no other method of prayer except mental prayer. They fail to realize that the very word "mental" indicates that this is only a type of prayer and not prayer itself. It is called "mental" prayer simply because in it we exercise our mental faculties in discursive reasoning, and not because prayer itself consists in mental exercises. Nor should it be a purely mental act; rather, it is an affective act, although it also implies an intellectual consideration of the truths of faith.

In other words, one who prepares himself for prayer with the right dispositions is already animated by the idea, even before he starts, that he is going to perform an act which is of utmost importance to his spiritual life. He is profoundly aware of his great need and misery and ardently desires to be freed from his imperfections and sins and to be purified and sanctified by the graces which God communicates through prayer. Moreover, he has a knowledge of God, according to the light of faith, which reveals to him the infinite greatness of divine mercy and goodness and how much God desires souls to turn to Him so that He may sanctify them, fill them with His gifts, and inflame them with His love. Wherefore, even before he begins to pray, a soul illumined by faith and desirous of sanctification implicitly performs many mental acts which are accompanied by great fervor. Consequently, it may very well happen that without any further preparation or any other means, he makes a perfect prayer simply through that loving attentiveness to God of which St. John of the Cross speaks.[1]

Does a beggar who presents himself before a kind and understanding rich man have to speak much or offer great arguments in order to make known his need? Do true lovers need many words in order to declare their love to each other? The same thing is true of this kind of prayer. The soul simply directs its gaze to God without discourses or violent efforts and sees Him as He is: an infinite treasury of goodness, mercy, and love. By the same token, the soul sees itself as an abyss of all misery, poverty, and weakness.

[1] *Ascent of Mount Carmel*, Bk. II, chap. 13.

By a simple glance the soul says all there is to say and God understands what it means, for He knows even the most hidden movements of our hearts. Hence the divine Master said: "When thou shalt pray, enter into thy chamber, and having shut the door [that is, the door which separates us from the exterior world and from our interior world of distracting thoughts and imaginations], pray to thy Father in secret: and thy Father who seeth in secret will repay thee." [2]

We can see from these words of our divine Savior that prayer is really a very simple matter for souls of good will who are not deluded and confused by strange ideas on the nature of prayer. We must not deceive ourselves; prayer is as simple and natural as the desire for health is to the sick or the lover's desire to communicate with his beloved. What we need is a hunger and a desire for God, a hunger and a desire for sanctification, a knowledge of our own wretchedness and the necessity of divine grace to attain perfection.

If as yet we lack this desire for sanctification, if we feel cold and insensible toward the things of God but very much attracted and attached to temporal things, then this fact should prompt us to give ourselves more to prayer, for this proves how much we need it. Moreover, it should arouse within us a holy and salutary fear of our condition and a vehement desire to overcome it, lest our distaste and coldness toward divine things increase and finally result in that disastrous state of lukewarmness wherein our wretched spiritual condition would no longer cause us anxiety or fear. So serious can this become that in time we may even look favorably upon our lukewarmness, for we shall no longer feel the pangs of conscience. May God deliver us

[2] Matt. 6:6.

from such false peace and tranquillity! Hence our first and foremost petition before God should be that He never permit us to have peace or repose outside of Him; that He enlighten our eyes that we may never sleep in death, lest at any time the enemy should boast of having prevailed against us.[3]

There is no need of many discourses to ask these things of God and satisfy these yearnings. It is enough to present oneself humbly and contritely before God and at the same time to be fully confident in His infinite goodness and love. All our good consists in being near Him and if our miseries take us to Him, then blessed are they, for they take us to our ultimate end and true good.

From what has been said one can readily understand what is meant by a general, loving attention to God in prayer. We wish only to add that this attentiveness does not exclude any explicit acts which we may feel moved to make in prayer. In this, as in everything else, our attention cannot remain constant and uniform. It has its moments of intensity and relaxation. It is the same as when we fix our gaze on an external object; we cannot maintain our attention on that object for a long period of time. Therefore, we should not try to preserve this loving attention in all its intensity, but should alternate it with different acts when we feel so inclined. We should pray as our heart moves us and not according to any preconceived method. Hence, the loving attentiveness of which we here speak should rather be understood as the general attitude which the soul should assume when it cannot or should not meditate, because it is occupied with other things which are better and more beneficial.

The same doctrine is taught by those two great guides

[3] Ps. 12:3.

and masters, St. Teresa and St. John of the Cross. Some have thought that there was a certain discrepancy in their teachings concerning this kind of prayer. Whereas St. John of the Cross advises the rejection of all images and representations, even those of our Lord and the scenes of His holy life, as well as all discursive reasoning and the exercise of our faculties, in order to preserve this general, loving attention, St. Teresa says that the images and representations which pertain to the sacred humanity of our divine Savior should never be rejected.

The apparent contradiction can be reconciled perfectly by distinguishing between the grades of prayer to which the two saints refer. St. Teresa refers to a grade of prayer in which the soul can still do something for itself, and therefore she does not wish that the representations and mysteries of the humanity of Christ be systematically rejected at that time. Through Christ's humanity all good has come to us; it is the door which leads to His divinity. But St. Teresa observes that when God wishes to elevate the soul to contemplation, wherein it can no longer do anything for itself, then it must not oppose or hinder the divine action by its own activity. In like manner, St. John of the Cross says that when the soul is able to do anything of itself it should do so. Therefore, St. John of the Cross does not systematically exclude images and discursive reasoning from prayer, nor does St. Teresa insist that we must never exclude the images and considerations which refer to the humanity of Christ.

The fact of the matter is that these two saints were considering the question from two different points of view which, nevertheless, are both true. St. Teresa was apprehensive lest as a general rule we exclude the humanity of Christ from our prayers, for this would be a grave error.

St. John of the Cross, on the other hand, feared that souls would strive to make acts of the imagination and reasoning when unable to do so because God was already giving them whatever they could possibly accomplish by their own efforts. Much to his sorrow, St. John had seen the trials and afflictions which souls suffer without benefit and even to their great detriment when they are obliged to meditate at a time when the Lord wishes to raise them to contemplation and suspends the exercise of their faculties. For that reason he tried his utmost to convince souls of the great harm and inconsistency of such a procedure.

This doctrine should serve as a light, a consolation, and an incentive to perseverance in prayer for all those who for some involuntary reason cannot meditate, especially those whom God places in a state of aridity wherein they feel that they are not accomplishing anything and that they are even offending Him because of their failure to pray. To oblige such souls to do what they cannot, is to increase the weight of their cross and to tempt them to abandon it altogether, for they will judge themselves absolutely incapable of carrying it. This is a danger that must be avoided at any cost. For the greatest evil that can befall us in the spiritual life is the abandonment of prayer and it is the source of many other evils as well.

If we forsake prayer we lose everything, but if we persevere in it, however great the trials and fluctuations of our spiritual life, we are on the right road and we may cherish the certain hope of arriving at our goal. That is why our divine Savior exhorted us to persevere in prayer. He knew that in it is all our good; that it is the secret of our salvation. Hence it is necessary that we persevere in prayer whatever way we are able: whether it be vocal prayer, meditation, contemplation, reading, or chanting. He who cannot do more, can pray simply by remaining in the presence of God, even if he says nothing and can only stand before God like a beggar before his benefactor or a sick person absorbing the rays of the sun whence he derives heat, health, and life.

Prayer, we repeat, is extremely simple, but by our discourses and imaginations we make it complicated. In the last analysis, if we cannot do anything more, it is enough simply to remain in the presence of God. To remain in God's presence and to persevere in prayer in spite of all the weariness and repugnances that one sometimes experiences, indicates very clearly what we seek. On the other hand, God knows the movements of our hearts and even anticipates our intentions. He knows very well what we wish and what our presence before Him signifies, even though we do not utter a single word.

It would, therefore, be a most grave error to forsake prayer because we do not know how to pray. We all know how to ask for what we need if we truly feel the need of it. And even if we did not know how to pray as we ought, this very deficiency should be an incentive to strive to pray as best we can, for then the Holy Ghost will teach us how to pray and will communicate Himself to us in prayer. The only thing required is that we approach prayer in a spirit of simplicity, trusting only in the Lord, forgetting about systems and methods of prayer, and using only those which unite us more closely to God and detach us from ourselves. In other words, we should not seek ourselves in our prayers; we should not look for light and sweetnesses and consolations or sentiments of any kind or description. We should seek only how to please God more perfectly, how to sanctify ourselves with His grace, and to be finally consumed in charity.

CHAPTER 28 🖎

Books on the Mystical Life

IN reading mystical literature, it is well to keep in mind certain benefits and dangers which may be encountered in such works. This is especially true if the meaning of any passages is vague or doubtful or if there is the possibility of doing harm to one's spiritual life. Many such books profoundly captivate the attention and heart of the reader by reason of their solidity, profundity, clarity, and even by their originality of treatment. Frequently one can see that the author speaks out of the abundance of his heart and is a true mystic, not a "mysticologist." However, we would not indiscriminately recommend all such books to souls dedicated to the interior life, lest they should fail to interpret the meaning of the author correctly and it should prove spiritually harmful to them.

In our opinion, the first stumbling-block souls encounter in reading mystical works is the danger of Quietism. Some writers presume an extensive knowledge in their readers and, consequently, they present the doctrine on prayer and contemplation in such a way that it could easily cause one to fall into that error. Indeed, the author may understand and correctly explain the exercise of prayer and infused contemplation but, judging solely from the way he writes, the inexperienced reader could very easily conclude that mystical contemplation depends entirely on our own efforts. He would believe that the Holy Ghost infallibly communicates infused contemplation to anyone who practices active annihilation, that is, anyone who by his own efforts rids himself of all sensible forms and species and all discursive reasoning and exercises of the faculties in order to become empty of everything and be able to receive the Spirit of God and be perfectly docile to His motions and impulses. All this could be an occasion of error and a reason for denouncing the author as a Quietist, unless it can be proved that he does not make mystical contemplation the fruit of our own industry and efforts.

Wherefore, in order to avoid all danger of error in the reading of such books, one must bear in mind that in the lofty contemplative state the soul usually cannot exercise its faculties or make acts of its own initiative, and if it does so, it is with great effort and violence and without any efficacy whatever. On the other hand, God gives the soul an irresistible desire for solitude and interior recollection and in the soul's emptiness and detachment from all things, even from its own senses and faculties, God performs the great marvels of His love, purifying, perfecting, beautifying, and filling it with His inestimable gifts. The soul in this state must take the greatest possible care not to hinder the divine action by its own activity; it must refrain from making acts of its own initiative, for they will only cause needless fatigue and impede the work of God.

It is here, and here only, that we may apply the rules given by St. John of the Cross and all true mystics concerning the soul's conduct when God calls it to contemplation. But until one reaches that state, these same authors say that it is necessary to make use of our faculties, to meditate, and to perform all the acts required to foster and practice prayer. To do otherwise would be to go against the will of God and to fall into that rightly condemned Quietism, which is the greatest of errors on the question of prayer. Quietism consists essentially in the attempt to apply the norms of contemplative prayer to ordinary prayer, in the belief that by this means true contemplation can be acquired.

It is necessary to affirm once and for all, in accordance with the doctrine of the Church and the saints, that there is no method, procedure, or rule whereby one may acquire or induce mystical contemplation. All that we can do is dispose ourselves so that God will communicate it to us when it pleases Him. However, in preparing ourselves we may, with the help of grace, do much to uproot and remove the obstacles which impede it. Indeed, if God does not grant this grace more frequently it is because few souls prepare themselves to receive it by renouncing self and detaching themselves from all things. For how can God communicate Himself to hearts that are filled with self-love and worldly affections?

In consideration of the soul's efforts to prepare and dispose itself for contemplation, we would admit the term "merited contemplation," but not "acquired contemplation." We believe that it is in this sense also that the partisans of the latter use the term; otherwise it would be impossible to reconcile the two extremes. In the supernatural order, acquired contemplation is either nothing at all or it is pure Quietism, subject to all the extravagances of the imagination and the devil. We cannot believe that authors who defend acquired contemplation in good faith understand it in such a sense. Rather, observing what generally happens to persons habituated to prayer, namely, that after a few prayers or meditations or any other active form of prayer, God elevates them, suspends their faculties, and introduces them into passive or contemplative prayer, they believe that the latter (passive prayer) is an effect of the former (active prayer). Yet, such is not always the case, for many times this does not happen, regardless of how much they may pray or meditate, while at other times God suddenly brings them to contemplation without any preparation whatever on their part. We do not mean to deny that there may be a natural contemplation produced by meditation on the truths of faith, but this is not the supernatural contemplation of which we are treating here. A natural cause cannot possibly produce a supernatural effect.

We stress this point because it would be a lamentable error indeed if souls were taught artificial methods dependent on our own industry for the atainment of contemplation, while the true way and proper disposition were forgotten. This true way and method is none other than that which Christ Himself taught His disciples, and all of us through them, when He told them how to pray and what to seek. It is incomprehensible that we should go about looking for someone to teach us to pray, or for methods of prayer, when He, by His own mouth, tells us what to do and what to ask. What better or more divine prayer can there possibly be than the *Our Father,* if said with the same meaning and affection with which it came forth from His sacred lips? To be sure, this supposes the most sublime and supernatural contemplation, for it would be a participation in that which He Himself enjoyed, who was perpetually absorbed in the love of His heavenly Father.

St. Teresa has aptly declared that by saying this prayer as it should be said, we could be raised to the highest contemplation. Blessed are they who are able to say the *Our Father* well at least once in their lifetime, with a truly childlike spirit and with dispositions and sentiments worthy of such a Father. That indeed would be a most perfect prayer and extremely pleasing to God.

Therefore, rather than seek the best method of prayer from books and teachers, we should exercise ourselves in that which He Himself teaches us by word and example. We should beg Him to grant that we may do it with His same Spirit: "Lord, teach us to pray! Communicate to us Thy spirit of prayer. Do Thou Thyself pray in our hearts, for we know not how to pray as we ought." When Christ shall live in our hearts, then we shall know how to pray, for then His Spirit will pray within us.

What we have said is not out of line with our purpose of cautioning souls of the danger of going astray by reading mystical books which describe in minute detail the various methods and kinds of prayer and the phenomena which are experienced in them. Such books can be very useful in giving light and reassurance to souls who are passing or have passed through the higher states and, above all, to spiritual directors who should know the various degrees of prayer and contemplation. They will also stimulate other souls to strive to dispose themselves to receive this grace, if the Lord wishes to grant it to them. But under no circumstances are such books suitable for impressionable souls who tend to reproduce within themselves all that they read on this subject; souls who pray with the imagination and believe they experience those effects and phenomena in prayer which are described in the lives of the saints.

Souls of this type are very solicitous in ascertaining their degree of prayer and they measure it by the sensible effects they experience in it. These are the deluded souls, inclined to deceptions and illusions, that St. Teresa referred to when she said that their raptures were nothing more than gape-gazing, and in order to bring them out of them one need only feed them better, occupy them in manual labor, and not give them more time for prayer than their health and duties call for. Souls such as these must be instructed in the nature of true prayer and the kind that is more suitable for them. They need a type of prayer that will help them become more humble, more simple, more obedient, more detached and mortified; a prayer in which they will not seek themselves, but how better to serve and please God. They must be taught that any prayer that does not produce fruits of virtue and perfection is pure illusion, and all the more so as it seems the more lofty.

In conclusion, mystical literature can be divided into two classes: that which treats of perfection or any other subject of the spiritual life from a doctrinal standpoint, aiming principally at the instruction and practice of that life, and that which principally describes the phenomena of the mystical life or of contemplation. The former is neither objectionable nor dangerous to anyone and, if properly used, is always beneficial; indeed, it constitutes one of the most efficacious means of attaining perfection. The latter, on the other hand, can be a source of danger and is in fact dangerous to such souls as we have described, who are inclined to be the toy of their imagination and fantasy and of the aberrations of their sensible nature.

CHAPTER 29 🖎

Seek Thyself in Me

A most efficacious help in striving for perfection was prevalent among the monks of ancient times. It consisted of conferences or collations in which subjects pertaining to the spiritual life were proposed and discussed in an informal, conversational manner; an exercise which rendered their recreations both holy and fruitful. This profitable and holy custom was revived by St. Teresa of Avila. With inimitable ingenuity she proposed themes pertaining to the spiritual life ("motets," as she called them), not only to her nuns but also to priests who, despite their holiness and theological knowledge, were often hard-pressed to answer her. On one occasion no less a personage than St. John of the Cross took part, together with other learned and spiritually minded men, and the theme was the celebrated maxim which heads this chapter.[1]

The answers which these holy men gave on so significant and stimulating a theme are known to us only from the clever judgment which St. Teresa wrote of them. However,

[1] We recommend this practice to all superiors and directors of religious communities and to sponsors of spiritual and pious associations, for we hold it as certain that one of the greatest obstacles to virtue and the interior life in religious communities is the misuse of recreation periods whereby the interior spirit acquired in the other pious exercises is totally lost or dissipated. That is why we consider it one of the gravest and most pressing obligations of superiors and masters of novices to take care that the recreations of those under their charge are conducted in such a manner as to be useful and profitable for the spirit as well as for the body; that is, they should be what the name indicates: a re-creation of body and soul.

as a critic she limits herself to pointing out the weak points in their views, without giving her own opinion or fully presenting those she criticizes.[2] She asserts that St. John of the Cross is excessively supernatural and lofty, for he presupposes the precise thing which is sought: union with God. However, she was in perfect accord with him on the fundamental point; namely, that man truly finds himself only when he finds himself in God.

In order to understand this, we must bear in mind that even in the supernatural order man seeks the full development and perfection of his being. This is in accordance with the fundamental law of all being: to seek the plenitude of its development and perfection. Some psychologists would call it a "superiority complex." In the natural order this desire for superiority obliges man to seek his greatest possible development and perfection within himself; in the supernatural order he seeks and finds it only in God. Again, in the natural order, we say that a man "finds himself" when he discovers the most suitable field for the development of his natural talents. We say, for instance, that a painter, a musician, or a writer finds himself when, aided by favorable circumstances, he discovers and cultivates his talents. Conversely, man seeks himself when he seeks the full development of his faculties and energies in the perfection of his being.

It is, therefore, by virtue of an inescapable law of his

[2] St. Teresa had heard interiorly the words: "Seek thyself in Me." She asked for an explanation of them from several people versed in spiritual matters, including St. John of the Cross, and a series of meetings were held to discuss the maxim, the nuns taking part. It was the Bishop who decided that the final explanations should be in writing and that St. Teresa should compare and criticize them. This she does in her delightfully ironical *Judgment*. See *Complete Works of St. Teresa*, Vol. III, pp. 215 ff. and 266 ff., Allison Peers trans. (Tr.)

nature that man seeks his own greatness: an unlimited, infinite greatness. The truth is that he seeks divinity, for he is made in the image and likeness of God. God abides within him and, as St. Paul says, in Him he lives and moves and has his being.[3] God has sealed his soul with the light of His countenance [4] and that is why man tends toward Him and seeks Him; that is why he finds himself only when he finds God, in whom is the root and substance of his being.

Hence, when man seeks himself within himself or in other creatures, as he does when he is misled by sin and error, he never attains his end and he strays all the more as he goes farther away from God, who is man's true goal. That is also the reason why in order to find God man must depart from himself and all creatures and enter into God and live in Him. Thus the law of total renunciation which is proposed as an indispensable condition in the spiritual life in order to find God. For the only way to find God is to renounce and abandon oneself and all things for His sake. When man does this, he finds again all that he abandoned for God's sake, but now greatly beautified and elevated. He finds light, love, liberty, peace, glory, and every good his heart ever yearned for, but all is raised to the level of the divine and the infinite. His light is divine light; it is that fountain of infinite wisdom which brings all good with it.[5] Divine wisdom, or the experimental knowledge which comes from intimate union with God, makes us so happy that we have nothing more to desire. It completely satisfies the intellect's craving for light and it fulfills all the longings of the heart, for it is a participation in the very light and glory of God. He who knows God with such a knowledge already possesses to some degree the substance of eternal beatitude.

[3] Acts 17:28.   [4] Ps. 4:7.   [5] Wis. 7:11.

Wherefore, if a man seeks perfect happiness, if he wishes to find himself, if he desires to realize the full capacity of his intellect by filling it with uncreated light and to enlarge his heart to the greatest possible extent so that it can be filled with infinite love, if, in a word, he seeks the fullest possible development and perfection for all his faculties and energies and his entire being, let him seek it in God, for there alone is it to be found. Man came forth from God and to Him he will return; for Him he was created and only in Him can he attain full perfection.

"Seek thyself in Me," God repeats incessantly. These words echo in the depths of the consciences of those who, in their feverish quest for happiness, run after the wretched goods of this world, goods which succeed only in exasperating more and more the cravings of their hearts. "Seek thyself in Me," He says also to many souls who seek Him, but not in the right way, for they seek their perfection in themselves; they make no effort to go out of themselves and lose themselves in Him. They seek His gifts, His consolations; they desire sensible signs of His love; they do not seek Him alone, nor do they serve Him, but rather serve themselves.

Serving God does not consist in feeling any particular sentiments in prayer nor in having any particular difficulties or temptations in the spiritual life or any special attraction to it. To serve God is simply to do His will. It means to believe in Him, to confide in Him, to love Him wholeheartedly. It means to rejoice that God is God, that He is infinitely happy, and that no one can deprive Him of that happiness; it means to rejoice that He is just what He is, with all His infinite attributes. To the soul that loves God it is enough for its happiness to know that God is who He is, even though the soul may consider itself the most wretched and miserable of souls and even if God should seem to deal harshly with it, for the soul loves Him so much that it also loves and adores whatever belongs to Him, including His infinite justice. It asks only the right and the grace to love and bless Him always, though it should be from the depths of hell, were such a thing possible. Such a soul looks only to its growth in charity: whether it is patient and kind; whether it "envieth not, dealeth not perversely, is not puffed up; is not ambitious, is not provoked to anger, thinketh no evil; rejoiceth not in iniquity, but rejoiceth with the truth; beareth all things, believeth all things, hopeth all things, endureth all things." [6] In a word, the soul that would know whether or not it truly seeks God and is approaching more closely to Him should examine whether or not it has grown in charity; that is, in the true love of God and neighbor, for in itself charity is nothing else but the love of God reigning in our hearts. Moreover, since love tends to make us like the object of our love, one who loves God is divinized and becomes like unto Him both in his being and in his actions.

CHAPTER 30 ✑

The Friends of God

ST. TERESA of Avila was wont to implore the Lord very fervently and earnestly on behalf of persons of her acquaintance who, because of their good dispositions and aptitude for His service, seemed likely to become good

[6] Cf. I Cor. 13:4–7.

friends of God and do much good for souls if only they had the courage to break the bonds that held them back and give themselves wholly to God. Whenever she met one of these persons she would importune the Lord incessantly saying: "Behold, Lord, how wonderful it would be to have this person as our friend."

In offering this delightful prayer, the Saint had in mind persons whom she hoped would be of great benefit to the Church and powerful instruments for the salvation of souls. Her zeal and greatness of heart were such that she always followed that divine ideal. That is why she esteemed men of great learning and intelligence so highly, for she knew that if to these qualities were added those of virtue and sanctity, they would make God's best instruments for the extension of His holy kingdom.

Besides such souls, however, there are many others who, although they seem to lack those qualifications and even seem to have quite contrary characteristics, would never-theless make good friends of God if they had someone to guide and enlighten them. Many sincerely desire to be good friends of God and it would be their greatest happiness to be so, but they dare not aspire so high, deeming themselves so unworthy as to be more His enemies than His friends. These souls should be enlightened so that they may take courage and fly to God who is inviting them with His friendship and grace. Indeed, no one is worthy of the friendship of God, for friendship implies a measure of equality, and who is equal to God? If we were to view the matter from that standpoint, realizing what God is and what we are, such an aspiration would be sheer blasphemy. But we should regard it rather in the light of the infinite charity and mercy of God, which are so great that He seeks and desires our friendship. "I will not now call you servants, but friends," [1] said our Lord to His disciples; and again, "You are my friends, if you do the things that I command you." [2] Friendship is a work of love and it is the love of God that in some way makes us equal to Him.

Who, then, would make good friends of God? We are not treating here of those who are already His friends, but of those who may become such: of those who at present may perhaps be His enemies and of those who may be standing at the very threshold of friendship with Him, but do not enter for lack of courage.

Regarding the former, we can say that humble sinners generally make good friends of God; those who sin, not through malice, but through frailty, and who do not justify and excuse themselves, but deplore their sins, contritely accuse themselves of them, and would like with all their heart to be freed from the bonds of Satan and from sin. Many of these souls lead a bitter life, constantly lamenting their sad lot and hopefully awaiting a friendly hand that will help them emerge from the mire into which they have fallen, a charitable soul who will understand and compassionate them and help them walk the path of their redemption. Of these we have two great examples in the gospel: Mary Magdalen and the Samaritan woman, great sinners who became friends; indeed, more than friends, spouses of the divine Bridegroom of holy souls. The fact is that they had the qualities necessary for friendship with God: they were noble, generous, and detached souls, capable of great heroism. Unfortunately, they fell into the snare of the devil and launched forth into the way of perdition with all the impetus of their generous temperaments, but once they heard the voice of the Good Shepherd calling

[1] John 15:15.   [2] John 15:14.

them back to the fold, they answered Him wholeheartedly.

We can also say that sinners who transgress through error and in good faith likewise would make good friends of God. Such are many heretics, schismatics, and unbelievers who, because they were born and bred outside the pale of the Church, live in darkness and in the shadows of death. Many earnestly seek the truth and are disposed to embrace it once they find it. When these souls are converted, they frequently make generous reparation for their former errors by a burning zeal for the Church and the service of God, for they are deeply appreciative of the great grace they have received. St. Paul is an excellent example of such zealous converts.

Another class of people who make good friends of God are the upright and simple of heart whose noble and elevated sentiments are concealed beneath the clouds of ignorance and a rough exterior. Such were the men Jesus chose for His disciples and apostles, and today this type constitutes the major part of the Christian people. When these people hear the voice of the divine Shepherd, they follow Him with steadfast determination even unto death. If they have someone to guide and encourage them, they are capable of attaining the highest sanctity. To such as these, Jesus referred when He said: "I confess to thee, O Father, Lord of heaven and earth, because Thou hast hid these things from the wise and prudent and hast revealed them to little ones." [3]

The realization that God places His love and friendship, which are the most precious things in heaven or on earth and the happiness and glory of the angels and saints, within the reach of every mortal, and especially of the poor and simple, cannot but deepen our appreciation of His im-

[3] Matt. 11:25.

mense goodness and mercy. So thoroughly was a holy Franciscan impressed by this that he cried out in ecstasy that the poorest and most ignorant woman could love God and, therefore, could possess as much wisdom as St. Bonaventure.

Finally, there are those timid and cowardly souls who ardently desire to be good friends of God but lack the courage to give themselves completely to Him. They cannot see how creatures as miserable as themselves could possibly aspire to anything so lofty and have a place among such noble and generous souls as those who constitute the "aristocracy," so to speak, of the court of heaven. To this class belong all those dedicated to the interior life who cannot bring themselves to take the final step. Actually, these souls are already friends of God, for they are in the state of grace, but they are not friends to the degree of intimacy that God desires and to which He invites them, lovingly manifesting to them His infinite goodness and tenderness and calling them to partake of the divine banquet of His love. When these souls respond to the call of divine love and abandon themselves totally to it, they will partake of a more intimate friendship and union with God.

To this end they must be admonished against a false humility which is only a mask for the most refined pride and subtle malice which greatly displease and offend God. For it is pride to cling to one's own opinion and refuse to believe that the love and mercy of God are great enough to admit one to friendship and union with Him. This unbelief implicitly supposes that such union and friendship depend more upon one's own merits than on the pure goodness and charity of God, which is a great error that goes against the very glory of God.

More greatly to be feared, however, is the possibility that

beneath this pretext of humility lurks a secret infidelity to grace, a reluctance to sever the last ties that bind us to our self-love, whether natural or spiritual. In this, as in all our works, we must not consider so much the immediate reasons for doing a thing as the deeper motives which prompt those reasons, for human nature easily finds reasons for doing or not doing what it pleases.

By way of summary we say that the qualities which make us apt for friendship with God are humility and nobility of heart. Those souls make good friends of God who esteem nothing of their own, and whatever is theirs they despise or think little of it, however great and praiseworthy it may appear. These souls may feel the full weight of human misery and experience all the temptations to which it is subject, such as pride, ambition, avarice, envy, sensuality, and all the other meannesses of human nature, but they recognize them, weep over them, and as far as possible endeavor to overcome them. Certainly, they never try to justify them.

This is the precise difference between those who make good friends of God and those who do not. Both are subject more or less to the same passions, inclinations, miseries, and pettiness, but the former admit their guilt, deplore their sins, and desire with all their heart to be freed from them. The latter, on the contrary, do not admit their failings; they think themselves good and irreproachable and suffer no one to advise or correct them. Rather, any advice or correction is taken as a personal affront.

True humility is always accompanied by nobility and magnanimity of heart, virtues which are never content with earthly, petty things, but only with the infinite treasures of God. Generosity and detachment naturally follow, because in despising all other goods we are disposed to renounce them in exchange for that infinite good which alone can fill our hearts. But he who lacks nobility of heart and clings to the goods of this world cannot enter into the kingdom of heaven, that is, cannot enjoy friendship with God. As Christ has said, "It is easier for a camel to pass through the eye of a needle, than for a rich man to enter into the kingdom of heaven." [4]

We should, therefore, ask God for humility and detachment, for these virtues are very pleasing to Him and indispensable for friendship and union with Him. Then we may be sure that although we feel ourselves to be the poorest and most miserable of mortals, we shall be admitted to intimate friendship with Him and enjoy His grace, and all the more as we confess ourselves to be the poorest and most miserable of all.

[4] Matt. 19:24.

PART V

Devotion

CHAPTER 31 ✒

Practices of Devotion

IT is interesting to note that mystics seldom speak of devotions. If we review the works of the great masters in the mystical life, such as St. John of the Cross, we shall find scarcely any reference to devotions, much less the recommendation of any one in particular. This fact seems all the more remarkable when we consider that it contrasts sharply with the attitude of ascetical writers, who are lavish in praising and recommending various devotions and manifest an eagerness and enthusiasm which is completely lacking in the mystics.

How can this be explained? Could it be that the mystics are less devout than the ascetics or that contemplation is incompatible with devotions? The explanation is simple and is based on the very nature of the spiritual life. By its very nature the spiritual life tends to an ever greater unity and simplicity, for it is a constant development or movement toward God who is consummate unity and simplicity. Moreover, the very repetition of interior acts makes for unity, as can be observed in all the phases of our psychological activity.

In the beginning of the spiritual life the tendency of souls is to perform a great many interior acts and to have recourse to many different practices, prayers, and methods. At this stage there is a fondness for devotions; indeed, they are the principal source of the soul's nourishment. Gradually, however, this activity becomes increasingly simplified until it is eventually reduced to one thing alone: the love of God, the goal to which all things are ordained. Then all devotions and spiritual exercises produce the same effect in the soul, for in their use the soul is absorbed in the one thing necessary: the love of God.

Devotions, therefore, are not opposed to contemplation; on the contrary, they are ordained to it. They habituate us to prayer by serving as a means and incentive to it and thus they help to dispose us for contemplation. But contemplation, when it is granted, is incompatible with any other exercise of our own initiative. Apart from this, devotions are useful and generally necessary for the development of the spiritual life, provided that they be wisely selected, adapted to the needs of our soul, and practiced for the right purpose and in the proper spirit.

The spirit with which we practice a particular devotion should gradually become more intensified and ever more elevated. In the beginning it may arise from personal and selfish, though spiritual, motives, but in time it should be prompted solely by zeal for the glory of God and a desire to grow in His love. This progress will take place if we endeavor to penetrate more and more into the meaning and substance of the devotions we practice.

Let us take as an example devotion to the Blessed Virgin, which is the most excellent among the devotions to the saints. At first it will consist of sentiments of filial piety toward her, manifested chiefly by praising, entreating, and thanking her. These acts tend to increase our love for the Blessed Virgin and to unite us more closely to her. But Mary is the personification of the love of God and she necessarily leads us also to the love of God. Thus our devotion to her is gradually transformed until the sole motive of our union with her is the better to love and glorify God. Then we shall no longer regard her principally as a protectress or advocate, but as the one creature who most perfectly loves and glorifies God, for the voice of her praise arises from the most sublime sanctity there is outside of God Himself.

That is what enraptures mystical souls; that is why they love and bless her. When they address themselves to her, they are forgetful of self and rather than entreat her on their own behalf, they tend irresistibly to unite themselves to her in order to love and bless God. Indeed, in reciting her litany, they would be delighted to substitute the words "let us love God" for the words "pray for us." It is as if they were to say: "Most Blessed Virgin, give me your heart so that I may love God more perfectly. I unite my heart with yours in order to love God more."

Thus we see that true devotion does not disappear as the interior life progresses; it becomes increasingly transformed and elevated until it attains the end of all devotion: to unite us to God in order that we may live in Him, love Him, and glorify Him as perfectly as possible. What we say here regarding devotion to Mary can be applied proportionately to devotion to any of the saints and to all devotions generally. For the sole end of every devotion, whether to the Blessed Virgin or to any of the saints, is to lead us to God and unite us to Him. That is why, when we attain this end, the saints and even the Blessed Virgin herself seem to fade away so that we may remain alone with God. In like manner, Christ Himself had to depart from the apostles so that the Spirit could come. But just as Christ departed and yet remained with them in a different manner, so also the Blessed Virgin and the saints fade away only to reappear in the soul in another, more divine form.

We believe that this explains why the mystics deal so little with devotions. They suppose that the reader has al-

ready passed beyond the stage of devotions and has attained
the end to which they are ordained, which is union with
God, or at least that God is initiating the soul into passive
prayer which, while in actual progress, is incompatible
with any other occupation of the soul.

In saying that the soul has passed beyond the stage of
devotions, we do not mean that it never again undertakes
devotional practices as long as the state of contemplation
perdures. For the *act* of contemplation is not permanent,
even when it constitutes the habitual state of the soul in
prayer. Therefore, once the contemplative act is completed,
the soul regains the active use of its faculties and it may
return to the devotional practices which are especially
conducive to the cultivation of interior devotion and
growth in the love of God. It is tnen that the Holy Ghost
moves these souls to acts of supplication, praise, or thanksgiving and it is then also that they make these acts more
perfectly, for the contemplation which they have just experienced has illumined their minds and inflamed their
hearts so that they are better able to understand the profound meaning of devotions, especially the liturgical acts
with which the Church celebrates the mysteries of our holy
religion and glorifies God in His saints. No one can imagine the torrents of light which these souls receive and
the ineffable sentiments they experience at the celebration
of the sacred mysteries and the exercises of divine worship.

It is also commonly known that God permits contemplative souls to be severely tempted at times so that they may
feel the full weight of their misery and unworthiness and
not indulge in vainglory. These trials make them realize
how poor and deficient they are of themselves and that
whatever good they may be able to do or experience, comes
not from themselves but from God. The more advanced a

soul is, the more profoundly does it feel its great misery. Then it is necessarily obliged to have recourse to devotions and to invoke the protection of the saints.

Such is the function of devotions in the spiritual life and how we are to make use of them. We should use them so far as they serve as a means of fostering our spirit of prayer and lead us to God. However, if we are already united with God in prayer and our soul is in that passive state wherein the practice of devotions and the exercise of our faculties distract us from our one and only object and are an obstacle to perfect union, then we should lay aside all devotions that are not obligatory. However, it is good to seek the advice of a prudent spiritual director in order not to fall victims of illusions. Our spiritual director should also indicate to us the devotions which would be more conducive to our spiritual progress, being mindful always of the rule of the masters in the spiritual life: *Few devotions, but much devotion.* These should be carefully selected, giving preference always to those which deal more directly with the worship of the three divine Persons and avoiding the monstrous error of those who load themselves with innumerable devotions to the saints and all but forget God, thus giving occasion for the statement that the saints of God are His enemies because they rob Him of veneration. Let us bear in mind that devotion of this type cannot possibly please the saints themselves and, indeed, it would offend them gravely if it were to hinder the soul from glorifying God and uniting itself to Him. Finally, we should practice our devotions with great fervor, avoiding routine, which is the ruin of every devotion and the reason why many apparently devout persons do not advance one step in the spiritual life.

What we have said applies to all persons who dedicate

themselves to the interior life and aspire to perfection. As for those who do not preoccupy themselves with this, it would be well for them to practice some particular devotion, regardless of what it is, whereby they can perform some act of religion and ask for the graces they need.

CHAPTER 32 ✍

Theological Devotion

Now this is eternal life: that they may know Thee, the only true God, and Jesus Christ, whom Thou hast sent.[1]

ALL true devotion should be directed to and should terminate in the knowledge of God, a "sapiential" or delectable knowledge whereby the soul, as it were, tastes the divine truths. We arrive at this delectable knowledge by means of habitual and constant prayer and not through study, unless we turn our study into prayer, as happens when we seek to know God in order to love Him. In that case, both study and meditation of the divine truths are a very powerful and efficacious means of fostering and deepening our spirit of prayer.

Nevertheless, although study and meditation are suitable and profitable means, they are not absolutely necessary nor indispensable. Many souls arrive at this delectable knowledge of God by means of affective rather than by discursive prayer. As as matter of fact, discursive prayer alone is incapable of attaining that end and must eventually give

[1] John 17:3.

way to affective prayer if we are to enjoy that delectable knowledge.

This fact should be very consoling to simple souls who for some reason or other are incapable of meditating or thinking discursively on spiritual subjects. It is also one of the greatest proofs of the infinite tenderness of the heavenly Father for souls: to conceal His ineffable secrets from the wise and prudent and to reveal them to the humble and little ones. We ourselves know from long experience that simple and humble souls who are generous and anxious to love God succeed in knowing Him more profoundly than most theologians. Indeed, their devotion is ultimately transformed into the most theological of all devotions. (We call that devotion "theological" which is nourished principally by the contemplation of the divine attributes, even those which seem most abstract and inaccessible.) It could not be otherwise, for the love of God in its most sublime degree is naught but a never-ending hymn of praise and adoration of His infinite perfections. All the happiness of the saints in this and in the next world consists in the unspeakable joy they derive from the consideration that God is God and from the contemplation of His ineffable attributes. In this way they fulfill their purpose as creatures, for the goal of every creature is to glorify God.

That is why St. John of the Cross places on the top of the Mount of Perfection the words: "On this Mount abide solely the honor and glory of God." It was undoubtedly while she sojourned upon this mount that St. Rose of Lima composed the "Angelic Exercise," a litany of the divine attributes wherein she praises and rejoices in God's perfections and renders Him the most perfect homage of worship and adoration. In this litany she refers even to the most ineffable of the divine attributes and to the most profound truths concerning God: His self-existence, His unity and trinity, His eternity, infinity, simplicity, goodness, omnipotence, and wisdom; the innascibility of the Father, the generation of the Son, and the spiration of the Holy Ghost. St. Rose was also joyously conscious in a very special way of the inner life of God, that is, of the activity of knowledge and love among the three divine Persons.

We refer to this theological devotion of St. Rose because it is a very pointed example of the possibility of the simple and uneducated to rise to the loftiest heights of contemplation, for she was of a poor family and without any training or education whatever, yet she attained a lofty knowledge of God and delighted in an exercise which to all appearances seems dry and abstruse. But the lover is never satiated with contemplating and delighting in the perfections of the beloved; it is the source of all his happiness and the only occupation which fully satisfies him.

Another element of theological devotion is the knowledge of Christ, as explained by our Lord Himself in the text quoted at the beginning of this chapter. As a matter of fact, no one can give glory to God except in and through Christ. All the praise and adoration and everything that creatures can offer to God would be absolutely devoid of value without Christ. It is He who spans the infinite abyss which stands between God and the creature, between created and uncreated being. His divine Person is the bond of union between these two beings which by their natures are infinitely distant from each other.

God can be worthily honored only by acts of infinite value and only God Himself can give such value to the acts of creatures who of themselves are nothing. This is precisely what Christ does and it is His specific mission, so to speak, in the divine plan of creation. In Him, with

Him, and through Him the actions of creatures can have an infinite value. Man can now turn to God and say to Him: 'In union with Thy well-beloved Son, Jesus Christ, I love Thee, I adore Thee, and I glorify Thee, for I know that my love pleases Thee and that my praises are acceptable and worthy of Thee."

What ineffable happiness it is for one who yearns to glorify God to know that he can now do it in a manner worthy of God. How utterly inadequate seem his protestations of gratitude to Christ for having effected so great a work and having so admirably restored the plan of creation that all creation glorifies God and man himself can now pay Him divine honor. Indeed, what would the world be without Christ? What would become of souls whose one and only end is to glorify God? Life would be a veritable hell, for souls could never satisfy their immortal yearnings.

But now in and with Christ they possess all good, for He is all theirs. It no longer matters that they are poor and miserable, for they have in their possession the treasures of Christ. The imperfections which are found even in their good works, the mediocrity and pettiness of their thoughts, the unworthiness of their actions before the majesty of God are things that no longer afflict them, for they have in their possession the justice, sanctity, merits, thoughts, and affections of Christ as well as His divine dispositions toward His heavenly Father, and these they offer to God with unspeakable joy. In Him is their life and happiness; in Him they find all the treasures of wisdom and knowledge hidden in God, especially the all-surpassing science of the charity of Christ. For these souls, to live is Christ, for they have no inclination or movement except in Him, through Him, and for Him. This is the object and end of all true devotion: to die to self in order to live in Christ and thus glorify His heavenly Father with Christ's own heart and spirit.

CHAPTER 33 🖎

Affective Progress of the Soul

THE progress of the soul's affections does not consist in their increased intensity but rather in their elevation and ennoblement, in their ever greater spiritualization and perfection. Greater intensity may be a sign of greater perfection within a given order or grade, but it does not of itself signify a greater perfection of all the affections as a whole, nor does it of itself constitute a distinct grade or degree. Thus, sorrow for sin that is founded on fear may be the more perfect as it is the more intense, but it will never be as perfect as the sorrow that arises from love and reverence for God. The reason for this is that the sensible affections do not constitute the essence of spiritual values, nor do they even necessarily accompany them. On the contrary, as they become more spiritual, they are usually less sensible or, as St. Paul says, they are above all sense.

It is an error, therefore, to maintain that progress in the spiritual life is in direct proportion to the intensity of the affections and that the greatest saints were those who were the more impetuous and ardent. At most, this ardor can serve as a criterion for the stages preceding the transforming union, for St. John of the Cross says that at that time the wine of divine love is still in the process of fermentation, bubbling and running over toward the senses. However, once this wine of divine love is well fermented, the soul no longer experiences the excessive effervescence and suffering. The reason for this is that the capacity and powers of the human senses, being limited, cannot embrace the infinite; therefore, as the latter is gradually revealed to the soul, the sense nature recedes until it dies altogether, although it comes to life again in a new and more divine form. That is why in order to see and rejoice in God it is necessary first to die: "Man shall not see me and live."[1] For that reason also the saints, after their transforming union, are intensely aware of their interior death and their utter nothingness before the infinite abyss of God. It is this supersensible awareness of their nothingness that gives them an ineffable knowledge or awareness of God. For one abyss attracts another:[2] the abyss of human nothingness draws unto itself the infinite abyss of the divine plenitude and is filled completely with God.

But we cannot gauge the progress of the soul by the sensible affections even in states preceding the transforming union, unless we consider the sentiments of desolation and bitterness, experienced by many souls in certain stages, as signs of such progress. So consistently and unremittingly is this desolation the portion of many souls that they would be tempted to think that those who speak of consolations and sweetness in the spiritual life are mistaken, or that everyone but themselves lives in a veritable Tabor, for they cannot remember ever experiencing anything but fears, darkness, hardships, and conflicts. Of course, this gloomy outlook is due in great measure to the darkness that envelopes them at the time, for on other occasions things will not appear so gloomy and dismal and they will even rejoice in their trials and tortures; after

[1] Exod. 33:20.   [2] Ps. 41:8.

all, they cannot help but see that they are suffering for God and that it is His love that torments them. They will realize that it is the divine hand that wounds them, that hand which, even as it wounds and torments, never fails to leave a trace of its ineffable sweetness.

Such is the interior life of many souls, and eventually all, to a greater or less extent, must pass through their "dark night" before they can arrive at union with God. It is expedient, therefore, that they be acquainted with this doctrine in order that they may know that the love of God does not consist esentially in sweet affections and that it is very possible for one's prayer to be most acceptable to God in the midst of spiritual darkness and inexpressible sufferings. Indeed, it is precisely in darkness and tribulation that souls are purified and their sentiments and dispositions are purged, transformed, and divinized. Hence, here also true progress of the affections takes place, for the affections are in direct relation to the state and perfection of the soul; they are faithful reflectors or manifestations of the soul's degree of nobility or perfection. In the measure that the soul is ennobled and perfected, in that same measure are its affections ennobled and perfected in regard to everything, especially in all that relates to God and His holy service.[3]

This explains the diversity of sentiments which the saints

[3] The progress of the affections always advances parallel with the purification of love, the life of the soul. Therefore, the purer the love, the purer and more elevated the affections it produces. For this reason, after union with God in the consummation of love, the saints experience a complete renovation of their thoughts and affections in the spiritual order. They no longer think, feel, and speak as children, as St. Paul relates, but as perfect men. All that is past seems baneful, low, imperfect, and altogether inadequate for the glorification of God. At this point they intone their new canticle, which they alone can sing.

experience in the various stages of their interior life, so diverse, indeed, that at times they seem contradictory. St. Teresa of Avila observed this phenomenon in herself toward the end of her life, when she had arrived at the threshold of the beatific vision. She used to marvel at the fact that she was no longer torn with an insatiable yearning to die in order to see God, for it no longer mattered to her whether she lived or died. Did this mean that her love for God had died or that she had grown cold? Quite the contrary. What happened was that she had arrived at that state in which she could sing with the spouse of the Canticles: "I found him whom my soul loveth: I held him: and I will not let him go." [4] She no longer felt that intolerable yearning because she had found Him whom she sought. Although she did not yet possess Him as she would in heaven, in such a way as to beatify her completely, she did possess Him in a way that completely filled her heart.

The Saint likewise marvelled at the fact that she no longer felt the horrible pain and anguish that she had formerly experienced at the thought of the offences committed against God. Not, as St. John of the Cross says, that she had ceased to realize their gravity and deformity, but because her very sanctity estranged her, so to speak, from the sentiment of sin and elevated her to the pure regions where peace and conformity to God's will dominate and eclipse every other sentiment. In other words, she lived in God, where the sentiment of sin cannot enter. Her sentiments were simply the expression of the sanctity of her soul.

These changes are similarly and proportionately experienced by all souls in the course of their spiritual life as they approach more closely to God. Their sentiments and dispositions undergo a process of transformation that causes

[4] Can. 3:4.

some souls to become dubious and apprehensive regarding their state, fearing that they are retreating instead of advancing or that they have strayed from the right road. For this reason it is expedient that they be instructed in this matter so that they may not fear that their sentiments and dispositions are becoming worse or, still less, that they are contrary. They should bear in mind that as they approach more closely to God, their sentiments and dispositions undergo a process of renewal which is proportionate to the stages through which they must pass in their journey to Him.

In the beginning the soul's sentiments and dispositions are directed primarily either to those things that separate it from God or those things that lead it to Him, such as hatred of sin, the love of virtue, or whatever contributes to one's spiritual advancement. That is why beginners so ardently yearn to be purified and desire repeatedly to renew their general confessions, to do penance, and to weep for their sins. Their soul necessarily demands this as divine grace moves them to clear away the obstacles that hinder its expansion and growth. Afterwards they tend principally to arouse sentiments of love through a consideration of benefits received and the ineffable manifestations of the infinite goodness and love of God. When they arrive at the state of union, such sentiments do not disappear but are elevated and transformed, despoiled of all attachment and spiritual self-love in order that they may be directed exclusively to God. Then they begin to love God truly for His own sake and not for any alien motives, not even because He is good to them, or because He is the source of all their good (unless by "all their good" we mean the very glory of God in Himself, for that indeed constitutes all their happiness). In fine, it is in the life of union that the sentiments and affections of the soul are fully spiritualized and perfected, for they no longer proceed from the soul's own life, but from the life of God within it. Who could fathom the height and depth of such sentiments?

From all that has been said, we should like to draw some practical conclusions concerning the spiritual life. The first is that sentiments and affections of piety and fervor should not be underestimated on the grounds that they do not constitute virtue and sanctity, for they are very powerful means of obtaining them. Moreover, not to esteem them when God gives them would be equivalent to despising His gifts. Affections of piety and fervor should, therefore, be sought and fomented in prayer by arousing what is called a movement of the affections. Further, we should investigate whether our coldness and indifference proceed from dissipation or lack of fidelity to grace.

Secondly, if we find no manifest culpability on our part and we sincerely endeavor to pray as well as we are able, then regardless of how dry and tedious our prayer may be, we may rest assured that it will be fruitful, and all the more so as it is the more tedious. Therefore, we should not allow ourselves to become distressed over our dryness of soul and, above all, never abandon prayer on account of it; on the contrary, it should be an incentive to even greater effort to persevere in prayer.

Thirdly, when our impotence in affective prayer or in meditation is due to that state which St. John of the Cross describes in the *Dark Night of the Soul* and is accompanied by the signs which he indicates as proof that one should leave meditation, then it will be useless and even harmful to endeavor by violent efforts to exercise our faculties. In such circumstances we should follow the interior impulse and practice prayer in a passive manner, being careful not to hinder the divine action. Prayer then demands only perseverance before God, patiently enduring the divine action of interior purification which is taking place. At that time everything depends on our accompanying Christ in the garden of Gethsemane and following Him even unto death.

Fourthly, when God calls us to a given kind of prayer and arouses in us certain affections, we should foster those affections without endeavoring by our own initiative to change to another kind of prayer, thinking it better for us and more pleasing to God. It would also be a grave error to think that because the soul is in a particular state of the spiritual life it cannot experience the affections proper to other states. Even the prayer of union, although permanent, is not always manifest and sometimes it is eclipsed to such a degree that the soul is obliged to have recourse to every available means in order to maintain order in its house and direct its faculties and senses back to their divine center.

Fifthly, it is expedient for all souls, regardless of the stage they may be in and even in the very beginning of the spiritual life, to evoke within themselves the purest and most lofty affections of the love of God, such as to love Him for His own sake alone and insistently to beg God for this purity of love. If they do this sincerely and whole-heartedly, they may be sure that God will soon hear them. For it is our indifference in desiring and asking that ties the hands of God and prevents Him from giving it to us as quickly as He would like. Sanctity is not a matter of time, but of disposition of soul.

Sixthly, sublime and lofty sentiments are not a reliable criterion for determining the soul's degree of perfection, unless they are accompanied by other signs. Many believe

themselves to be very exalted in virtue and sanctity because they have lofty and sublime thoughts and sentiments
concerning God and the things of God, whereas they may
be deceiving themselves; their exalted virtue may very
probably be founded on nothing more than their imagination. Many speak with facility and eloquence about holy
things and yet the magnitude of their imperfections could
almost be measured by the loftiness of their speech.

However, there are certain signs whereby we can tell
with a high degree of certitude whether the affections are
a true expression of the state of the soul. We are not speaking here of the interior testimony of the Holy Ghost who
testifies to His own that they are the sons of God.[5] The
interior testimony which souls have in the transforming
union carries the conviction of truth itself; its certitude is
something ineffable. It does not proceed from human reasoning nor from proofs or external lights; it is itself a
light that illumines all things. However, for those of us who
do not possess that light and certitude, the proof that the
loftiness of our spiritual sentiments is a true measure of
our perfection lies in our works, above all in the work of
our purification and interior detachment: the death of our
self-love. This death, if it is true and definitive, is indeed
positive proof; and that it *is* true and definitive is, in turn,
demonstrated by our humility and self-contempt. Another
proof of the sincerity and veracity of our sentiments and
their worth as a true expression of our interior state is
when they habitually and spontaneously arise from our
soul without the need for discursive methods.

In conclusion, we wish to remind the reader that these
rules are meant more for the purposes of instruction and
direction than for one's particular use. There is nothing

[5] Rom. 8:16.

more dangerous than to attempt to probe into our interior state in order to ascertain our progress. Let us serve God wholeheartedly in whatever stage we may be, taking care not to go backward, and leave the rest in His hands.

CHAPTER 34 🖋

The Pure Love of God

THE most sublime ideal and most ardent yearning of souls hungry for justice and sanctity is, without doubt, to attain to the pure love of God; that is to say, a love absolutely unalloyed by any other love. That is why they implore God with the greatest earnestness to "sanctify them in truth." [1] This great desire also moves them frequently to examine their interior in order to discover the ambushes of the enemy and escape his plots and snares. What would they not give, especially in time of contradictions, to know what is the most pure love of God, what would be most agreeable to Him, and how they could truly please Him!

Much has already been written to supply this need and to clarify this point which is so important in the spiritual life and it is not our intention to repeat it here. Nor do we intend to discuss the historical errors which already have been refuted a thousand times, such as that of the semi-Quietists who, by reason of their erroneous concept of the pure love of God, fell into many other errors. We wish only to observe that in justly condemning this error, the Church did not condemn the pure love of God, but the "state of the

[1] John 17:17.

pure love of God." To put the matter more clearly, the Church condemned two errors: first, that the pure love of God is incompatible with interest in one's salvation; secondly, that there is a state of perfection in which the soul is always moved to love God alone with the pure love as defined by the semi-Quietists. Under the appearance of sanctity and holiness, these errors concealed a danger which was all the greater by reason of the fact that it tended to seduce the most noble and generous souls. Under pretense of disinterestedness and greater purity, they threatened to undermine the solid foundations of the fear of God in the spiritual life.

It is necessary, therefore, emphatically to affirm that the true love of God is not contrary to a legitimate interest in our own salvation. On the contrary, this interest, if properly understood, increases in proportion as we grow in the true love of God. For the latter elevates the concepts of self-interest, salvation, and eternal happiness and places them all in the one and the same love. Thus, although at one time we may have placed our beatitude in some other kind of happiness, eventually we neither know nor can we imagine any other beatitude or happiness than that of the love of God. Therefore, to renounce or ignore this happiness is absurd and diametrically opposed to the true love of God.

Moreover, even if we were to consider this self-interest according to the common notion of escaping hell and gaining heaven, it is not opposed to the true love of God. For this aspiration is an expression of human nature's fundamental law of self-preservation, and grace does not oppose the legitimate aspirations and tendencies of nature. All that the love of God does is direct these tendencies to more lofty ends, orientating them to God and despoiling them of all servile and petty egoism. The whole point, therefore, lies in placing our interest in the possession of God or divine love, thus fulfilling the famous axiom of St. Teresa: "Seek thyself in Me."

Finally, the state of pure love, as understood by semi-Quietist authors, actually does not exist, because there is no state in the spiritual life in which the soul is always actually moved to love and to act solely from pure love, to the exclusion of all other motives. We speak, of course, of a *state*, and not a privilege which God could confer upon a particular person. We say that no such state of perfection exists, because even the most elevated states attainable in this life are subject to disturbances in which the soul is obliged to act upon the motives of fear and hope in order to maintain itself firm in that state.

God permits conflicts and tempests to assail the soul even after having bestowed upon it the highest favors, in order to keep it humble and cognizant of the source of all its good. Even in the state of transformation and union (which state never entirely disappears but remains substantially the same) disturbances are apt to arise on the surface of the soul, so to speak, and temporarily eclipse the light which illumines it. At such times the soul is obliged to have recourse to every means in order to keep itself firm in its adherence to God.

In a word, true love does not disdain any motive which will serve to unite the soul more closely to God and avoid being separated from Him. As St. John of the Cross says, true love incites the soul to seek in all things, the high and the low, the natural and supernatural, motives to love God more ardently.[2] In other words, love transforms all things into love. Let us now clarify some misconceptions on the

---

[2] *Ascent of Mount Carmel,* Bk. III, chap. 26.

love of God and consider a few fundamental notions whereby we shall be able to discern the nature of the true love of God.

There are two errors into which those dedicated to the interior life and to the attainment of the love of God often fall. Some maintain that the love of God lies primarily in the affections and others, in works. We say "primarily" because, of course, no one totally excludes the contrary point of view. We could even add that neither of these two classes of souls hold contrary spiritual principles or doctrines on this point, but that in their spiritual life they are influenced by one or the other of these two concepts of love. Nor is it strange that this should be so, for almost everything that is said or written regarding the love of God is expressed in such terms as to give one, especially simple souls, the idea that it consists in affections and sentiments (elevated, to be sure, but still in the sensible order) or in heroic deeds or extraordinary works. If, for example, we read the lives of the saints, we shall see that the authors almost exclusively take either the affections or works of their subjects as the measure of their love for God. He who has the most tender affections, the most ecstatic raptures, the most ardent zeal, the greatest manifestation of the "divine folly"; or he whose works are most extraordinary, whose penances are the most astounding, and he who has accomplished the most magnificent projects for the glory of God and the Church; he, without doubt, is the most holy.

To be sure, such sentiments or works are generally the marks of charity and sanctity, but they are not charity and sanctity itself. It is important to observe and emphasize this point, because very often those who hear or read such descriptions are prompted to imitate them. Consequently, if they dedicate themselves to prayer, they concentrate all

their efforts on evoking within themselves tender affections
and ardent sentiments of devotion. If they fail in this and
find nothing but aridity and repugnance, they believe
their prayer fruitless and the time lost that is spent in it.
Likewise, when they consider how poor and insignificant
their works are by comparison with those described in the
lives of the saints, they lose heart and even condemn their
own spiritual lives. They conclude from all this that since
their affections and works, or their interior and exterior
lives, are so far from resembling those of the saints, surely
sanctity is not for them and God is not leading them by that
path.

This is indeed a very great evil, for it estranges souls
from God instead of leading them to Him. It is, therefore,
of prime importance repeatedly to affirm the true doctrine
and with St. Paul to proclaim in very definite terms that
the love of God, or charity and sanctity, does not consist in
tender affections or extraordinary works and that it has no
other distinctive signs than those which the Apostle himself
enumerates in describing it.[3] Wherefore, as far as sensible
affections of devotion and fervor are concerned, he who
should persevere for a lifetime in prayer of desolation
would reveal greater sanctity than another whose prayer
was a continuous ecstasy; and he who for the love of God
conformed himself to a humble and despicable life would
be a greater saint than another whose life was studded with
brilliant and marvelous deeds in which he took satisfaction.

Would that we could learn to love poverty of spirit for
the love of God! That we could desire to be nothing in order
that He might be our all! Wisely has that great saint of our
time, the Little Flower, exalted and stressed this important

[3] Cf. I Cor. 13.

virtue. Indeed, the principal affection or disposition aroused by the true love of God and the surest sign whereby we may discern it, is death to self, a total detachment from all that is not love. This affection (let us call it so, for although it is supernatural, it is somewhat perceptible) is not the passion of love, even in the most noble sense of the term, but a feeling of death, annihilation, alienation, and transformation.

This supernatural transformation is the touchstone whereby we may discern the true love of God, inasmuch as it is its essential and exclusive effect; the love of God alone can produce it. It is, therefore, a most certain and unmistakable sign of the true love of God, because it implies the destruction of the old man and the emergence of the new. Moreover, these two beings, the old man and the new, are so diametrically opposed to each other that he who undergoes this transformation cannot possibly doubt it; indeed, sooner would he doubt his transformation from a child into a man. Furthermore, by its destructive and renovating effects, this transformation is accompanied by a supersensible awareness of its supernatural character, for it is above all the forces and laws of nature. He in whom it takes is fully aware of the marvelous and inexplicable spiritual and moral change he has undergone: a change which is manifested in a new way of acting and living. He feels that the language whereby men express their judgment and appreciation of things has become incomprehensible to him, not to his natural reason, but to his spirit. The reason for this is that he no longer esteems human or temporal values but only the divine and eternal, and this is so not only in his judgment and appreciation of things in the natural order, but even more so of those in the supernatural or spiritual order. In the latter, he no longer esteems anything but the glory and interests of God, and in this he finds all his delight and happiness.

A similar change takes place in his attitude toward the virtues. They no longer have any value for him as means to an end, for he has already attained that end. However, he does appreciate the value and necessity of the virtues in obtaining the end he has attained or as expressions of what the Spirit has already wrought in him. He also acknowledges and realizes their need when God permits him to feel his frailty, as He sometimes does in order to keep the soul humble. It is impossible for us to describe all the effects of this transformation, but one can read descriptions of them in classical works of mystical doctrine.

Finally, we wish to emphasize two very important conclusions. First, in reading descriptions of the state of union or transformation in works on mysticism, we should guard against the false notion that those who have attained this state have been completely freed from the miseries of this life and from the frailties of human nature. They are subject to physical miseries the same as every other mortal, although they experience them as something totally exterior to themselves which cannot destroy their interior peace and happiness. These miseries may indeed eclipse their peace, making it temporarily imperceptible to them, but they cannot destroy it altogether.

Likewise with regard to moral frailties and miseries, souls in the unitive way are able to feel them when God so permits, and perhaps even more vividly than others, for the reason that their souls are more delicate and accustomed to live in such lofty regions. But however great these evils and sufferings may be, they cannot affect the interior depths of the soul nor penetrate into that innermost recess where they are securely sheltered under the divine wings.

Rather, such frailties and miseries deepen their love for God, strengthen their union with Him in a remarkable manner, and enable them to rejoice all the more in Him as they see that He is thereby magnified and glorified in them. Their frailties serve also to keep them constantly vigilant, lest they be surprised by the enemy who is ever ready to snatch the treasures they bear within them.

Human nature never dies completely and the devil never sleeps. Indeed, both human nature and the devil will do their utmost to confuse the divine with the human or the human with the divine and to make souls misuse the very gifts they have received from God. But if souls are vigilant this will not happen, for they will be able to discern between the movements that proceed from both the one and the other. The wisest course, however, is not to feel secure and to remember that without an exceptional privilege from God no one is confirmed in sanctity. This is true even of those who arrive at the highest degree of union with God. What, then, must be said of the rest? How many souls have been deceived into believing themselves to have reached the most sublime sanctity, whereas it was but a fantastic dream and a deception of the devil! In some cases there may, indeed, have been some degree of sanctity, but they thought it more exalted than it was, became careless and proud, and fell miserably to earth. Is this not the history of all the spiritual disasters that have been recorded?

Secondly, inasmuch as the unmistakable sign of the true love of God is one's interior transformation, let him who wishes to ascertain his progress in the spiritual life look to this transformation within himself. Let him observe whether the love of God has greater and greater sway over his way of thinking, feeling, and acting. Let him see whether he is more detached from the things of earth and more fond of those of heaven. Let him consider if in his appreciation of things he is guided more by the criterion of the saints and the mind of Christ than by that of the world. Let him see if he is becoming more and more humble and if he is learning to relish the fruits of the Cross. In a word, let him observe if he now finds joy and spiritual contentment in conquering, denying, and sacrificing himself for Christ. For these are the signs of the true love of God. In order to attain this, let him not seek consolations in prayer, but the virtue and strength to detach himself from all consolations. In all his actions let him seek solely to please God, doing His holy will in all things. This is the true love of God.

CHAPTER 35 ✄

Interior Peace

WITHOUT fear of exaggeration we could say that no other element is considered of such great moment or is so highly recommended for the spiritual life as interior peace. Experience has amply demonstrated that interior peace is an indispensable condition to progress in the way of perfection; without it, all perfection is exposed to grave danger of shipwreck or, at least, of losing much of its vigor and beauty by reason of the many imperfections and defects which proceed from a lack of interior poise and equilibrium.

Every fault and imperfection is possible in the midst of turmoil and confusion. That is why Satan invariably employs the tactics of disquieting souls or taking advantage of their perturbed state as a previous disposition for his assaults. This is, in fact, an efficacious procedure in all warfare: before launching the attack, steps are taken to disconcert the enemy or surround him with a smoke-screen. Such tactics enable Satan to hide in the least suspected places, conceal from us his traps and snares, and attack us surreptitiously at our weakest point in order to make us fall. This is one of the many reasons why the preservation of interior peace should be the earnest endeavor of every pious soul. It should not only be preserved but increased, if possible, until finally it is firmly fixed on the most solid and permanent foundation: God Himself.

This means that there are various kinds of peace, even apart from the false peace of the wicked which we do not treat here. In the first place, it is important for us to distinguish between sensible peace and peace of conscience. The former consists in the lack of interior and exterior conflicts; the latter, in the testimony of our conscience that we are doing what we should at all times. It could perhaps be expressed more clearly if we said that sensible peace consists in the feeling of peace, and peace of conscience in the knowledge that we are conducting ourselves well. However, we must note that this knowledge is sometimes so veiled and concealed as to deprive us of any feeling of interior peace. This fact is of prime importance in the spiritual life, and persons who are tempted or perturbed should never forget it, for it is one of the most powerful means of preserving interior peace.

We should also remember that it is not always possible to have sensible peace and that there are many things that can perturb it without any fault of our own. Consequently, there may be true peace of conscience in the midst of the greatest confusion, temptations, and exterior conflicts. Moreover, when these temptations and disturbances are not voluntary, God permits them for our greater perfection and sanctification. Even more, the sacrifice of sensible peace is one of the most agreeable sacrifices that perfect souls can offer to God. Hence it is said that God abhors the peace of those He destines for war. The sacrifice of sensible peace not only does not destroy true peace but it augments and strengthens it, because it supplants the fickle and variable sensible peace with that which is purely spiritual and secure against assaults.

It is this spiritual peace, or peace of conscience, which we can and should always seek. Whatever be our situation, we should always strive to do what we believe in conscience to be the most perfect thing. This should be the constant and earnest desire of everyone seeking perfection. Where there is a sincere will to do at all times what seems best and most pleasing to God, neither the present, the past, nor the future can disturb one's true peace of soul, for He Himself has promised it to souls of good will.

Regarding sensible peace, we should remember that although its sacrifice is very pleasing to God, this is so only when it is He who imposes that sacrifice; that is to say, when the causes that disturb our peace are not the result of our own volition. We ought on our part carefully to avoid every occasion of sensible disturbance or perturbation. If we were to do otherwise and were the cause of our own disquietude, we could no longer enjoy true peace of conscience. Moreover, it is undeniable that disquietude of itself is never good and if it ever has a good effect, it is because God in some cases makes it serve His holy designs.

However, we should at all times, even when the disturbance is evidently ordained by God, endeavor to avoid every voluntary contribution to it and do all in our power to maintain perfect peace, both interiorly and exteriorly. Various means are recommended for this end. The first is not to propose the attainment of peace as the goal of one's interior life, but simply to love and serve God. With this uprightness and purity of intention, we shall not oblige God to prove us by trials calculated to disengage us from that attachment which arises from a disguised spiritual egoism. The second means recommended is not only to avoid an anxious solicitude for peace, but to resign ourselves to live without it during our whole life if it so pleases God.

The third means is to watch and control our thoughts and sentiments, however good they may seem to us, for as the Holy Spirit says: There are ways which appear good to man but they lead to death. We do this by simply applying the rule which our divine Savior gave for discerning false teachers and doctrines and which can be applied to all kinds of frauds, sophisms, and falsehoods: "By their fruits you shall know them." [1] By the fruits which our desires and sentiments produce and by the action to which they incline us, we shall know if they are good or if our malice or the devil have distorted them to serve evil ends.

Good souls should be especially vigilant about the third norm, for it is not so necessary to be forewarned about those things which are patently evil. Let them examine attentively how many times they have erred or fallen into imperfections and perhaps into sins by allowing themselves to be carried away by sentiments which seemed very just and holy. All too often it happens that upon recalling their past sins for the purpose of stirring their conscience to greater remorse, souls fall into temptations and disorders which they should avoid at any cost. Again, prompted by extrava-

[1] Matt. 7:20.

gant aspirations for sanctity, for instance, they frequently allow themselves to be carried away by fancies which take them as far from the reality of life as from true sanctity. Or, under the impulse of a misguided zeal, they launch forth into projects which God does not approve. Often they wound charity, are filled with resentment, and are poisoned by rash judgment because they set themselves up as supreme judges in the cause of God. They deceive themselves again and again, thinking they act upon just and holy motives, whereas their passion conceals from them the true motives from which they act. Indeed, it would be an interminable task if we were to undertake to indicate all the deceptions and disorders which arise in these matters. We can, therefore, only repeat: "Watch your thoughts and feelings; do not take their goodness for granted and allow yourselves to be carried away by them. Observe closely how they incline you and examine the fruits they produce."

This does not mean that we should stifle every thought and feeling however good and noble it may seem. On the contrary, we ought to foster in our heart whatever is noble and holy, for it is the only good we have and the most clear sign of our divine origin. The only thing we wish to emphasize is the necessity of vigilance over our interior, especially when we have a disquieting thought, so that the impulses and inclinations of our soul will not become distorted and perverted.

The fourth means for preserving peace consists in striving not only for interior peace, but also for exterior peace, as far as lies in our power. We shall attain this exterior peace if we try to live as "angels of peace," that is, as *peacemakers*. It is not sufficient that we be meek and patient; we must make positive efforts to bring peace to our surroundings, endeavoring by every means to live in peace with everyone and that everyone around us may also live in peace. Exterior peace or composure is a powerful influence on our interior peace and he who makes no effort to preserve it or who actually destroys it will not delay long in suffering the consequences. However, it is possible that even observing all that we have thus far pointed out regarding the means of preserving peace, there will be times when we shall be disquieted and upset through no fault of our own. On such occasions, the following norms should prove helpful:

1) Seek the advice of a spiritual director or, if this is impossible, of a virtuous and prudent person.

2) Ascertain the causes of the disquietude in order to eradicate them, especially if they spring from vices and passions.

3) If the matter can possibly be deferred, do not make any resolutions when in this condition. If no delay is possible, then do not let your decision extend beyond the present necessity. Every day we see the fatal consequences of imprudent steps taken under such circumstances.

4) Have recourse to fervent prayer, the universal remedy of our ills, asking God by His power to bestow peace.

5) If in spite of everything the tempest continues, do not on that account fail to do what in conscience you believe to be right. Above all, do not fail to bless God and humble yourself before Him, trusting that in spite of your sins He will have mercy on you.

6) Do not seek peace by trying to elude the will of God, that is, by wishing to change situations or abandon your duties and obligations on the pretext that they are the cause of your disquietude and the faults you commit or believe you commit. On the contrary, resign yourself to live without peace your whole life through, if that be the

will of God. In order to persevere in this resolve, remember
that this resignation is the principle means for attaining
the most sublime degree of peace, the peace of God.

This ineffable peace "which surpasseth all understanding" [2] is founded on our detachment from self and our
union with God, whence it proceeds as a participation in
His own immutability. Indeed, the last degree of detachment is that of peace. We ought never to lose it wilfully—
that would be monstrous—but if we fail, in spite of all our
efforts to obtain and preserve it, let us resign ourselves into
the hands of God and from Him alone hope for our welfare
and salvation. Thus we shall cooperate with His designs for
our sanctification, for the end which God proposes in such
trials is none other than to make us cease to depend upon
ourselves and rely upon Him alone. His intention is to
detach us from all spiritual egoism in order to give to us
Himself and His very life.

Manifestly, this does not in reality require a sacrifice
of true peace; we merely exchange our peace for another
which is incomparably more perfect. It is then that peace
of conscience also becomes perfect, for it no longer consists
merely in the testimony that our works are in accordance
with reason, but also that our reason and spirit are in conformity with and united to God. This peace is the greatest
of all possible blessings in this life and we should strive
to attain it, but we shall not find it by seeking it directly,
but only by seeking first the kingdom of God and His justice.

[2] Phil. 4:7.

CHAPTER 36 ✍

Poverty of Spirit

Disciple: Master, will you please explain poverty of spirit to me? I am perplexed and confused regarding this subject which is so important to the spiritual life. Although I have heard and read explanations of it and I myself have meditated much on it, I am still dubious concerning certain points. In fact, my acquaintance with the subject thus far has only added to my confusion, for I am so inept at understanding spiritual things. Please tell me exactly in what poverty of spirit consists, how far it extends, how it is recognized, and what are its principal effects.

Master: I shall be very happy, my son, to pass on to you whatever light God will accord me on the subject. For spiritual matters such as this are above human reason and judgment and, therefore, we should not depend too much on these human means concerning them. In striving to dispel spiritual darkness, we must first of all humble ourselves before the Holy Spirit and ask Him to illumine us. Then, remaining firm in our faith, we must confidently trust that at the proper and opportune time He will enlighten us and continue to do so ever more and more, transforming us, as St. Paul says, "from glory to glory." [1]

Now to answer your question: Poverty of spirit is the same as the spirit of poverty. This may sound like a platitude, but it is not, and if you will but reflect on it a little, you will see that it dispels all the errors and clarifies all the ambiguities concerning poverty of spirit. It dissipates at

[1] Cf. II Cor. 3:18.

once the error of those who confuse poverty of spirit with the lack of natural and supernatural gifts and who apply the term "poor in spirit" to the foolish and incompetent. Taken in this sense, they could with greater reason apply the term to sinners, for these are indeed poor in spirit, taken in this erroneous sense, inasmuch as they are wanting in grace and all its riches.

Poverty of spirit, taken in the sense that Christ spoke of it, does not presuppose nor require the privation of any gift, natural or supernatural. On the contrary, these gifts, if rightly employed, are a very efficacious means of attaining it. Moreover, poverty of spirit itself is the best disposition—indeed, an absolutely indispensable disposition—for the possession of God Himself, the highest good, in whom is every good and every treasure.

Speaking even from a human standpoint, poverty of spirit requires great virtue and profound wisdom. Hence it is said that the truly wise man is always humble. It could also be said that he is poor in spirit, for he knows better than anyone the vanity of all human power and wisdom. Notwithstanding all this, the poverty of spirit to which the wise men of this world can attain is infinitely removed from the spirit of poverty which Christ taught us; for the detachment which the latter causes is also infinitely greater, inasmuch as it is produced by the total death to self. The detachment required by the former is merely human; that of the latter is divine. Hence, however penetrating their wisdom, the wise men of this world will never attain divine detachment unless they humble themselves and for the sake of Christ submit their understanding to faith.

Therefore the wisdom of this world, generally speaking, is more of a hindrance than a help in comprehending the spirit of Christ, for those who possess it become infatuated

with their wisdom and insist on judging everything according to their own reason. Because of this pride God condemns them to the "reprobate sense,"[2] and they err more
than other men in matters of morality, even in the purely
natural order. What, then, must be the result in the supernatural order? Have you not heard, time and time again,
from the mouth of these wise men, errors which would put
a child to shame? Have you not noticed the great uproar
they make and the satisfaction they derive when they succeed in distorting or perverting the meaning of a verse of
Scripture or a sacred doctrine, adapting it to their egoistic
and worldly standards? One would think they had discovered a new world by the way they carry on when they
believe they have succeeded in substantiating their errors
(so they think) with a sacred text. Oh, how greatly we are
indebted to Christ for having given us in His Church a
mother who educates us and teaches us the divine word,
giving us its true meaning and guarding us against such
folly!

Disciple: Indeed, the blindness of the proud is a sad and
lamentable thing, but perhaps that of the simple and humble who sincerely seek the truth and who nevertheless fall
into error is even more so; for the blindness of the former
is a just punishment for their pride, while that of the latter
seems more of a misfortune without possible justification.

Master: There is no doubt that this is one of the greatest
misfortunes that afflict fallen humanity. However, for our
consolation, we may be sure that the errors of humble souls
who sincerely seek the truth will never be like those of

[2] This reprobate sense signifies a worldly and egoistic manner of
judging all things, and is opposed to the *sensus Christi* or mind of
Christ, of which the author spoke previously. Similarly, we say that
carnal prudence is opposed to Christian prudence. (Tr.)

the proud, nor will God permit that they be as fatal. On the contrary, in the divine plan these errors serve for their greater merit and crown, if they take steps to deliver themselves from them, accept them as a humiliation, and seek light in the source of all light. To the humble, as to them that love God, "all things work together unto good," [3] and everything turns out favorably.

But let us not deviate from our subject. What other questions and doubts do you have concerning poverty of spirit?

Disciple: The main one is that some simple or uninstructed souls, among whom I count myself, believe that poverty of spirit, or the spirit of poverty as you say, refers solely to the material goods of this world and not to spiritual goods, as the authors of mysticism affirm and as Christ probably meant.

Master: It cannot be denied that such is the obvious meaning of the term and the one most commonly accepted, but it cannot be admitted that Christ did not intend also to give it a spiritual significance. Indeed, it could not be otherwise, for He is the light that illumines all things. However, many who heed the words of Christ and listen to His disciples are still much given to material and earthly things; hence they can appreciate naught but earthly values and they esteem virtue only in relation to these things. Therefore, one cannot exact more from them at first. That is their starting point: their first step toward total detachment, which is perfect poverty of spirit.

This initial step is of transcendent importance in the spiritual life. Without it, no progress is possible nor is it possible to enter into the kingdom of heaven. According to the words of our divine Savior: "It is easier for a camel to pass through the eye of a needle, than for a rich man to

[3] Rom. 8:28.

enter into the kingdom of heaven." [4] Moreover, detachment from temporal goods is a powerful aid in the practice of more complete detachment, for the very reason that it costs us more and also because God, who will not be outdone in generosity, rewards it with the grace of higher degrees of detachment which are as numerous as are the higher degrees of sanctity.

The term "poverty of spirit" has primary and direct reference to temporal goods, inasmuch as these goods, or rather our attachment to them, is our first and greatest obstacle to entrance into the kingdom of Christ; however, it also has reference to spiritual goods.

Disciple: That is a difficult thing to understand. I can see how detachment from material goods is necessary in order to attain the spiritual; but that detachment from spiritual goods should also be necessary is difficult to comprehend, for they are life's only real benefits and without them we would be absolutely bereft of all good.

Master: We would be bereft of all personal and individual good; better still, we would be bereft of the ownership of such goods; that is true. But we would not be deprived of the use of them as something conferred upon us by God. In other words, we would have their use, but not their ownership, for this belongs to God. It is the spirit of ownership that is diametrically opposed to the spirit of poverty and deprives us of the possession of God; for, inasmuch as God is infinite, He cannot exist in conjunction with something that is not Himself. Do not doubt, therefore, that detachment extends even to spiritual goods, so far as these may become the object of selfish ambition; so far as we may covet them as our own possessions. Moreover, poverty of spirit is a work of love, a love which despoils us

[4] Matt. 19:24.

of all that is not pure love; that is to say, it despoils us of all self-interest, of all egoism, and in exchange gives us the interests and the very life of Him whom we love.

But if you still do not understand this, let me tell you that attachment to goods, of whatever order they may be, should not be confused with esteem and appreciation for them. Although poverty of spirit is opposed to the attachment to any kind of goods, it is not opposed to esteem and appreciation for their substantial value. Indeed, no one esteems and appreciates goods, especially spiritual goods, as much as they who are poor in spirit, but they appreciate them at their true value: as means to union with God, the supreme good, in whom and by whom all good consists. But since spiritual goods are such so far as they serve as a means of attaining God and being united to Him, they who are poor in spirit especially appreciate the gifts and graces that dispose us to possess God: humility and charity, or poverty of spirit and love.

All other goods of nature and grace they appreciate as gifts of God, to whom it belongs to give or not to give, according to His good pleasure, and holy souls conform themselves perfectly to whatever God gives them, be it little or much. Thus, if God gives them great talent, many natural gifts and the means to develop them, they are grateful to Him and they use these gifts for His greater glory. However, they are always disposed to return them to Him who gave them, if it is His will to take them away. If they have received little or nothing by way of natural gifts, they glorify God in their poverty and give thanks to Him for the gifts He has granted others as if He had bestowed them upon themselves. In a word, they rejoice above all in the dispositions of divine providence, for their greatest love is the divine will.

This same disposition animates them also with respect to supernatural gifts. Thus, in their exercises of piety or penitential practices they seek nothing for themselves except union with God and whatever is necessary to attain this end. Apart from this, they desire neither peace nor rest nor knowledge nor virtue nor perfection nor anything in heaven or on earth. In their heart they repeat the words of the prophet: "What have I in heaven? and besides Thee what do I desire upon earth? Thou art the God of my heart, and the God that is my portion forever." [5]

If the Lord wills that they live in the greatest spiritual desolation, deprived of all sensible light and consolation and the pleasure which generally accompanies the practice of the interior life; if in spite of long years spent in the practice of virtue, they are ever more keenly aware of their frailty and miseries and they seem to be growing worse instead of better; if all their struggles and efforts to attain perfection seem to end in the most bitter failure; they do not on that account become discouraged and abandon the struggle. Rather, they persevere, hoping against all hope and blessing God in their abandonment as they repeat with Job: "Although He should kill me, I will trust in Him." [6] Furthermore, their desire for humiliations is such that they even rejoice in their misery, inasmuch as it prevents them from indulging in self-complacency, serves to increase their self-knowledge, and is a means of glorifying the love and mercy of God. Far indeed are these souls from aspiring to anything extraordinary in their spiritual life, for even in the ordinary things they are perfectly content to be treated as the least of the servants in their Father's house.

Disciple: Master, you have touched upon a point that I should like to have explained more clearly, for it is rather

[5] Ps. 72:25, 26.　　　　　[6] Job 13:15.

confusing. How can you reconcile the hatred for and struggle against faults and imperfections which the authors in the spiritual life teach and the love of one's misery which these authors also counsel. For it is our very misery that is the source of our faults and imperfections.

Master: In spiritual works authorized by the Church, one always supposes the correct meaning of these terms, even though it be insufficiently explained. It would be an interminable task to stop to define every term and phrase at every step. The meaning of the terms you now refer to is quite generally known and accepted, so that its repetition at every step is unnecessary. However, should an author undertake to define them and fail to do so clearly, the reader should nevertheless suppose the correct meaning.

Only a stupid person would believe that holy souls love their sins and defects as such, for no one detests and combats them more than they. Love of one's misery is what St. Francis de Sales called love of self-abjection, that is, love of the humiliation that is caused by one's wretchedness. Above all, however, it signifies the love of God's glory which is so magnified in the remedy and cure of that wretchedness. In the same sense our holy Mother the Church also refers to the sin of Adam as a "happy fault."

This is what frequently prompts holy souls, who are in love with God and not with themselves, to use expressions which at times seem not only exaggerated but even offensive to pious ears, inasmuch as they give the impression that they are rejoicing over their sins. Nothing, of course, could be farther from the truth; at the very thought of their past sins, their whole life becomes an act of deepest contrition. But this does not prevent their contrition from becoming a transport of joy and praise when they think of God's infinite charity. The consideration of God's immense love for them despite their great unworthiness intensifies the sense of their own nothingness and inasmuch as this latter sentiment is synonymous with the spirit of poverty, it also is intensified beyond measure. Furthermore, since we possess the kingdom of God in proportion to the extent and depth of our poverty of spirit, the saints loved this virtue almost to excess and uttered holy foolishness in its praise.

The whole matter, therefore, is reduced to this: what the saints love is God, and if they love poverty of spirit and even their own misery, it is only because these destroy their self-love, which is the great enemy of the love of God. That is why they extol this poverty so highly and sing hymns of praise in its honor, hymns which only those who know what it is to love God can understand. That is why St. Francis of Assisi espoused himself to Lady Poverty and in her honor committed such holy folly. For he knew very well the great good that poverty holds; it made him lord and master of all things, inasmuch as it put him in possession of the Lord of all.

If men only realized what it is to love God, how easy it would be for them to understand poverty of spirit. Then they would see how divine love makes us infinitely poor and infinitely rich! Then they would understand also that the poverty that comes from love is what redeems us from our slavery and makes us infinitely free, even as God Himself is free. They would understand that it is this poverty which sanctifies us, disengaging us from all things and filling us with the spirit of wisdom, that wisdom which is folly to the world and a scandal to the proud. Finally, they would understand that it is poverty of spirit that puts us in possession of the kingdom of heaven and all its ineffable riches.

With this I conclude, for it is not possible to describe

all the marvels and riches contained in poverty of spirit. Neither can they be learned by words or discourses. No human intelligence can comprehend them fully; divine love alone can reveal them to us. Love; then you will see and understand how poverty of spirit is the measure of love.

CHAPTER 37 🖎

Our Daily Gift

OUR Lord Jesus Christ, in order to keep us from becoming apprehensive, teaches us to ask for our daily bread and in return He asks us for our daily gift to Him. In the spiritual sense, our daily bread is the divine grace which God gives us every day, or at determined intervals, for our sanctification. Our daily gift to Him is our faithful correspondence to that grace in the measure that it is given us.

This truth is founded on the doctrine of the economy of grace, according to which God does not, ordinarily, give all His graces nor the full measure which He has destined for each individual person, all at once. Grace is dispensed to us gradually, according to the needs and dispositions of our soul and, above all, according to what God has determined in His adorable designs. For this reason He does not demand perfection from us all at once; He merely asks our faithful correspondence to the grace of every moment, as it is imparted to us. For the ways of God, or of grace, are not spasmodic and abrupt, but regular and constant, as we see manifested in nature as it advances toward its perfection.

For this reason the process of our sanctification is more or less lengthy, according to the designs of God and our own dispositions. It is always longer than we would wish. No one becomes a saint suddenly, just as no one becomes a reprobate suddenly, in accordance with a norm which prevails as much in the supernatural as in the natural order. One who wishes to cooperate faithfully with the inspirations of God must necessarily adhere to this norm. We would like to become saints at once; not so much because of our love for God, but because we find the labor fatiguing, the sacrifice irksome, the delay wearisome. God, however, whose ways are infinitely perfect and who is not in any such hurry, seems purposely to delay the realization of our hopes in order ultimately to give Himself to us more bounteously. During the long wait, the soul is endowed with the invaluable riches of humility and patience; it yearns for divine love and learns to esteem at its true value the inestimable treasure of the kingdom of heaven.

What should we deduce from all this? Simply that we ought never to anticipate grace, but always to follow its every inspiration faithfully. To this end, we must be attentive to the voice of God and hear what He asks of us every day and every moment in order not to deny Him anything but to give generously all that He asks. We should dedicate our attention every day to this supreme and most noble endeavor of serving God and sanctifying ourselves, applying to it all our faculties and senses, all our heart and soul. At the same time, we ought cheerfully to make any sacrifice and embrace whatever sufferings our Lord may send. This is what it means to give God our daily gift.

If we see that our works are not as perfect as we should like or as those we have heard or read about concerning other souls, we should not despair, but be patient. Many souls become discouraged at the thought that total renunciation or surrender to God is necessary for sanctity. They are so conscious of their frailty and misery, and the struggle which they experience between nature and grace is so intense, that they despair of ever being able to renounce themselves completely. If the triumph of grace depended on our own powers, then indeed, we would have cause to despair. But that triumph comes from God, and He gives it to one who perseveres in the struggle to the very end, despite wounds and blows. We already know that the triumph of grace lies in the defeat of self-love.

Souls who are thus tempted to despair should remember the philosophical axiom that the first thing intended is the last thing achieved. Thus, the total surrender which is indispensable for sanctity has two aspects: the first concerns the intention or disposition of soul, and the other, the actuality or execution of that intention. The former of these two, or one's disposition to give oneself to God, is the indispensable requisite for sanctity; and even this disposition is gradually strengthened and perfected as the soul progresses in the interior life.

Whatever the degree of perfection a man may possess, the disposition of his heart and soul should always be one of complete surrender to God. This is certainly within every soul's capacity and God asks it of us all. There is no room here for excuses of frailty or impotence, for it is not a question of exterior works or real sacrifices, but merely of the surrender of the heart. This is what our Lord solicits with such loving importunity. "My son, give Me thy heart!" [1] God asks this of us because the heart is, in a manner, the whole man, and eventually draws with it all the rest. God knows very well our weakness and impotence,

[1] Prov. 23:26.

and therefore He requires no more of us than our powers permit. The surrender of the heart, however, He always demands, for it is within our power and its denial implies ill-will.

As for the gift of ourselves in actuality, that is, the sacrifices He asks and the sufferings He sends, it is enough that we be disposed to accept whatever each day brings, embracing it as it comes. In a word, it is enough that we give Him our daily gift. We can apply here the rule which our Lord Himself gave us in order to enable us to endure the evils of life with greater resignation: "Sufficient for the day is the evil thereof." [2] So also, sufficient for the day is the sacrifice thereof, without worrying about what He will ask of us tomorrow. We do not know what He will ask, but whatever it is, we do know that He will give us the grace and assistance we shall need in order to accomplish it. The will of God is that we confide in Him blindly and leave all our cares to Him, being solicitous only that we sin not against this confidence, for that is what wounds and offends Him most. Thus, without any cares or efforts other than cooperating faithfully with God's action in us and being faithful to His grace and following His inspirations at each moment, we shall imperceptibly advance toward sanctity and the possession of the divine treasure of the kingdom of heaven and with it, all the treasures of grace and sanctity. Thus, total surrender to God is realized and perfection is consummated.

We should not falter, therefore, when we hear that sanctity requires total renunciation and death to self-love, for this is the work of divine love, a work that is accomplished in us in the measure that this love takes possession of our hearts. If we find ourselves far from the summits of sanc-

[2] Matt. 6:34.

tity, let us not lose heart. Let us humble ourselves in our nothingness and ask God in His merciful love to regard our littleness and misery, for one glance from Him can raise us to the highest summits. Let us not cast envious eyes upon the lives and sanctity of others, however sublime they may be, but let us rather attend to our own life, however humble, and to the grace which God has given us whereby to sanctify it. This is God's gift to us and in it is the secret of our sanctity, for it is an expression of His most holy will.

Let us, out of love for the will of God, embrace and conform ourselves to our own life as it is at this very moment, with all its labors, pains, and sacrifices, even though we ourselves may be the cause of the bitterness of our present situation, offering it all to God in expiation of our faults and for His greater glory and our sanctification. Let us, in this, imitate the good thief who, when he was about to die, did not look at his past life save to turn away from it with deepest contrition; nor did he look to the future, for he had none; but he embraced wholeheartedly the present moment, painful as it was, in satisfaction for his sins. Then, responding to the grace of the moment, he humbly asked Jesus to remember him when He entered His kingdom. This was enough to justify him and open the gates of heaven to him the very day he expired. Oh, if we would thus sanctify our present moment! What great graces, what ineffable treasures, what sublime sanctity we would attain!

This admirable example of the good thief should serve as an encouragement to us never to hesitate to accept and offer to God all the pains of our present life, even though we may realize that we ourselves are the cause of them. For if we detest our faults and firmly resolve never to fall into them again, their bitter consequences will be for us a powerful means of sanctification and the infinite glory of the merciful love of Jesus will shine forth in our lives. Indeed, the foremost reason why God permits the faults of men is that His glory may be manifested in their cure; and if God is glorified in us, what does anything else matter? In conclusion, let us sanctify the present moment by embracing it wholeheartedly, for it is the manifestation of God's will in our regard and in it is the grace whose fruits we must return to God. This is our gift of every day and of every moment.

PART VI

The Wisdom of the
Tree of Life

CHAPTER 38 🕿

True Happiness

"SEEK ye therefore first the kingdom of God, and his justice, and all . . . things shall be added unto you." [1] These are the words of eternal truth and, as such, are infallible. Man seeks happiness with great eagerness and, consequently, fails to find it, for nothing drives happiness away so much as the immoderate desire for it. Man's first and foremost desire should be, not happiness, but perfection; for happiness is a consequence of the latter, not vice versa.

To seek happiness primarily and directly is to foment egoism, which is the antithesis of perfection. The latter consists in the annihilation of egoism, whereby we attain the full expansion of our being and prepare ourselves to reach our last end: the possession of the infinite good, God Himself. Therefore, he who would find happiness must not seek it directly, but seek only the attainment of perfection, leaving the matter of his personal happiness in God's hands. In other words, he should disengage himself from all things in order to annihilate self-love and make himself capable of receiving the plenitude of infinite goodness. Self-love makes us incapable of any good; it separates us from God and closes the door to happiness. To love self is to reduce oneself to the nothingness that we are, for every man becomes in some measure what he loves, and his love is in proportion to his self-detachment.

Do you wish to be happy? Then, die to self and to all things for the love of God. This is the only happiness there

[1] Matt. 6:33.

is in life, for only contact with the divinity can fully satisfy and delight the heart of man. He who loves God loses the desire for any other happiness outside of God, for that divine nutrition so completely satisfies him that he has no desire for anything else; indeed, it contains every other delicious savor, every other delight.

The conditions of the present life do indeed prevent the full possession of this supreme happiness, yet it can so completely satisfy and rejoice the heart of man that he has nothing more to desire than that he be not impeded in the enjoyment and possession of so great a good. Nevertheless, the miseries of the present life are a hindrance and although they cannot deprive the soul of the possession of the supreme good, they can at times overshadow its fruition and joy. Therefore, we should not aspire to the impossible or desire that earth become heaven. In this life we shall always have to suffer in many ways. But for those who love God this suffering becomes a fount of joy and a most delectable spiritual sustenance. The love of God makes all things sweet, delightful, and desirable to the heart of man.

He who is united to God is fortified by the divine power and knows that the evils of this life cannot approach that high and secure refuge where he abides under the protecting wings of divine omnipotence. All the angry waves and tempests of life break and dissolve at his feet, while he remains immovable as a rock in the midst of the angry sea. All the evils of life are like foam; they disintegrate and vanish as something that has no real substance. Moreover, they all take place on the surface, in the region of the senses; they never penetrate into the interior sanctuary where dwells the supreme goodness and beauty which is the delight of the saints. His happiness is indestructable. He is beyond what men can conceive as good or evil; he abides in the most intimate and profound depths of his being. He is firmly rooted in perfection, justice, and sanctity.

To be happy is to realize that one is good with the goodness of God, just with the justice of God, holy with the holiness of God, free with the freedom of God, peaceful with the peace of God, wise with the wisdom of God, strong and powerful with the strength and power of God; it is to be filled with all the divine treasures. This is the only true happiness in life. Without it, even though we were to possess everything imaginable, we would be unhappy and miserable. If at any time we should think otherwise, it is only because of that perfidious illusion which makes us take the idols of this world for our God. But that illusion can last only as long as illusions are wont to last, and even while it lasts it cannot make one truly happy, for it is utterly unsubstantial. Only contact with God can give us the "supersensible sensation," so to speak, of that infinite happiness which completely fills our heart. In a word, only the love of God can make us happy. Therefore, if we wish to be happy, let us seek, not happiness, but love. And if we would find love, let us detach ourselves from all things for the sake of love.

CHAPTER 39 ✒

Holy Joy

THERE are many kinds of joy, but in the spiritual order they can all be classified as either worldly joy or holy joy. Worldly joy consists in the enjoyment of earthly or sensible goods as such. Were we not fearful of being guilty of pedantry, we would say that it consists in taking pleasure in the pleasure of those goods; in taking satisfaction and placing our happiness in those goods as if they were our last end. This, and not merely the enjoyment itself is what really distinguishes worldly joy, for holy joy also can take pleasure in earthly and sensible goods, although not so much for their own sake as for God's sake. Moreover, holy joy does not place man's last end in these goods, but subordinates everything to God. From this radical distinction arise the different natures, contrary effects, and manifestations of these two kinds of joy.

Worldly joy is as ephemeral as the foundation which sustains it and it can endure only at the cost of a voluntary or unconscious blindness concerning the true values of life. It is a grotesque caricature of true joy, a mask which hides the miserable state of those who give themselves over to it.

Man cannot live without a sentiment of happiness and when he does not find it within, when he does not even dare penetrate into his interior and see himself face to face for fear of the disgust such a sight might cause him, he endeavors to go out of himself. With closed eyes he plunges into the whirlwind of worldly pleasures with all the more fury as his state is the more desperate, hoping thus to make himself insensible to the heart-rending cries of his sick soul.

How utterly foolish and absurd are mundane pleasures! Their very frenzy proclaims the horrible misery which they try to conceal. There is nothing sadder to a thoughtful man than those tumultuous manifestations, that riotous feasting and merrymaking of worldly pleasures; they are suggestive of orgies in a cemetery. But the saddest thing of all is that, far from obtaining what they desire, the poor wretches who give themselves over to worldly pleasures succeed only in aggravating their misfortunes, eventually becoming their own executioners. Their mind becomes more and more clouded, their soul more confused, so that eventually it can no longer find any light that will guide it in that whirlwind. Their heart becomes obdurately attached to those perishable, illusory objects which they shall have to abandon when they least expect it. Thus, they are forever escaping the sad realities of life, closing the eyes of their body to the heart-rending spectacles these realities present and the eyes of their soul to the bitter truths which they contain.

But escape is impossible. Those realities spring up everywhere; they pursue the soul ever more closely, ever more relentlessly, until they can be evaded no longer, and the soul falls into their clutches. Then comes disgrace, sickness, or death, and with them the hour of retribution. Every vicious pleasure has to be paid for at a frightful rate of usury. The soul will suffer, not one, but a thousand cruel deaths for each and every one of the forbidden pleasures which it has ever enjoyed.

Assuredly, this is a sad picture, but sadder yet is the thought of the blindness and folly it supposes. For the evil is not in the enjoyment of pleasures, but in the inordinate manner in which they are enjoyed. Man may enjoy every pleasure God gives him without incurring any guilt or having to fear any reprisal whatever. It is necessary only that he observe due order, as God Himself teaches us by means of our reason and faith.

In no sense do we infer that God condemns pleasure. He Himself is joy eternal and everything He does, He does with infinite joy. He pours it forth in torrents throughout the world, over every being, and especially over the heart of man. When God enters within a man, His first greeting is a divine effusion that makes a man tremble with joy, and as long as He remains there, the soul is ever rejoicing in the celebration of that perennial banquet of which Sacred Scripture speaks. If, therefore, God is joy, felicity, supreme happiness; if where He is there is every good, every sweetness, and every delight; then what greater error than to think that He is an enemy to such things or that He loves sadness!

Joy in itself is divine; sadness is satanic. Joy in man is the daughter of sanctity; sadness, the daughter of sin. If there is anything wholesome about sadness, it is not because of the sadness as such, but because of its effects: when it purifies us from sin and leads us to sanctity, which is true joy.

The good man is always joyful, at least in the depth of his heart, and the man who is always joyful is good. The characteristic of Christian joy is that it is immortal; it is unalterable. Yet he who possesses it will not be exempt from all the miseries of life. He may suffer them all; he may even suffer greater and more terrible torments and injustices than the rest of mankind. Nevertheless, the fount of his joy is never exhausted. He can indeed say in imitation of St. Paul: Who will deprive me of my joy, my happiness, and contentment? I am sure that neither death nor life

nor height nor depth nor any other creature can deprive
me of my joy and happiness.[1]

It is plain that according to this disposition of spirit only
the true Christian is disposed to rejoice with the greatest
intensity, for the very reason that he rejoices in everything
in all its purity, just as God made it. By "true Christian"
we mean one who participates fully in the benefits of the
redemption; one who is redeemed from the slavery of sin
and from every sinful slavery; one who is purified and clean
of heart. Such a man divinely rejoices in all things, for in all
things he sees and feels God. This is the man who is rapt in
ecstasy in contemplating the stars, the flowers, the immensity of the ocean; he rejoices and delights in the singing
of the birds, the sobbing of the wind, and the murmuring
of the brook. The whole universe is to him a stupendous
picture sketched against infinity and speaking of infinity;
it is a divine symphony which lulls his heart with the sweet
accents of love. His spirit lives in perpetual adoration before uncreated Beauty. Everything within and without re-
minds him of the Lover of his soul who embraces him with
an ineffable caress of divine tenderness. Every entity,
every delight and beauty, every love of earth is for him despoiled of all ugliness and impurity and vested in glory and
immortality. Therefore does he rejoice in them to the full,
for he rejoices only in the divine element within them.
But even if all this were lacking, he would not therefore
cease to be joyful and happy, for he has within him the
substance of all joy and happiness: God.

This is Christian joy, holy joy, true joy, perfect joy. In
order to find it, we need but look for it in its source, which
is God; not in creatures, for these have only what they re-

[1] Rom. 8:35–39.

ceive from God and they withhold even that unless we seek them in God. He who does not proceed thus but seeks in creatures that which only God can give, causes a disorder and falls into sin. He will then be justly punished by his own inversion of values, which converts into his executioners the very things that were created for his happiness.

If only man would seek his happiness in God; if only he would renounce forever those bitter and disastrous joys and delights which cost him so dearly and which will some day be his undoing! If he but knew and realized what holy joy is! If he would learn to rejoice with a pure and holy joy as he should! Then he would know true happiness; he would know what it is to live and to rejoice. He would perceive the folly and absurdity of worldly souls who place their happiness in creatures, and the wisdom of the saints who detach themselves from them all in order to find God; for, in finding Him, they find the eternal fount of all joy, of which it is said, he who drinks thereof will not thirst forever.[2]

CHAPTER 40

The Art of Suffering

MANY people are intent on probing into the causes of suffering and are assailed by temptations against faith when they see its extension and magnitude in the world, for it seems to be irreconcilable with an all-good and loving God. Assuredly, for those who lack faith or disdain its light, for

[2] John 4:13.

those who heed only the light of reason and consider the natural order as supreme, for those who regard the natural goods of this life as absolute, for such as these, pain has no possible explanation. Neither can it be explained satisfactorily to those who regard suffering as an instrument of the intellectual and moral dignity of man in the natural order, for it seems to have no adequate compensation; it does not even seem necessary, for all creatures attain their natural ends without such costly assistance.

Only in the light of the supernatural order do we find the key to the solution of this mystery. Actually, the natural order is not supreme and absolute; its goods have a purely relative value, as do its evils, which are merely privations of those goods. Wherefore, those very evils may be valued as good, inasmuch as they are or may be the source of greater good. God may permit such evils in order to obtain greater good and this is what He has done.

It is not so important to know the reason for the existence of good and evil in the world as to know whether in that good or evil there shine forth an infinite power, wisdom, and goodness. The works of God can have no other purpose than the manifestation of His glory. And what we should seek to know is whether that glory shines forth in all things: whether we see His goodness, justice, wisdom, power, mercy, and love everywhere: in heaven, on earth, and in hell.

Assuredly, as long as we are enveloped in the darkness of this life, as long as the sun of eternity does not shine upon our souls, we shall not be able to contemplate these divine attributes clearly; but even in the midst of the darkness of faith we perceive brilliant gleams of light which fully satisfy our hearts. If we were to consider the infinite good we gain through suffering, we would change our lamentations into hymns of joy and exultation to our God who works such great marvels.

We shall understand this better if we bear in mind that, although the divine plan is not subject to man but that man is subject to the divine plan, nevertheless, when man subjects himself voluntarily to this plan, it seems, admirably enough, to be ordained solely for man's good. As St. Paul says: "To them that love God, all things work together unto good." [1] "Even sins," add the commentators, but perhaps more than anything else, suffering.

After Christ died on the cross and sanctified suffering, He infused divinity into it, so to speak, and made it a kind of sacrament by means of which the graces of heaven descend upon earth. Suffering is the living cross on which and through which every man must be redeemed and saved. Christ redeemed us by giving us the power to redeem ourselves by means of His grace and His Cross. Every Christian is another Christ and as such must suffer and die in order to attain the glory of the resurrection.

This is the economy of suffering. Through it, all things are restored; the order of justice is re-established; man is reconciled with God, is re-instated in His friendship and grace, and attains sanctification. Suffering is, therefore, the eternal executor of the redemption of the world. The fact is that suffering is the great agent of our purification. Nothing defiled can enter the kingdom of heaven. No one can enter into the possession of God without first detaching himself from all that is not God, and that is what suffering effects in our hearts.

Suffering is the father of love. If we should ask all the saints the secret of their sanctity, they would answer that it was suffering. They would all say: "I myself did nothing;

[1] Rom. 8:28.

it was suffering that did it all. All my works would have been worth nothing if God had not come to my assistance by means of suffering."

However, we must bear in mind that these marvelous effects are produced by suffering provided it is sent by God and accepted from His hand; that is to say, provided we suffer as Christians and in union with the spirit of Christ. It matters not if it comes to us as a consequence of our sins and in expiation of them. God does not want sin, but He does desire its punishment as reparation to His justice. Thus, His mercy and love make use of punishment as a most efficacious means for our redemption and sanctification.

What the masters of the spiritual life say regarding these truths so often proved by experience is already well known. When one wishes to erect a high edifice he fixes its foundation deep into the earth. So also, when God wishes to elevate a soul to a high degree of sanctity and glory He may permit it to fall into great sins or at least into great misery. Indeed, there are certain petty weaknesses which humble man even more than great sins, for they make him more aware of his frailty and impotence. Because of a tenacious and dangerous attachment which she was unable to break for many years, St. Teresa of Avila learned her absolute impotence for good and her capacity for evil, had not God held her in His hand. All the saints, however pure and innocent, acquire this practical self-knowledge in some way or other. We regard as exaggerations their sentiments of humility and their tears and lamentations over their slightest faults, but they well knew what those faults signified and, therefore, they were absolutely sincere.

From all this we can deduce a truth which is very consoling to all who suffer in any way: Christian suffering sanctifies all things and divine love sanctifies all suffering. There is in this life no suffering so profound, no disgrace so irremediable, no misery so great that it cannot be compensated and sanctified by divine love. To achieve this, it is necessary only to bear them humbly, in the spirit of expiation and in perfect union with the divine will. One act of perfect union with the divine will suffices to blot out all the sins of the world and one perfect act of love would suffice to make us saints. When I see a man in the profoundest depths of degradation and misery, I think of how all that could be changed into sanctity with one equally profound act of humility and love of God.

The best way of repenting one's sins is by accepting their consequences, especially the humiliation and pain, in the spirit of expiation. Sorrow for sin is the firm base of the pedestal of a saint. Out of your past sins you must lay the solid foundation for your future sanctity, by humility and distrust of self and by love and confidence in God. When you truly love God and not self, you will rejoice at your past sins, not as offenses against God but because they have deepened the abyss of your nothingness and made you capable of receiving in greater measure the fullness of His love and mercy. In a word, you will rejoice because He is more glorified in you.

Every new imperfection and misery you discover in yourself is a new treasure of sanctity, if it serves to humble and unite you more closely to God. To be humble is to accept wholeheartedly what we are, realizing what we are. Pride is the absolute evil; God therefore permits all other evils, and even sin, in order to destroy it. Will to be humble if you do not wish to be humbled against your will. Humility is the best shield against all the evils of the world, because the humble man is always carried in the arms of God, even as an infant is carried in the arms of its mother.

We are not asked to embrace suffering, but the will of God which is manifested in suffering. The whole science and art of suffering consists in suffering with and for the sake of love. That is the whole secret of suffering. Wherever God is, there is happiness and blessedness. Suffer for God and you will be blessed. Do not expect me to pity you in your sufferings, whatever they may be, even though you yourself be their cause; if you can offer them to God, they are your soul's greatest good. I pity only those who in their suffering do not know how to turn to God. Truly, if the angels could feel envy, they would envy us one thing only: our ability to suffer for God.

Nevertheless, it is necessary for us to learn how to suffer without causing suffering to others. Some sufferings are avoidable; others, unavoidable. Regarding the latter, it is necessary only to prevent them from fostering self-love in us by seeking consolation inordinately, by indulging in self-pity or desiring sympathy from others, or by believing that our sufferings make us worthy of special considerations and favors.

The best way to suffer is in silence and alone with God, pouring forth our heart to Him alone. He will be sure to give us the suitable external and internal relief and strength. To seek consolation outside of God is like seeking water outside its fount. Above all, we should avoid all sufferings that are not inevitable; that is to say, those which we ourselves may occasion.

Whatever has been said of the benefits of suffering is true only if and when suffering is a divine instrument for our sanctification. Of itself, it is neither good nor does God

desire it, save for our sanctification. There are many sufferings we could avoid by avoiding their causes. Who doubts
that the sinner is his own executioner? The majority of our
sufferings arise from our repugnance to mortification, our
vanity, pride, and sensitivity, our immoderate desire for
pleasure and recreation; in a word, from our egoism.

It is fitting that they should suffer who feverishly go
after pleasures. It is likewise just that they should suffer
who worship themselves; who love vanities and lies; who
disregard God and desire to find their happiness outside of
Him; who idolize pleasure, riches, ambition; who think the
world was created for themselves alone and become ir-
ritated and indignant when things do not turn out to their
liking; who do not recognize the rights of others; who have
no compassion for their neighbor; those merciless hearts
who tolerate not the least defect in their neighbor. It is
right and just that the scourges of mankind should suffer
and pay the price of their malice.

He who desires to avoid useless and dangerous sufferings
should examine his heart, observe the idols that reign
within him, and endeavor to destroy them if he does not
wish them to destroy him. Above all, he must control the
imagination, that "great rambler," which is a prolific cause
of useless sufferings.

Dispose your soul to receive all that God may send you;
but do not torture yourself wondering what He will send
you. "Sufficient for the day is the evil thereof." [2] To desire
to foresee and forestall all the future is to usurp divine
jurisdiction. The best way to prepare for the future is to
live the present well. Do not torture yourself over what has
happened to others, thinking it might happen to you, for
everyone has his own role to play, and just as there are not

[2] Matt. 6:34.

two people with exactly the same features, so there are not two lives exactly the same. Do tranquilly whatever is within your power and leave the rest confidently in the hands of God.

Wheresoever you may turn your head, you will not find a more steadfast or sweeter rest for it than the Heart of Christ. Absolute faith and confidence in the bounty and love of God are and ever will be the immovable basis of life's equilibrium and the only refuge and support of human frailty and misery. Even though everything should come to naught, God will abide forever and His word will never fail. Outside the will of God for us, things in themselves have no more value or importance than that which we may wish to give them. The only good man can do is not to hinder the divine action and to follow it readily and with docility. Do not concern yourself with either the benefits or evils of life, but love and adore God sincerely in all things, and you will find happiness in and above all things.

Suffering is a miraculous wand which, by breaking the hard rock of our hearts, brings forth from them torrents of life and sanctity. "He that hath not been tried, what manner of things doth he know?" [8] It is suffering that makes us penetrate the profound secrets of the wisdom of God. Suffering sums up all the blessings of earth.

To console the grief-stricken is an act of mercy; but for the grief-stricken to console is an act of the most sublime charity. To resist suffering is to kick against the goad. Do not attempt to shield from suffering him whom God desires to suffer, but rather help him to suffer as God wishes him to. Be patient toward all, especially toward yourself; for if you love sanctity, you yourself will be your greatest cross.

Only victims are redeemers. What mortifies most is what

[8] Ecclus. 34:11.

sanctifies most. Christian suffering knows only one word: *Fiat.*

To one who has a pure intention, the approbation or disapproval of men matters little. Resist vigorously the first movements of passion and you will avoid innumerable sufferings. Die to all things before they die to you, and you will find death sweet. Do not ask God to relieve you of your cross but to give you strength to bear it.

CHAPTER 41 🖋

Testimony of a Christian Soul

I BELIEVE in God, I hope in God, I love God in all things, above all things, and against all things. My greatest aspiration and motto is: "All in God, all for God, God alone."

I recognize nothing good in me but the ardent and sincere desire to be so. I would not believe in my perfection even though the whole world should swear to it, but I do believe myself to be less hampered by pettiness than the generality of men. My only ambition is to be loved with divine love.

I expect nothing from men save that which God wishes to communicate to me through them. I have never been disappointed because I have never placed my faith and hope in creatures. I do not demand from anyone what he cannot give of himself. I do not think evil of others; nevertheless, I do not put my trust in them.

The errors of the holiest of men do not surprise me; God permits them in order to remind both him and ourselves that, after all, he is but a man. I am not scandalized at anything, and when I see defection and diffidence spread, I place my confidence in God and say: "Even though all should stray, I shall not."

I have a blind faith in the triumph of God and of good even though everything should seem to fail and come to naught. When I look at man I am a pessimist and a skeptic, but when I look at God I am an optimist.

I am grieved at those who are depressed by failure and elated by success. Such attitudes seem to me to be proper to children, but not to men. I distrust enthusiasm and have faith in conviction.

I believe that God has no need of us except to make us happy, saintly, and blessed with Himself. For me there is no greater beauty than the beauty of divine goodness. For me there is no greater good fortune than to have much in order to give all.

My greatest happiness is to see those whom I love happy. My greatest sorrow is to witness the misfortunes of others and be unable to assist them. My greatest delight is to deal with those with whom I am one in heart and soul.

The rule of my life is not to annoy anyone. My greatest torment is to have to correct and reprimand others. I prefer to teach men to love God in order that they may not sin, rather than try to destroy sin in order that they may love God. I desire no other reward or recompense for my work than that men be made better and love God more. Services rendered with selfish motives are a torment to me, and nothing is so repulsive to me as self-interest disguised as love.

I value my liberty and independence above everything in the world. I attribute so little value to human judgment and opinion that I do not even feel contempt for them. I delight in simplicity and detest affectation. I abhor vulgarity, above all the vulgarity of being singular. I find nothing so insufferable as having to deal with small, niggardly hearts. No sound is so harsh to my ear as the word that wounds charity. Nothing is so repugnant or hideous to me as a man in a fit of passion.

I do not know what either hatred or pardon are, for I have now no personal enemies. I have an irresistible sympathy for all who are unjustly persecuted. I wish that everyone would feel as I feel, but not do as I do. No one humbles me so much as he who asks my pardon. There is for me no sweeter vengeance than to do good to him who has injured me.

Nothing is so sacred to me as the duties inspired by love. There is for me no virtue so desirable or so necessary as meekness. The only thing in which I should like to excel above all other men is nobility of heart. These and many other things manifest not so much what I am as what I should like to be. What I am, I do not want to say, for the world is already full of bad examples.

CHAPTER 42 ✍

Simplicity and Sanctity

MAN invariably complicates things. He is a stranger to simplicity and seems to delight in amassing difficulties in order afterward to have the joy of overcoming them. At times, however, he amasses so many and he upsets things so thoroughly that there is no way of resolving his problems.

What is more simple than sanctity? Sanctity is the perfect goodness that comes to us from God, and is there anything simpler than goodness? To the upright, sincere, and unselfish man who loves the truth and is noble and generous of heart, who does not act from selfish motives but in all things sacrifices himself for the good of others, who seeks not his own glory or advantage in anything, who acts not by reason of any extrinsic cause but is impelled by the very goodness and nobility of his heart: to such a man, is there anything simpler than to be good? Goodness is equivalent to uprightness and nobility of heart. Is this a very complicated thing?

However, here we are faced with a difficulty. If uprightness and nobility of heart are to be perfect, they must come from God. It is not enough that they be human, for then perfection would be very limited, whereas it must be divine. This means that the heart of man must be sanctified so that it will be good and holy with the goodness and holiness of God. And what is needed in order to sanctify it?

Even here sanctity is the simplest thing possible. One thing alone is needful to sanctify the heart of man: the grace of God. And in order to obtain that grace man needs but one thing: good will. The man of good will profits from everything and acts as he should in all things. He needs neither great science nor study in order to act with an upright intention and to look to God in all things.

It is the lack of this uprightness and purity of intention that complicates the way of sanctity. We seek ourselves, not God. Why are we so preoccupied with our own feelings in the service of God? Why so many doubts, so many fears, so much examining of our interior state? Why do we not leave that dark abyss of egoism, and rivet our attention solely upon the accomplishment of our duty for the love of God? Why do we so solicitously seek ways and means of ridding ourselves of the weight of our cross, above all, of the cross of ourselves and our state in life, and neglect the one true way which consists in embracing everything wholeheartedly for the love of God? Why so many impossible aspirations and fantastic notions about sanctity and perfection when there is no other sanctity or perfection than that of desiring to be nothing for the love of God and of not performing any work save for God?

As St. John of the Cross says, it is not by accepting, but by denying that one approaches God; [1] that is, not by complicating things, but by simplifying them. God is unity, and the way that leads to Him is the way of unity; a way which becomes ever more simplified until eventually we see only Him in all things.

Why, then, are we so solicitous about inventing methods and exercises that will lead us to Him? The suitable means for each and every one of us are already indicated by our religion and state of life, and God will give us whatever others we may need without our inventing them. Let us comply well with our duties as Christians or as religious in our relations with God, our neighbor, and ourselves, and we shall need nothing more. Let us do this with the sole intention of doing the will of God and of sanctifying ourselves.

"But who will teach me to do the most perfect thing among so many and so diverse circumstances of life?" you will ask. Your own heart or the Spirit of God will teach it to you if you are always disposed to follow the inclinations and inspirations of an upright spirit. And if you do not always succeed in discerning what is the most perfect thing,

[1] *The Complete Works of St. John of the Cross,* Allison Peers trans., Vol. III, p. 246.

do that which seems so to you, humbly praying God that you may succeed. If you should not succeed, humble yourself and ask Him to rectify your mistakes, and do not be distressed, for there is not a little presumption in wanting always to succeed. Bear in mind that God does not ask the impossible and if, in spite of our good intentions and sincere efforts to do the most perfect thing, we fail, He well knows how to repair our mistakes to our advantage, for He permits them that we may become humble and distrustful of self.

Still you will say: "All that is very true, but in order to attain sanctity one must know how to pray, how to make the general and particular examens, how to receive the sacraments properly, and other things about which many books have been written and which presuppose much study and meditation. Moreover, do we not see in the saints themselves how much they did and how many methods they used, how often they examined themselves and consulted others in order to make sure they were on the right path? All this proves very clearly that the attainment of sanctity is not so simple."

To this we shall reply in parts. In the first place, we do not treat here of the extraordinary paths of sanctity, but only of the ordinary, observing that what matters is the attainment of sanctity, irrespective of particular paths. Furthermore, the extraordinary elements do not necessarily prove a greater degree of sanctity. True, God does lead some souls along extraordinary paths, not because it is absolutely necessary, but in order to manifest His tender love for all of us and His great solicitude for our welfare. He knows that in our weakness we are more impressed by such manifestations. Moreover, since the coming of Christ, there is really but one way: Christ Himself.

Some saints consulted others, examined themselves, and studied considerably, but they did it because they had no one to guide them in the most secure and practical way. Had they found such a guide, doubtless he would have taught them what we here indicate: simplicity and again simplicity; detachment from everything, even from the very gifts of God; forgetfulness of self, being mindful only of His glory. Indeed, those very saints, after they were sanctified, zealously recommended this path. Read St. John of the Cross and you will see to what heights this Saint takes total detachment or, what is the same thing, holy simplicity.

I say that simplicity and detachment are the same because to become detached is to become simplified, unified. Thus we see what constitutes the spirit of simplicity. It does not consist so much in the lack of a variety of exercises as in practicing them simply. Truly simple souls neither need or relish a multiplicity of exercises and they always choose the most beneficial and important in order to practice them with greater efficacy and intensity. If they are obliged to undertake exercises that are not of their choosing, they perform them in the same simple manner. Their prayer is simple, their examens are simple, their confessions are simple, as also are their devotions. They have no need for long discourses or reflections because their heart teaches them everything. They do all with love and for the sake of love. This is the great secret of simplicity. He who loves God and seeks sanctification or he who seeks only to please God in everything, thereby simplifies all his acts into the only one necessary.

He who loves God has a blind faith and confidence in Him, and therefore he rests tranquilly in the arms of His loving providence. He sees everything as coming from the divine hand and his only care is to conform in all things to God's holy will. And even this he does calmly, lovingly, without distress or excitement, as one who serves a tender Father who well knows our frailty and who exacts nothing from us save that we give Him our heart.

In conclusion, we repeat that sanctity is the simplest thing possible because everything is reduced to but one intention: pleasing God and disregarding every selfish intention or interest. Selfishness complicates sanctity and renders it difficult by seeking its own interests: all the desires and loves we may have outside of God. Therefore, if you desire to know how much progress you have made in the way of perfection, observe your progress in simplicity, being certain that the greater one's sanctity, the greater also is his simplicity of spirit.

CHAPTER 43 🖋

The Nature of Sin

"I FEEL as much a man as anyone," St. Francis de Sales used to say. The saints not only do not cease to be men, but they are even more so than anyone else, for the reason that they are such with greater perfection. When it is said that the saints are not men or that they are not human, the meaning is that they have not the carnal spirit of the world with all its disorders and evil inclinations. Assuredly, the saint is a divine or deified being, but not because his human nature has disappeared or has been destroyed; rather, because it has been purified and elevated to the divine level. Sanctification does not destroy nature but despoils it of all that is extraneous and enhances it with celestial beauty.

The saints, therefore, retain their human nature integral and unimpaired; they are possessed of a heart and soul; they have their sensibilities and inclinations, aversions and loves, attractions and repugnances; their ardent desires, hopes, joys, fears, anxieties, worries, together with all the sentiments and motions proper to an exquisite, delicate nature. They have, or can have, certain defects of character and temperament. They are as thoroughly human as anyone else. Finally, their nature has absolutely the same functions as that of other men. To be sure, through the exercise of virtue and the aid of divine grace, their passions are, so to speak, domesticated, but they are not dead or annihilated, nor can they ever be.

As a matter of fact, within their proper limits, the passions are good and necessary. If they are not generally so considered, it is because the word "passion" is now used almost exclusively in reference to disordered movements which, being uncontrolled by reason, give one the impression that they belong solely to the animal nature. But when rightly ordered, the passions are good and contribute much to the beauty of life. What would an insensible and impassive man be like; a man without love or fear, without desires or enthusiasm, a man insensible to joy, sadness, pleasure, pain, and lacking every emotion? He would be a monstrosity; the very antithesis of a saint. No one is farther from that insensibility than the saint, and all the more so as he is the more saintly. The saints love much, and it is already known that love is the source of all the heart's movements. He who loves much also fears much, hopes much, rejoices much, suffers much. This is clearly seen in the Saint of saints, Jesus Christ. Has there ever been a more intensely dramatic life than His?

It is necessary, therefore, to lay aside that false idea about the saints. If mortification of the passions is taught and counseled for the attainment of sanctity, it is not with the object of destroying them, but of domesticating them and subjecting them to the spirit. For when the spirit has taken control, it moves and commands them and makes them serve life's highest ends. Wherefore, nothing is more erroneous than to consider all the movements of the passions as sin.

There is so much ignorance prevalent in this regard that no few persons dedicated to the interior life are much grieved because they experience emotions which they believe incompatible with sanctity, even when such movements are perfectly legitimate. For instance, they feel very grieved or joyful at the absence or presence of loved ones; ingratitude and calumny wound them; success exalts and failure depresses them; the approbation of others elates and humiliation saddens them; or they crave sympathy and are pleased with applause. All these and an infinite variety of other emotional reactions are only natural and, therefore, in themselves are not sinful. It is foolish to look for sin where there is none, seeing that we already have so many real ones. Moreover, all the saints experienced those emotional experiences to a greater or less degree.

Neither are natural defects sinful. What useless lamenting! "Oh, I am so sensitive, irritable, violent, lazy, timid, affectionate, disagreeable, fussy, forgetful, suspicious, tenacious, unstable, open-hearted, reserved, etc. I like comfort, luxury, and diversion, etc." Even here there is no sin. At most, it may be a natural defect of character or temperament, but as long as the will does not enter in, it is not a

sin. Who does not like the good and dislike the evil? That
and other things also the saints experienced.

In what, then, does sin consist, and how do saints differ
from sinners? Sin consists in impurity of heart and it is in
this that saints differ from sinners. By their purity of heart,
the saints are detached from all inferior things. The saints
experienced the sentiments of which we speak, but they
were not slaves to them. They were detached from them,
dead to them. They felt them as if they were not their own.
Their spirit did not partake of them save to elevate them
to the region of purity and sanctity in which they dwelt.
Even more, those sentiments and movements shared, so
to speak, in the saints' purity and sanctity and helped to
unite them more closely to God. The saint sees everything
in God, feels everything in God, and elevates everything
to God. By "everything" we mean just that, be it exterior
or interior: heaven and earth, angels and men, the good
and the bad, the sad and the joyful. The fact is that everyone interprets things and acts in accordance with his nature and since the saints are divine or deified beings, everything about them is clothed in divinity.

That is why the saints are incomparably happier than
other men and they live so much more intensely. No one
has ever penetrated so profoundly into the heart's depths
as they; no one has ever rejoiced so thoroughly in the allur-
ing beauty of God's creation as they; no one has ever delighted so exuberantly in the harmony of the universe as
they; no one has ever been as happy as they, for always and
in all things they felt in their soul the ineffable caress of
divine love. They were far from finding either within or
outside themselves the horrible deformity of sin, for they
were clothed in the purity and sanctity of God. If they saw
within themselves some vestige of the ravages original sin

has caused in our fallen nature, that very fact served to unite them more closely to God by strengthening their humility and helping them to appreciate the infinite and incomprehensible love which joins itself to such miserable creatures. It gave them a knowledge of their own frailty and of the goodness of God, who is the soul of all sanctity.

The saints feel their misery, but this does not deprive them of their peace of soul nor hinder them from rejoicing in the perennial banquet of divine love. For they realize that although they may be subject to misery, it is not theirs, for their heart is detached from all things and established in that most high refuge, God Himself, where no sin or other evil can approach.

Do not grieve, then, if you still feel within yourself the effects of your mortal and earthly condition. Examine your heart and see if you are detached from earthly things and if they are no longer obstacles to you; see if, on the contrary, they serve to unite you more closely to God by making you aware of your infinite unworthiness and of the infinite love of God. If such is not the case; if your heart and spirit are still the slaves of vanity and of falsehood; if earthly things attract and drag you down; if your passions dominate you and impose their law upon your soul; if your senses are distracted and turn away from God; if you still do not feel divinity within you but are purely human; then you must fight without respite, you must deny yourself in all things and plead day after day at the door of divine mercy that your heart may be purified of all its dross and that He will sanctify you with His grace and holiness. Never weary of the battle for sanctity; in it is your redemption, your liberty, and all your happiness on earth and in heaven.

Oh, if men knew and felt what it is to be redeemed from the slavery of sin and free with the freedom of the children of God, they would not hesitate to sacrifice a thousand lives and a thousand worlds in order to attain that freedom.

CHAPTER 44 🖎

God's Sovereignty

GOD is absolute Lord and Sovereign of all creation; obedience to Him and worship of His infinite sovereignty is the supreme law which constrains all creatures. It is impossible to escape that law, and sooner would the whole universe crumble rather than that this law should cease to be observed.

All the world's ills arise from a refusal to render to God the cult due His infinite sovereignty and every hell is wrought by rebellion against it. But even if this rebellion should beget a thousand hells, God cannot renounce that right. In doing so, He would cease to be God. Wherefore, he who rebels against the divine sovereignty makes his own hell, just as he who reveres it makes his own heaven.

We are alarmed at the evils of the world and even scandalized because God does not put an end to them. What useless fretting! As long as man will not humble and resign himself, he will find no other mercy than that of pain in order to open his eyes and make him turn back to God.

Although the sovereignty of God is absolutely one and unique, nevertheless, the worship that it exacts from man has various manifestations, according to the various divine attributes. The first is that of faith, whereby man yields his judgment and reason upon the altar of infinite truth, honesty, and wisdom. This is the worship of the intelligence. We fulfill this law and practice faith when we adhere firmly to divine truth despite the battles and combats that would wrest it from us.

Faith is absolutely certain in itself and in its content, but it may be encompassed by darkness within our spirit. Wherefore, our adherence should be to faith itself and not to our way of understanding its truths. Faith infinitely surpasses our powers of comprehension, although it becomes ever more clear and comprehensible as we progress in the spiritual life. But total comprehension will be possible only when the sun of eternity shall appear on the horizon of our souls.

The clarification of the truths of faith comes to us by means of our intellect; yet not as a product of our intellect, but of the divine light; and the more we humble ourselves, the more enlightened we shall become. The supreme act of faith is made in the supreme degree of obscurity.

The subjective act of faith should not be confounded with the objective act, or the effect of our faith. The former blinds us, so to speak, but the latter illumines us. Objectively, the proper effect of faith is to illumine, for in this sense it contains God Himself.

He who believes regardless of everything and in spite of everything is perfect in faith, just as he who hopes against all hope is perfect in hope, and he who loves despite everything that opposes love is perfect in charity.

Although on first thought it seems absurd, he who believes without faith and hopes without hope and loves without love has attained the summit of perfection, for perfection consists in objective reality and not in sentiment or feeling.

Reverence for the sovereignty of God as infinite goodness

exacts of man an unconditional and absolute confidence. Since God is infinite goodness, He has an infinite right to be trusted by us from the moment we turn to Him. The perfect act of confidence is made in the supreme degree of abandonment.

The homage due the sovereignty of God as infinite justice exacts from us a reverential attitude in all that happens, both within and without, regarding everything as just and holy, inasmuch as it comes from God.

Love for and union with divine justice is sanctity itself. The happiness of the creature does not consist in joy nor in anything proper to self, but in union with the justice of God, for happiness and perfection are one and the same thing.

If the condemned could love the justice of God in their punishments, they would thereby be blessed. Eternal beatitude is nothing more than a never-ending hymn to the justice and sanctity of God. Our justification consists in accepting our lot and adjusting ourselves to the place assigned to us in the universe according to the divine plan.

In order to fulfill all justice and render everyone his due, self must be reduced to nothing in homage to the divine All. God has all the rights, we have none but the right to be all His. To belong to God means that God abides in us. God possesses us through life, that is, by absorbing our life into His and transfusing His life into ours. He who is possessed of God understands with the light of God, loves with the love of God, and acts by the power of God. Reverence for the sovereignty of God is reverence for the sovereignty of love. He who renders homage to this sovereignty has himself become sovereign in all things.

CHAPTER 45

Points for Meditation

JUST as it would be impossible for us to have any idea of the present life before birth, so is it impossible to have a true realization of the future life before death. It is enough for us to know that both are the work of God and that if the temporal and mortal life is so enchantingly beautiful, what must immortal and eternal life be like?

It is not enough to see the reason for a thing in order to feel and experience the force of that reason. For the former, the intellect suffices; but the latter requires the proper disposition of the heart. Therefore, if you want to convince a man, dwell not so much on what convinces you as upon what impresses him. Explanations, yes; arguments, never.

If you want to justify yourself, do not be eager to make excuses, but give proof of your goodness. Your conduct will justify you.

We can never know a man completely, for in order to do so, we would have to place him in every possible situation.

Never is a man's pettiness so patent as when he is exalted, for nothing is more difficult for a man than to be truly great in an exalted state.

Treat a man according to what you desire him to be, for he will always try to live according to the opinion in which he is held. If you treat him as a beast, he will be a beast; if you treat him as a man, he will be a man; if you treat him as an honorable person, he will be honorable; if you treat him as a criminal, he will be a criminal. The greatest injury that can be done to a man is to treat him as though he were irresponsible. The effect of such treatment is most demoralizing. Heaven and hell give us the measure of God's concept of man. He treats man as a god, so to speak.

All great errors arise from our taking a relative truth as absolute. A truth is not false because it is relative; the falsehood lies in taking it as absolute.

Many get very excited and accomplish little; others remain calm and accomplish much, for excitement squanders the energies which should be applied to the work in hand.

It is said that the passions have been given us for our help, but in the present state of human nature, such are the inconveniences they bring, that the wise man will do well to dispense with their assistance as far as possible and act on pure reason.

If you want to be good, place yourself in a situation where you will have to be so.

Do not indulge in self-pity if you do not want to debase yourself.

An indomitable will is equivalent to no will at all.

The stability of nature's laws demonstrates how perfectly God fulfills the law. Man marvels that the universe should continue its unchanging course as much in his misfortunes as in his prosperity. He forgets that the universe was not made for man alone.

When I see that man still believes in justice, truth, virtue, and love, in spite of how greatly these have been abused, I cannot but marvel at the intensity with which God has engraved these sentiments in his heart, and I have to conclude that the works of God can withstand any kind of attack.

It seems that God has permitted sin in order to prove the solidity and marvelous structure of His works, for these are so made that nothing can destroy them and every deterioration carries in its wake a more perfect reparation.

When we consider the disruptive forces at work in the heart of man, and still more in the bosom of society, we see clearly that the greatest miracle in the world is the existence of humanity after so many centuries.

It is not strange that he who does not find God in his heart should not find Him anywhere. In order to see God one does not need great ingenuity, but purity of heart, i.e., detachment from self and all creatures.

If you want to give God something, give Him your littleness, for that is the only thing that you have and that He does not have.

They say you think chastity impossible, and certainly, your environment and the way in which you live make it impossible. If you want to win, never carry the battle to your enemy's territory.

Pride brings confusion; humility brings understanding. If men loved God, they would not find it difficult to understand one another.

I did not make the world; therefore I must accept it as it is.

Never make resolutions in time of distress. Everything in its good time. Await an opportunity, but do not fail to take advantage of it when it comes. Neither our conscience nor our responsibility are the fruit of the moment. They are a result of all our acts of the past combined with present circumstances. Experience is not an infused gift and it is useless to expect it from him who does not have it. Of all that I may tell you, you will really understand only that which you have experienced.

You say you have never met a saint; the reason is that it is more difficult to be a saint in man's opinion than in God's. Do not call him a saint who pleases you in all things, but him who pleases God. If God Himself has not succeeded in pleasing all men, you are foolish to attempt to do so.

An upright heart rebels against nothing so indignantly as against the humiliation of human standards. The free heart has the infinite arrogance of submitting to none but God. Ever since I came to know myself, whenever I judge man for what he is in himself, I esteem him as nothing. But in God everything is ennobled and made beautiful, even man.

True love is based, not so much on our neighbor's goodness, as upon our own.

The saint does not differ from the sinner in what he has of himself, but in what he has of God.

If you want to be a good judge, put yourself in the place of the culprit. No one is a good judge of others if he is not a good judge of himself.

Pardon is the strongest bond of friendship. The truly good man does not do good for extrinsic reasons, but because he is impelled to it by his own goodness, even as God lavishes his benefits upon the good and the bad. To attend always to the interests of one's neighbor rather than to one's own is characteristic of a great and noble heart.

Our difficulty in understanding God and His way of acting is due to the fact that we are not God. Man's understanding comprehends only what is in some way within man himself. For the understanding is nothing more than man himself in a state of enlightenment. That is why what he comprehends of God is due to what he has of God, and what he does not comprehend is due to what he has of self.

The impious man denies God because God is beyond comprehension, that is, he denies God because God is God. It is one thing to prove the existence of God and another to manifest God Himself. Reason can do the former, but the latter can be done only by God revealing Himself to the heart. Purity of heart, not reason, is the means by which we see God.

If everyone were what he ought to be, all problems, social and individual, would disappear.

It is strange that man can control everything except himself.

It is sad to see how lightly men speak of love when it should be spoken of only on one's knees. Love is by nature divine and it alone can teach us to love as we ought. To love is to abide in and dwell in God.

Religion neither defends nor condemns property. It defends the right to it when it is justly possessed and condemns it when it is unjustly acquired.

Religion supposes the natural order and its purpose is not to create it, but to sanctify it.

To be free is not a right but a duty.

The union that hatred engenders is not a union of cohesion among those who hate, but a union of opposition against another.

God decreed punishment in order to destroy sin. Therefore, he who accepts punishment seconds God's decree and is sanctified.

Fear of death is reasonable, but terror of death is irrational.

We should treat the passions as we would wild animals: first they are domesticated, then they are used to advantage.

What morally constitutes a man is the unyielding determination to sacrifice one's life on the altar of duty.

Every disorder brings within itself a punishment, and he who proposes life as the end of life turns life into a living death.

All man's rights with respect to God are based on man's littleness and on what God owes to Himself.

Unity is the distinctive note of the divine attributes. Unity in duration is eternity; unity in being is infinity; unity in life is love; unity in light is truth; unity in action is omnipotence; for unity signifies undivided totality.

Where reason ends, charity begins.

If you want to find consolation in grief, apply yourself to assuage that of others.

In your battles of self-love versus love of neighbor, always put yourself on the side of your enemy if you want to be the victor.

CHAPTER 46 ✍

The Disguises of Evil

THAT sinners should sin is not surprising; but that the just should fail in charity and sin, and do so under the appearance of good, that is something which demands sad and serious reflection. More than all the disorders and scandals of the world, this fact gives us some notion of the immense evil which original sin has caused in human nature. To derive good from evil is proper to God, but to derive evil from good is proper to man—to fallen man. That the latter should do evil knowingly and should derive evil out of evil is, to a certain extent, natural; but that he should do evil under the pretext of doing good and that he should derive evil from good is disconcerting and disheartening.

The only consolation we have in this matter is the thought of the wisdom and mercy of God who well knows to what extent we are responsible for our ignorance and how worthy of compassion are creatures subject to such misery. We are also consoled by the thought that it is undoubtedly an admirable disposition of His love and wisdom to leave the just man to his misery so that he will not trust in his own justice, take pride in his own goodness, or exalt himself above others; in a word, that the just man may remain always humble and not fall into the sin of sins, pride. This thought, moreover, is a powerful incentive for us to be cautious and vigilant in order that the weed of egoism may not take root and feed on our good works.

Generally, the just, those who have resolved to do good

at any price and are disposed to sacrifice everything for the
sake of a good conscience, have no reason to fear the evil
which presents itself to them as such, but rather the evil
which presents itself under the appearance of good: wicked-
ness which hides beneath the cloak of virtue, the angel of
darkness transformed into the angel of light. The devil is
too clever to present himself to holy souls under his true
colors. He knows that they would reject him immediately.
Consequently, he assumes the appearance which is most
agreeable to them, for he knows that the tree always falls
on the side toward which it is inclined. The person much
given to penance he incites to self-destruction; the one inclined to obedience he makes a slave to the human judgment of his superiors; the soul given to humility he fills
with shyness and cowardice; the one inclined to works of
zeal and charity he incites to give itself to such works inordinately so that it will become distracted and dissipated,
lose the religious spirit, and become totally worldly.

To enumerate the deceptions which we see every day
would be an endless task, even if we were to mention only
the principle ones. We see so many falls, defections, blun-
ders, and sad predicaments even in the spiritual life! Today
you will hear remarkably wise comments on charity, peace,
or poverty from a person who to all appearances seems
upright and sincere and even well experienced in such
things; a little later you will hear that same person complain and become exasperated because he lacks some object
for his use, because those about him have failed to interpret his will, or because they have uttered an unkind word
to him. He will make such a display that you will wonder if
it is the same person.

The saddest thing of all is that these persons are seldom
aware of their defects, however obvious they may be. They

are very apt at justifying themselves, formulating the most logical arguments concerning their duty and the glory of God. They must comply at all cost with what they believe is their duty, their charge, or their office, and they believe that this justifies the violation of any virtue. They always allege some reason or some right which they believe inalienable. Oh, how such persons need to remember the divine model, Jesus Christ, who said of Himself that He had come, not to be served, but to serve and to give His life as a redemption for many.[1]

What shall we say of the murmurings, contentions, conflicts, and strife which certain persons incite when, under the guise of religion, they unduly emphasize and promote the excellence and importance of some particular pious exercise, of a certain religious institute or association, or even the cult of some saint? Can there possibly be a more deplorable evil than that of fomenting strife and discord among the just in the name of religion?

But that is not all. We find many persons, otherwise truly good, who mistakenly believe that they must be scandalized in certain cases and even to the point of doubting the salvation of their neighbors, thinking that in this way they more effectively defend the integrity of their religious principles. They confuse the sinner with the sin and include both in the same anathema. One would think from this that the goods of life harm rather than benefit man and that it would be better to deprive him of them entirely. But this would be a foolish solution, as foolish as it would be not to eat or not to construct buildings because food sometimes makes us sick and buildings sometimes collapse and kill us.

The solution lies in being prepared and armed against

[1] Matt. 20:28.

the dangers to which our sinful nature is subject in the practice of virtue. We should endeavor not to use goods wrongly nor practice virtue defectively. We already know that, according to the philosophers, virtue lies in the happy medium. Every extreme and exaggeration vitiates and destroys virtue and, in our case, it is all the more vitiated and deformed as it deals with more elevated objects. What greater deformity than to violate charity in the name of charity, to violate justice in the name of justice, or to offend against religion in the name of religion? Wherefore, let us be on guard and remember that self-love feeds on everything, the good as well as the bad. There is no remedy against it other than to let it die of hunger by not letting it feed on anything.

The spiritual life is a labyrinth of illusions and dangers for those who do not know how to abandon self and take refuge in God. He who wishes to avoid these illusions and dangers will do so only by way of holy detachment and simplicity of spirit. If you wish to escape error and deceit, flee from self. If you wish to live in truth, take refuge in God. Apart from God, love neither virtue nor religion nor wisdom nor sanctity nor perfection nor your soul nor your life nor yourself nor your neighbor; apart from God, nothing, nothing, nothing.

Bear in mind also that you can neither know nor love nor esteem what God is in Himself, for He is beyond your comprehension. Therefore, detach yourself from everything, however good and holy it may seem to you. Do not attach yourself to anything, thinking that you thereby unite yourself to God. Only in the denial and detachment of self are you safe from error. Remember that to love God is nothing else than to detach oneself from all things for His sake. This is also the only way of possessing God and of possessing all things in God. Thus you will avoid all self-deception.

CHAPTER 47 🖎

The Divine Magnet

THE great secret of sanctity consists in having one's heart divinely magnetized. God is truly a divine magnet of hearts. As iron is magnetized by contact with natural magnets, so hearts are magnetized by contact with God. But even as the magnetization of iron requires that there be no extraneous substance between it and the magnet and that contact be repeated frequently, so also, in order for the heart to be magnetized there must be no impurity or extraneous substance between it and God which may impede contact; moreover, contact must be repeated frequently. It is necessary to detach the heart from all things and unite it to God by means of frequent and even constant holy desires and aspirations and by every other means of maintaining communion with God.

In the measure that the heart is magnetized, it acquires a divine orientation which enables it without any effort and by its own impulse to direct itself always toward God and remain united to Him. It directs and ordains everything to Him: the senses, faculties, affections, thoughts, and works. It does all this not only without effort, but even as if by natural instinct; as if drawn to it by a most sweet violence that it cannot possibly resist. Then it can be said that all the work of the heart's sanctification is finished.

Everything that is yet to be done costs it no effort, for it is all done by the divine power that dwells within it.

Once a heart is magnetized, it is in turn converted into a magnet which attracts other hearts, not toward self, but toward God; for it acts not by its own power, but by the power which God has communicated to it. This is how God attracts hearts unto Himself: some hearts through others, thereby forming a great spiritual current in the world of souls.

The center of that system and the first heart directly magnetized by God was the Heart of Christ. The latter is, so to speak, what the natural magnet is to other magnets. Its magnetism is not participated but is its own, and it is by contact with that divine Heart that other hearts are magnetized. Contact is the most efficacious means to that end and it is achieved principally and directly through Holy Communion. Thus, Jesus in the Blessed Sacrament is the great magnet of hearts and Holy Communion is the great means of acquiring a divine magnetization, for there we contact His humanity and divinity both physically and spiritually.

After Christ comes the Blessed Virgin who, being nearest Him, participated more fully in that divine power. Under Christ, she is the most powerful magnet which attracts souls to God. After her, come the saints in heaven and then the just upon earth who have attained divine union. All these possess that divine power in a greater or less degree and are centers of attraction drawing souls toward that universal Center which is God. This comprises the true communion of saints and society of souls which are united to each other and to God.

CHAPTER 48 🦋

The Love of Charity

MANY believe that the love of charity is simply the love of compassion and they would be much offended if they were told that they were loved out of charity. The reason for this is that the most notable characteristic of the love of charity is its disinterestedness, for it is a love founded, not on the merit or goodness of another, but on one's own goodness. But such a love is generally directed toward those whom the world calls unfortunate or who in the eyes of the world have no claim to love. Consequently, the love of charity is confused with that of compassion and regarded with a certain disdain. Nevertheless, the love of charity is the only true love. Every other love is in reality more egoism than love, because it is founded on the gifts and qualities of the person loved.

There is but one real and true love: God. "God is charity." [1] God is love, personally and substantially. God is love in its proper, physical nature, so to speak. Therefore, he alone who abides in charity and possesses God, actually and truly possesses love; consequently, he alone really and truly loves. Just as it is impossible to live without life or think without intelligence, so is it impossible to love without Love.

He who loves God loves all things with a real, physical, true love. He loves them because he has love within him and because in all things he sees love. He has no need of reasons in order to love, for he does so from necessity; his

[1] Cf. I John 4:16.

very life impels him to it. But if he does look for reasons, he finds them without number, although they are all comprised under that of beauty. And what greater beauty and enchantment can there be than that which divine love gives to all things? He who loves sees the object of his love everywhere, and this is all he needs to be held spell-bound by their fascinating beauty and enchantment.

So it is that divine love alone teaches us to love. It is divine love that orders charity within us. The disorder of love comes from not loving what one ought or as one ought. But divine charity loves in all things what it ought: God; and it loves Him as He ought to be loved: infinitely, according to man's capacity.

Charity neither destroys nor disdains the order or motives of human love. It simply elevates, sanctifies, and divinizes it. Thus, the natural love of parents, children, husbands, wives, brothers, and friends, far from disappearing because of charity, is elevated and ennobled by it even unto divinity, for that order also was established by God Himself. But since the love of charity is above and independent of all things, it desires them only so far as God desires them. Therefore, it does not attach itself to creatures nor is it the slave of any creature, however much the heart may naturally feel the greatest possible affection for it. No one can know how all this takes place if he has not learned it from experience; and, although it may seem to us inexplicable and incomprehensible how one can love thus, we may be sure that if we could experience this love, we would hold it as the greatest possible happiness to love and to be loved with divine love.

CHAPTER 49 🖋

Liberty of Spirit

THERE are some who think that liberty of spirit consists in having a lax conscience or in scorning the misgivings of a delicate conscience. Undoubtedly, as a general rule, a noble, sound, and upright heart acts with greater freedom than one which is not so by nature but yet wishes to act virtuously. But to believe that liberty of spirit consists in disregarding the qualms of conscience is a most grave error. When conscience accuses us, we must give it our attention, at least in order to see if its accusations are well founded. He who disdains the voice of conscience and disregards it in his actions does not possess liberty of spirit, but is a libertine at heart.

Sin is not in things but in impurity of heart. That is why the Apostle says: "All things are clean to the clean." [1] He who is clean of heart sees and loves God in all things and they all serve to unite him more closely to God. Just as every living thing lives by its operations, and as operations follow according to the nature of things, so also the pure and holy heart does all things in holiness and purity. This purity of heart proceeds from the soul's detachment from all created things and its union with infinite holiness. Wherefore it is written: "Where the spirit of the Lord is, there is liberty." [2]

This is one of the greatest joys of the children of God in this world: to feel in their heart this infinite and holy liberty; to see themselves liberated from the chains of sin;

[1] Titus 1:15.   [2] Cf. II Cor. 3:17.

to be able to rejoice holily in everything that God has created; to see that everything helps them to love and glorify God more; and that, far from being an occasion of fear and scandal, this freedom greatly increases their exultation and joy. Such are they who are truly free and completely redeemed.

CHAPTER 50 🖋

The Peace of God

"THE peace of God, which surpasseth all understanding," [1] does not consist in being spared the battles and trials of life, not even those which take place in the inferior part of our soul. The peace of God resides in the most interior and profound part of our soul, where God Himself abides, who is life and the eternally changeless One. True, we should do everything within our power to preserve the peace of the sensitive order, dominating our passions and self-love and avoiding everything that can give rise to disturbance. But to renounce the satisfaction of a sensible peace for the love of God is a sacrifice most acceptable to His divine Heart, most salutary for our own soul, and also a most adequate means of attaining the true peace of God.

An immoderate solicitude for peace is the surest means of losing it. God does not wish peace in those whom He predestines for the crown of triumph, for nothing is so beneficial to us as the war which we ourselves do not provoke or which wages within our heart in spite of ourselves.

[1] Phil. 4:7.

"He that hath not been tried, what manner of things doth he know?" [2] The peace which has not been attacked is a most precarious kind of security. That peace alone is secure which has been won through war. Such a peace is the fruit of abandonment to the divine will.

Our peace hardly enjoys a moment of stability and is continually exposed to disturbance by every interior and exterior event of life, but the peace of God is as unchanging as God Himself. The more detached we are from ourselves and the more united to God, the more clearly shall we see the difference between our personal peace and the peace of God and how independent the latter is from the former. The stability of the peace of God is proved in the midst of all the waves and tempests that can agitate our heart. This stability is absolutely constant and constitutes one of the greatest joys of souls in divine union. In this stage souls understand that this peace is absolutely impregnable, for neither the world nor all hell nor they themselves, with all their frailties and miseries, can destroy it. The soul united to God is like a rock in the midst of the ocean before which the storms and tempests which would assail it disappear as foam. He who unites himself to God enjoys the immutability of God. The peace of God is a participation in His changeless, divine repose and is the effect of the detachment of the heart and of its union with God.

[2] Ecclus. 34:11.

CHAPTER 51 🖋

Spiritual Fruits

THE gift of spiritual fecundity is the most precious of the divine gifts and the one that makes us most like God, for it is a participation in the attribute of His goodness, which is essentially communicative. Wherefore, the gift of fecundity is exclusively the fruit of the soul's union with God, as our divine Savior has said: "He who abideth in me, and I in him, the same beareth much fruit." [1]

All our works are worthless unless they are made fruitful by God's blessing, whereby He communicates His grace to them that they may be productive of good. And although a soul of itself may do nothing, God could produce good through that soul and diffuse goodness in the measure of its union with Him. To be fruitful, the only work that is truly necessary on the part of the soul is sacrifice, complete self-immolation on the altar of infinite love. Life is born only through pain and the divinely fecundated soul communicates life to other souls only at the cost of much suffering. Just as natural birth is not possible without pain, so there is no supernatural birth without suffering.

When souls already have this life, it does not remain inert within them but is renewed and diffused by means of a constant generation and expansion whereby it is communicated to other souls. Such souls are centers of divine life and ardor and, however hidden they may be, they radiate their influence throughout the world. All vital organs are hidden, and the more vital they are, the more hidden.

[1] John 15:5.

These souls no longer live, work, or suffer for themselves but for those whom God has entrusted to them and who will one day be their crown. That is the greatest glory and dignity to which God can elevate a soul, for that is what most likens it to the Savior of the world and makes it a veritable cooperator in the great work of redemption. The soul completes that divine work so far as it completes the sufferings which Christ must suffer in His mystical body.

God, then, has no greater grace or glory with which to enrich a soul in this world than to raise it, so to speak, to the selfsame glory and dignity of His only-begotten Son. Then it is that souls truly merit the name of spouses, for they are constantly giving Him children for heaven. Moreover, they merit the name not only of spouses, but even of mothers, a title conferred on them by Christ Himself, for they give birth to Him in hearts. Thus He said: "Whosoever shall do the will of My Father that is in heaven, he is My brother, and sister, and mother." [2]

When the Lord communicates to a soul the gift of fruitfulness, He also gives it, at the proper time, the affections of paternity and maternity toward souls; that is, He gives it such sentiments of tenderness and love that no father or mother could suffer and sacrifice themselves to such an extent for their children as these souls do for those whom God has entrusted to them. Then they well understand the words of St. Paul: "Who is weak, and I am not weak? Who is scandalized, and I am not on fire?" [3] and how he would even desire to be anathema for his brethren, whom he considers his glory and his crown.[4] Or again, the words of St. John: "I have no greater grace than this, to hear that my children walk in truth." [5]

[2] Matt. 12:50.   [3] Cf. II Cor. 11:29.
[4] Phil. 4:1 and I Thess. 2:20.   [5] Cf. III John 1:4.

Assuredly, such souls no longer work or suffer for themselves, but how many labors and sufferings they endure for others! Yet, since such sufferings give rise to a greater good, these souls can still say that their joy superabounds in their tribulations.[6] Only by suffering can one be a redeemer. It is useless for him who does not wish to suffer to aspire to such glory or to hope to do good on earth.

CHAPTER 52 ✎

The Better Part

WHEN Christ said: "Whosoever shall exalt himself, shall be humbled: and he that shall humble himself shall be exalted," [1] and "He that findeth his life, shall lose it: and he that shall lose his life for Me, shall find it." [2] He expressed a universal law of the spiritual life and the invariable norm which should be followed by all who aspire to gain His kingdom. Indeed, anyone destined for a place of honor in that kingdom and anyone who aspires to attain it, must subject himself to that law and always choose what is most lowly and contrary to the selfish tendencies of human nature. God will constantly furnish him with occasions for such a practice.

The most patent and unmistakable signs of God's predilection are crosses and humiliations. Thus we see that He gives the most sufferings to those whom He wishes to raise to the highest degree of glory. He shows Himself lovingly cruel and exacting toward such souls, punishing their

[6] Cf. II Cor. 1:5.   [1] Matt. 23:12.   [2] Matt. 10:39.

slightest faults with the greatest rigor. He may give them great gifts, but He takes care that they are afflicted with certain miseries which humble them in their own eyes, and the more so as His gifts are greater. Sometimes He even hides from them their spiritual gifts so that they may see in themselves nothing but wretchedness and sin. As a consequence, they are most profoundly humbled. At every step they discover new roots of evil inclinations and unfathomable abysses of iniquity. They may not accede to such tendencies, but God puts them before their eyes and makes them realize that it is only by His grace that they are not overcome by their own evil propensities.

The same thing occurs in their exterior life. Everything seems to conspire against them so that they are unable to enjoy a single moment of perfect peace and contentment. Everything seems so disposed that their life is a perpetual cross and martyrdom. Such is the life of God's chosen souls: they are marked with the sign of the cross.

To a greater or less extent they can all repeat the words of St. Paul when he recalls the trials, labors, sicknesses, persecutions, fears, anxieties, dangers, battles, contradictions, humiliations, injustices, and manifestations of ingratitude which he experienced.[3] Whatever can wound, mortify, and torture a delicate soul is, so to speak, their daily bread and perpetual sustenance. To experience this, one need not live a life like that of St. Paul; God knows very well how to conceal great crosses beneath simple appearances. He has control of the innermost parts of the world, of creatures, and of our very heart, and He knows very well the heart's most sensitive fibers.

Interior souls especially chosen by God realize very keenly that if they were to judge according to their natural

[3] Cf. II Cor. 11:24-29.

sentiments, they would maintain that in the distribution of the goods of life they had received the worse part. However, the divine light that burns in their heart shows them that in reality that they received the better part, and they would not exchange it for all the treasures of the world. As St. Paul says, the joy of their heart superabounds to such an extent in the midst of all their tribulations that these become lovable and desirable above all delights. Each new suffering is a new surge of living water "springing up into life everlasting," [4] the discovery of a new source of treasures and celestial lights which obliges them to say: "That which is at present momentary and light of our tribulation, worketh for us above measure exceedingly an eternal weight of glory." [5]

Taught thus by experience and understanding the infinite value of that "eternal weight of glory" which is all the greater as the sufferings and tribulations are greater, souls learn to esteem the latter as a most divine gift and as the greatest proof of God's predilection. That is why such souls are always eager for crosses and humiliations, and when God sends them, they receive them as the greatest gifts and the best goods of life that they could possibly receive.

All good souls should proceed thus, and they would if they knew how to evaluate God's gifts correctly. Every time they are offered a cross, a contradiction, or an affliction, they ought to adore it and embrace it as one adores and embraces the Cross itself. And whenever, according to the eyes of the flesh, they receive the worse part in work and sacrifice, they should esteem it as the better part and as the greatest gift that God could possibly confer upon them, rejoicing that they have been thus chosen.

[4] John 4:14.   [5] Cf. II Cor. 4:17.

PART VII

The Interior Life and the Apostolate

CHAPTER 53 🖎

The Saints and the Apostolate

THE great enterprise undertaken by the holy founders of the apostolic orders—St. Dominic, for instance,—of uniting the active and contemplative elements of the religious life and blending them into one, is well known and appreciated in its external aspect; that is, so far as it signifies the union of the monastic life with the apostolate. Formerly the two kinds of life had been separated and, at least in their social aspects, they were considered mutually incompatible. However the fact that these two kinds of life form but one supernatural life and are distinguished solely by the predominance of one or the other method of operation, is not so well known or appreciated. Nevertheless, this is the most transcendental and important aspect of the work of the founders of the apostolic orders and the profound significance of the sublime motto: *Tradere aliis contemplata,* "To give to others the fruits of contemplation." [1]

According to this concept, the active life of the apostolate should be a spontaneous and natural fruit of the contemplative life or a prolongation of the same, whereby the contemplative life is completed and perfected. The contemplative life, in its turn, should be the fruit and normal term of the active life in its ascetical aspect.

In order to understand this it is sufficient to remember that the supernatural life, as St. Thomas teaches, is not divided or distinguished in itself but in the individual who

---

[1] Motto of the Dominican Order, taken from the *Summa Theologica* of St. Thomas Aquinas, IIa IIae, q. 188 a.6.

possesses it, by reason of its distinct mode of operating in him.[2] Accordingly, the active life differs from the contemplative in that the first refers principally to man's exterior actions and the second to his interior actions. But exterior activity can be considered under two aspects: as directed to one's own salvation and sanctification or that of others. In the first case the active life blends with the ascetical life and precedes the contemplative; in the second, it follows the contemplative life as its proper and natural effect. In every case, however, these two kinds of life always go together and are united to a greater or less degree and under different forms.

The first part of this strictly theological doctrine has always been well understood and appreciated, that is, that the active life in its ascetical aspect should precede and accompany the contemplative life. Such is not the case, however, with regard to the second part; namely, that the active life of the apostolate is a consequence and natural fruit of the contemplative life or a prolongation and complement of the same.

Many believe that contemplation, especially in its most lofty degrees, is the final term and the most elevated goal of the supernatural life. That is not true, however, save in certain exceptional cases in which God disposes otherwise in accordance with His high and inscrutable designs. In speaking here of the contemplative life we refer to the formal element of that life, that is, to the habitual union with God, and not to certain transient states or extraordinary phenomena such as ecstasy or visions which sometimes accompany that life but are not essential to it.

Normally, therefore, the contemplative life should end in the active life, expending itself in some form of the

[2] Cf. *Summa theol.*, IIa IIae, q. 179.

apostolate. It should at least tend in that direction, although it may not always be possible for a soul to be active as are the preachers and apostles of the gospel, for this will depend upon the circumstances in which God has placed the soul and what His will is in regard to that soul. But a soul in this state will always feel the impulse to do everything possible to further the glory of God and the salvation of his neighbor.

It is reasonable that this should be so, for good is diffusive by its very nature and it is in the contemplative life that one attains, through union with God, the most perfect possession possible of the highest good. Wherefore, he who truly has attained to the contemplative life cannot help but feel this divine impulse to communicate it to others. This, indeed, is one of the most characteristic signs of the contemplative life and we find it in all the saints, especially in the great apostles and ministers of the gospel, although at times it may not be externally manifested, due to a life spent in solitude or in the cloister or because of other circumstances of one's state in life. But all these souls have felt themselves inflamed with zeal for the glory of God and the good of souls and have done all that they possibly could or whatever was permitted. They felt this impulse so intensely that doubtless their greatest sacrifice was to restrain their zeal in compliance with other duties and thus render themselves incapable of giving full expression to the ardent desires and aspirations of their soul.

St. Teresa teaches the same doctrine when she says that this is one of the surest signs whereby we may know the soul has entered the seventh mansion. "What surprises me most is this. You have already seen what trials and afflictions these souls have suffered because of their desire to die and thus to enjoy our Lord. They have now an equally strong desire to serve Him, and to sing His praise, and to help some soul if they can. So what they desire now is not merely not to die but to live for a great many years and to suffer the severest trials, if by so doing they can become the means whereby the Lord is praised, even in the smallest thing. If they knew for certain that, on leaving the body, they would have fruition of God, their attitude would not be affected, nor is it altered when they think of the glory which belongs to the saints, for they do not desire as yet to attain this. Their conception of glory is of being able in some way to help the Crucified, especially when they see how often people offend Him and how few there are who really care about His honor and are detached from everything else." [3]

Thus we see that the contemplative life, even the most lofty and extraordinary, terminates in the active life and is the life and soul of the apostolate. We see also the gross error of those who say that the contemplative and active lives are incompatible or that the contemplative life fosters slothfulness and that it is totally disinterested in the good of others. We see how badly some people interpret that passage of the gospel in which our Lord praises Mary for choosing the "better part," as if He thereby meant to establish two kinds of spiritual life, distinct and independent of each other. What our Lord wanted to teach us in this passage is that of the two aspects of the spiritual life, the better and more important is the interior or contemplative part, for it is the soul of the whole spiritual life, and that we must first and above all things attend to our own sanctification.

He also wished to teach us that when duty or charity do not dictate otherwise, it is better to apply oneself to the exercises of the interior life, which in themselves are more

[3] *Interior Castle,* seventh mansions, chap. 3.

excellent than exterior works, and that we should not apply ourselves to the latter with such great solicitude as to perturb and prejudice our souls. That is why He reproved Martha's excessive solicitude and praised Mary's attitude. For in this instance the latter truly chose the better part, although the other was also good. The right thing to do on that occasion was to take advantage of the opportunity to listen to the divine Master. On the other hand, if during the scenes of Calvary and the Resurrection, Mary Magdalen had been at home rapt in prayer, she surely would not have merited the praise of Jesus. On the former occasion, however, she was the most active of all, for then she loved most and love is the source of all activity, both in the natural and supernatural orders. That is why she merited that the Church should call her the "apostle of the apostles."

Thus we see clearly how the active life of the apostolate follows the contemplative life and is an effect and natural consequence of the same. We see also that the ascetical phase of the active life precedes the contemplative. For, as St. Teresa says, before Mary Magdalen sat at the feet of our Lord to listen to Him, she had already renounced the world and had suffered its maledictions and persecutions on account of her renunciation. Moreover, she had done penance for her sins and completely transformed her life, dedicating herself exclusively to the service of God and the salvation of souls.

Following these sublime doctrines and examples and moved by that same fire of divine love, St. Dominic, St. Francis, and the other founders of apostolic orders united the active and contemplative lives in their institutes in a way that was most appropriate and efficacious for the formation of great apostles. With this in view, St. Dominic and St. Francis established a rigorous monastic life which would be directed entirely to the apostolate and St. Ignatius formulated a strict ascetical life, as is stated in his memorable book of the *Exercises*.

Thus, those who are to be the example and light of the world are exercised in all the practices of the regular and ascetical life and they consecrate themselves in a special way to prayer and contemplation, endeavoring at the same time to acquire all the science necessary for preaching and defending the truths of our holy religion. In that way they learn the divine art of winning souls and directing them to heaven. Thus, religious houses, and especially the houses of formation and preparation, are the training camps for the militia of Christ where the soldiers are trained for the battle of the faith and the expansion of the kingdom of God. There they set themselves to acquire that wealth of virtue, supernatural zeal, and divine light which are necessary to fulfill such a sublime ministry. There they ought to warm their hearts at the fire of divine love so that it will make them die to every other love and all human interests, that is, to all that is not the pure glory of God and the good of souls.

The ministry of the apostolate requires such great sacrifice and detachment, abnegation and patience, constancy and fortitude, that only a love stronger than death can bear it and exercise it with the greatest possible perfection and efficacy. To launch upon the apostolate without due preparation and without the necessary spiritual provisions and, above all, with but a smattering of the interior life, is to tempt God and to risk becoming apostles of Satan rather than of Christ. For we cannot give what we do not have, and when we give, we have to give of what we have. If we possess the spirit of God, we shall communicate that spirit to others, but if we have the spirit of the world, we cannot but communicate a worldly spirit to others. That is why the saints did not want their disciples to go forth to preach and teach others what they themselves had not learned and practiced in the ascetical and contemplative life. They wanted them to be apostles of truth; not of abstract truth which is acquired through pure speculation, but of the truth actually lived and made incarnate within their hearts. They wanted them to communicate the divine word which is life and spirit, a flaming dart which penetrates into the deepest recesses of the heart.

So also we should strive to communicate to others our hearts transformed by the love of Christ; we ought to give them Christ Himself enclosed within our heart and hidden, so to speak, beneath the guise of our burning love of charity. Such is the idea of the apostolate according to the saints, the apostolate in its most elevated and perfect expression.

This does not mean that there are no inferior grades of apostleship. We already know that practice makes perfect. If, prompted by holy zeal and guided by an upright and holy intention, we dedicate ourselves to the apostolate after a sufficient preparation according to our capacity, and if, moreover, we do it under obedience or because it is our duty by reason of our state in life or, at least, with the good pleasure and approval of our superior or directors, then we may be confidently certain that our apostolate will be fruitful for others and for ourselves. But this will be so only on condition that we take every measure and precaution to ensure that its exercise will not be a cause of dissipation or relaxation.

The apostle must be especially mindful of the dangers that surround him in his dealings with the world and in his battles against all the powers of evil. He has so many temptations to contend with! His enemies lay traps and

snares for him at every step, and with what fury do the
demons strive against him! Then, there is his own frailty
and misery. Ah, there is nothing greater or more sublime
than the battles for the faith and for souls! Neither is there
anything more terrible than the fury with which the powers
of hell guard the prey which they are about to lose. But in
spite of all that, success is certain for those who never turn
away from the supreme commander, Jesus Christ. For He
Himself said to the apostles: "These things I have spoken
to you, that in Me you may have peace. In the world you
shall have distress: but have confidence, I have overcome
the world. The prince of this world is already judged and
now shall be cast out." [4] The apostle may, therefore, hurl
himself into battle confident of winning, but only on condition that he fight under the banner of the Redeemer. He
may be sure that he will bear much fruit as long as he remains united to Christ, but without Him he will accomplish nothing. [5]

This means that the apostle, more than anyone else, has
great need of prayer and the interior life. These are the life
and soul of every apostolate and without them he will bear
no fruit, however much he may work or however brilliant
his enterprises and apparent successes may be. The apostle
ought always to keep his spirit attuned to his ministry. He
must ever keep his heart and attention fixed on God, doing everything for God's honor and glory and for the good
of souls and never descend from the supernatural and divine plane on which he is placed by reason of his mission.
He must forget self and selfish interests and be constantly
vigilant lest there enter into his works or intentions the
slightest personal interest or self-love. In a word, he ought
to sacrifice all: comfort, health, life, and reputation for

[4] John 16:33, 11; 12:31.   [5] John 15:5.

the sublime ideal to which he is consecrated. These are the fundamental dispositions required for a successful exercise of the apostolate.

Further, in order to bear fruit among souls, the apostle must be filled of the spirit of God, and this he will attain only through an intensive life of prayer. This does not mean that he must spend all his time, or even the greater part of it, in this holy exercise, to the extent that it requires special attention in a determined time and place, but regardless of time or place, he ought never lose sight of God and should remain united to Him either by means of ordinary prayer or, as St. Francis de Sales says, by means of the prayer of works: doing everything for the love of God and with the intention of serving and glorifying Him. Whatever the form of the ministry of the apostolate, whether it be the activity of the spiritual or the corporal works of mercy, it offers abundant material for this kind of prayer. If these works were performed with the interior spirit which should animate them, that fact alone would suffice to make us saints.

There is no greater happiness for one who truly loves God than to know that he can offer Him something that will please Him, something that is infinitely gratifying to Him, and such are our works of mercy toward our neighbor. That is why, according to St. Catherine of Siena, God gave us our neighbor: so that through him we might be able to offer God these services and gifts, for He Himself has need of nothing. This is one of the greatest manifestations of His goodness: to accept as a gift what of itself is owing in strict justice.

Although at first we may not have the virtue and sanctity required for a perfect apostolate, if we perform our works in this spirit, we shall reach that state gradually. Our interior spirit will grow more and more from day to day and we shall produce increasingly greater fruit. For it is certain that we shall produce more fruit as our interior spirit is greater and our union with God more intimate. And when our union with God shall have become fully and permanently habitual, the active life of the apostolate in all its forms, whether it be preaching, teaching, the spiritual or corporal works of mercy such as caring for the sick, for children, or for elderly people, will not only cease to be a hindrance to the contemplative life, but it will be its best complement and will afford it abundant food with which to satiate that hunger and zeal which devour it. For then everything becomes a greater incentive to a closer union with God, especially those works which are so pleasing to Him. Then God showers with torrents of His lights and graces the souls who thus sacrifice themselves for love of Him. In this way they attain to a state similar to that of Christ in His own active life. Although they are bodily in this world and work and suffer here, they are no longer of the world. Their heart and soul are no longer on earth, for they live in heaven with Christ who is their treasure.

CHAPTER 54

The Fruits of Contemplation

IT is generally believed that the active life is inferior to the contemplative and that they are mutually incompatible. The first part of this statement is true if by active life we mean ascetical life, but it is not true if by that term we mean apostolic life. So St. Thomas states that the work of the active life which proceeds from the fullness of contemplation, such as teaching and preaching, is more excellent than simple contemplation.[1]

In order to understand this we must observe that the active and contemplative lives can be considered under two aspects: first, immanently, so far as the terms refer to the operations of the interior life of the soul, in which case the terms "active" and "contemplative" are synonymous with the ascetical and mystical lives, or "active" and "passive." Secondly, these two lives can be considered in their transient aspects wherein the terms have reference to the exterior works and exercises proper to each of these kinds of life. According to the first acceptation, the active life is undoubtedly inferior to the contemplative, even as the ascetical state is inferior to the mystical. However, in the second acceptation, it is necessary to make a distinction: the external works referred to are either a means for attaining perfection or they are the exercise of perfection already attained. If the works are a means to perfection, then those of the contemplative life, generally speaking, are considered superior to those of the active life. If the works are

[1] Cf. *Summa theol.*, IIa IIae, q. 188, a. 6.

those of perfection already attained, then those of the active life, at least the works of the apostolate, are preferred to those of the purely contemplative life.

This also clarifies the question of the apparent incompatibility of the two kinds of life. For if they are considered from their external aspects, inasmuch as the contemplative life is dedicated almost exclusively to meditation and prayer in retirement and solitude and the active life to preaching, teaching, and so forth, then undoubtedly they are incompatible. But such is not the case if one considers their intimate nature, for then the contemplative life is the best disposition for the fruitful exercise of the apostolic life.

We have already said that the perfect contemplative life is fundamentally the same as the passive state of the soul or the mystical life; therefore it is equivalent to the life of permanent union, the supernatural life, the plenitude of the interior life, habitual contemplation, the mystical, unitive, or contemplative state, and other similar expressions which signify a permanent, supernatural state of the soul. In other words, it is the interior life developed to perfection. It is necessary to remember this in order not to confound the contemplative life with certain contemplative states or with certain phenomena which accompany contemplation.

Many cannot reconcile the notions of contemplation and action because they imagine the former to consist solely in an act of ecstatic rapture before the divinity wherein all the faculties and senses are suspended. But this is not essential to the contemplative life, at least as refers to the suspension of the faculties and senses. Indeed, the saints consider this suspension as an imperfection resulting from the frailty of our nature, indicating that the latter is not yet strong enough to receive the divine communications.

However, once the soul is given the disposition and necessary strength, it generally no longer experiences such things. We observe this in the lives of the saints: their ecstasies and other extraordinary supernatural phenomena gradually disappear once they have attained constant and effective union with God. The phenomena of contemplation, then, do not constitute the contemplative life in its intimate reality. They are extraordinary effects of certain divine communications which God could produce without such phenomena.

The contemplative life consists in an intimate communication with God, or in the soul's stable union with God. To be sure, such a union implies the habitual contemplation of divinity, but it is a mysterious and ineffable contemplation which does not bind the understanding or the other faculties of the soul and make it impossible for them to act, but on the contrary, it makes them all the more ready and alert. There is no ecstasy of the senses, but an ecstasy of the heart and spirit, an ecstasy of faith and love.

Thus do we see how the contemplative life is the best disposition for the active life. For a soul that enjoys this most intimate communication with God, encounters no obstacles whatsoever from the natural order; on the contrary, it operates even more perfectly and it possesses, so to speak, the plenitude of divine and human efficacy at one and the same time. That is why great apostles have always been great saints and all truly contemplative souls eventually become apostles. It matters not whether they live in retirement and solitude or within the walls of a cloister. God will bring to them, even by extraordinary means if necessary, the souls He wishes to sanctify and save through their instrumentality. And even should they be unable to communicate with anyone, they would still be apostles through prayer and sacrifice. For the Holy Spirit Himself infuses into them the spirit of the apostolate and the plenitude of their interior life inclines them to it with all vehemence. It is, so to speak, the irresistible urge of the law which governs their present state.

Indeed, the process of the development of the supernatural life is similar to that of the natural life. Thus, just as all the powers and energies of our natural life before maturity are concerned principally with the growth and development of the individual and then afterwards tend rather to the diffusion of that life, so also, before spiritual manhood is reached, all the supernatural energies are directed principally to the development and perfection of the individual, but afterward they tend more especially to the diffusion of that supernatural life.

Such is the experience of those who possess the supernatural life. Upon reaching spiritual maturity they undergo a crisis and a change of orientation. They no longer value their own interests but only the divine. They are no longer preoccupied with self, but only with the extension of the kingdom of God throughout the world, that His Name may be loved and glorified by all men, beginning with themselves. All their prayers, petitions, works, and sacrifices are directed principally toward this end and they are converted into invisible channels through which the graces of heaven descend upon earth. Such were the apostles and St. Mary Magdalen and even the Blessed Virgin herself after our Lord's Ascension. That is why the saints, particularly St. John of the Cross, advise the cultivation of the interior life in preference to exterior works; not that they condemn the latter, but because it is an error to give preference to their material efficacy rather than to the efficacy of the spirit, which is the soul of the apostolate.

This does not mean that one may not undertake any work of the apostolate unless he possesses the plenitude of the interior life, that is, unless he has reached spiritual maturity. The division between the two states is not so definite and absolute that each one does not share some of the qualities of the other. But as a general rule, the efficacy of one's apostolate is in direct proportion to the degree of perfection of his interior life, and as long as his interior life has not attained the plenitude of perfection, neither will his apostolate.

It also follows that the principal exercises of the contemplative life, such as prayer, study, meditation, and other pious practices, are not opposed to the exercise of the apostolate, but are its basis, its support, and its very life. Therefore, the apostle should always give preference to the practices of the interior life as a means of increasing the efficacy of his apostolate. For although we have said that the works of the apostolate are to be preferred to those of simple contemplation, this is to be understood, as we have already indicated, only so far as the former works are informed and animated by the contemplative life. For that reason it is necessary to give the greatest possible attention to the contemplative life and take care lest exterior works lessen or eclipse it. This can be avoided readily enough by means of "active" prayer, which consists in performing exterior works with a most pure intention, with a magnanimous spirit, and with an ardent desire to fulfill the will of God; in a word, always to act with a profound love of God.

Then the apostolic life will not only not be opposed to the contemplative life, but it will be the best means of developing it and of giving it its greatest expansion. In this way the heart of the apostle is dilated to encompass the hearts of all those who are united with him in Christ. Thus there is created in him a new mystical personality which enables him to love and glorify God with the hearts and souls of those who form but one heart and one soul with him. Wherefore, far from being mutually opposed, the contemplative and apostolic lives complete one another. They are fused together in such an intimate union that the works and exercises of the one become the works and exercises of the other, thus mutually enriching one another until they portray the full and perfect life in all its beauty.

Nevertheless, we must acknowledge that the principal beauty of the perfect life comes from within and from within also come its value and efficacy. Without this, all else would be like a body without a soul; it would be what St. Paul says the most heroic actions are when done without charity.[2] On the other hand, the most humble and ordinary actions of a man who is filled with God have an influence and efficacy that are truly divine. His deportment and manner of life diffuse a supernatural aroma which profoundly affects souls and permeates them with the perfume of religious unction. His mere presence is sufficient to raise hearts to God.

That is why only that active life which proceeds from the contemplative life truly merits the name of an apostolic life, for only then does the latter possess all its efficacy. We also say that the contemplative life is the best disposition for the exercise of the apostolate, not only because of the abundance of lights, gifts, and graces which are proper to that life and are so necessary for the salvation and sanctification of souls, but by reason of the dispositions which that

[2] Cf. I Cor. 13:1–3.

life arouses in those who possess it and which are the most
adequate for the apostolate.

The life of an apostle requires consummate selflessness
and detachment from everything, a holy freedom of spirit,
an unshakable faith and constancy, and a limitless charity.
The apostle should be totally dead to self and seek only
the glory of God, but only in the way that God desires.
There is, therefore, no self-interest in his works and enterprises, nor does he manifest any personal preference for
one work rather than another, but only for those which he
knows God has especially confided to him. It matters not
to him whether he is here or there or whether he is occupied
in this or that ministry, as long as it is the one that God
has marked out for him through obedience or by means
of the circumstances in which He has placed him. Everything is a matter of holy indifference to him. The only
thing to which he aspires is to accomplish well the mission
which the Lord has confided to him and to do all the good
possible within his sphere of action.

However, in order to preserve this disposition and spirit,
he needs an unshakable faith and constancy. Better still,
we should say that he needs a divine strength that will
sustain him in the bitter trials and battles to which his
faith and constancy are exposed. In order to know what
these dangers are it is sufficient to recall that all the powers
of the world and of hell strive against the work of the
apostle, and as if that were not enough, his own human
frailty wages war against him. What would happen if he
were not sustained by divine power?

It is therefore necessary for him to be in intimate union
with God in order to defy and triumph over all the powers
of evil. Only then will he be able to exclaim with St. Paul:

"If God be for us, who is against us?" [3] It is this very union with God, or divine charity, that will crown his victory over the spirit of evil. "Many waters cannot quench charity, neither can the floods drown it." [4] And when all the sins and malice of the world fall upon him like a deluge, far from discouraging him, they will rather stimulate and inflame him all the more. No doubt the devil will endeavor to cool his spirit by arousing in his heart sentiments contrary to charity, by flooding him with all the ingratitude, injustice, and perversity of mankind. He may even incite him to rebel against God as the author or accomplice of such monstrosities. But all this fades away and vanishes like smoke before the piercing and supernatural zeal of a soul united to God.

Perhaps it is for this reason that the power of divine grace never shines so brilliantly as in the life of the apostle, for he does not on that account cease to be a man or cease to experience the frailty and misery of humanity, but in spite of all that, he must endure the most cruel trials, the most frightful battles, and the most painful sacrifices. God wants it so for the apostle's own good and for His greater glory: that thus His power, wisdom, and goodness may shine forth all the more, since through so frail an instrument He effects so marvelous an undertaking as the salvation of the world.

It is a law of the omnipotent Creator to turn nothingness into account in the creation of worlds. And to nothingness must the apostle humble himself if he is to be an apt instrument in the work of redemption, which is infinitely greater than the creation of the universe. He must retain nothing of self: neither ambition, nor interests, nor preferences, nor his own personality, soul, or life. He who is

[3] Rom. 8:31.   [4] Cant. 8:7.

to become all things to all men in order to save all [5] must sacrifice everything for the sake of the divine ideal. But who can arive at such utter selflessness and detachment? Only he who is totally possessed by the Spirit of God; he who can say with St. Paul: "I live, now not I; but Christ liveth in me." [6]

We see, therefore, that the contemplative life is the best disposition for the apostolic life and that the latter, in its turn, is the best means for the exercise and expansion of the contemplative life. They mutually complete one another, thereby bringing to its highest degree of perfection the accomplishment of the fundamental law of the Christian life: "Thou shalt love the Lord thy God with thy whole heart, and with thy whole soul, and with thy whole strength." [7]

CHAPTER 55

Our Holy Mother the Church

VERY few Christians, even of those who have made religious profession and live the religious life, have a clear and complete idea of what the Church is in itself, what its relation is to us, and, consequently, what our relations and duties are toward the Church. The generality of Christians have no other idea in this regard than that which they learned in the catechism: "The Church is the congregation of all the faithful on earth, united under one visible head." But this description is incomplete; it does not embrace

[5] Cf. I Cor. 9:22.   [6] Gal. 2:20.   [7] Deut. 6:5.

the whole concept of the Church, but merely its visible body. It tells us nothing of the bonds that unite us to her and the duties that these bonds imply. In addition to the definition expressed above, the Church can be considered under three fundamental aspects: as the mystical body of our Lord Jesus Christ, as His spouse, and as our spiritual mother.

As the mystical body of Christ, the Church is composed not only of the congregation of the faithful on earth, but also of the souls of the blessed in heaven and of all those who are united to Him by faith and grace. Moreover, it extends throughout all time, from the beginning to the end of the world, and will endure for all eternity. According to this concept, the Church is a great spiritual family whose head is Christ. It forms a truly organic body made up of various members animated by the same spirit and life and provided with the same means of development and of attaining perfection in accordance with the end which God has marked out for them.

From this arises the division of the Church into militant, triumphant, and suffering, and the further division of the Church militant into teaching and taught. From this also proceed the various categories of members which constitute it, with the diversity of functions, ministries, and graces enumerated by St. Paul. Hence also the communion of saints, for inasmuch as all the members form but one body and all are animated by the same spirit and life (that of Christ), so all share in and possess as their own what all the other members possess individually and collectively. This is the perfect union of which our Lord spoke at the Last Supper and which is verified by the indwelling of the three divine Persons in the souls of the just: "That they all may be one, as Thou, Father, in Me, and I in Thee: that they also may be one in Us." [1]

As the spouse of Christ, the Church continues His work for the redemption and salvation of the world. Her mission is to spread the gospel, to preach it to every creature, and to make Christ known, loved, and adored by all men. In this way the Church, as a true spouse, manifests her burning love for Christ. How greatly she suffers and labors for the extension of His kingdom and the glory of His holy Name! With what care and solicitude she guards the treasures He has confided to her: His words, His example, the memories of His holy life! Never does she tire of singing His praises, of proclaiming His goodness, of celebrating the episodes and mysteries of His most holy life! Who would remember Christ or His life if the Church did not continually bring Him before us by her preaching and the celebration of her rites and solemnities? Who would teach us to weep and to suffer, to rejoice and to be glad when Christ weeps and suffers or when He rejoices and triumphs? Who would teach us to elevate and offer our hearts to Him as a holocaust to His infinite love? Doubtless, if it were not for the Church, scarcely any remembrance of Christ would remain among men, and certainly the divine fire He brought to earth would have been totally extinguished centuries ago.

This title of spouse of Christ is intimately related to the third, which is that of our spiritual mother. Indeed, Christ gives life to our souls through the instrumentality of the Church. From her we receive faith, baptism and the other sacraments, and spiritual helps ordained to develop and strengthen the life we receive in the first sacrament. The Church is, therefore, our true mother in the spiritual order.

[1] John 17:21.

She it is who gives us life and receives us into her arms upon our entrance into the world, and she never abandons us until she has conducted us to heaven and placed us in the arms of our heavenly Father and Creator. She is our teacher in the life of grace; she educates and teaches us, encourages and guides us, and defends us from our enemies. She watches over us constantly lest we stray from the right path; she shields us from the errors and dangers that surround us in the way of salvation. Lastly, she nourishes and fortifies our souls with the graces communicated by means of the sacraments and other spiritual aids which she lavishly dispenses from the inexhaustible treasures which Christ has placed in her hands.

Moreover, like any true mother, the Church does all this at the cost of incredible sufferings and sacrifices. Who could fittingly appreciate what it has cost the Church to give us life in Christ and to transmit to us in all their purity the faith and religion which we profess? What torrents of blood and what horrible tortures of so many thousands of martyrs! How many and what atrocious persecutions by so many tyrants, apostates, and heretics, and by all the powers of hell intent on her destruction! What assiduous study, endless vigils, and unremitting labor on the part of her fathers and doctors! What great care and solicitude, anxiety and anguish in her prelates and pastors! What great trials and tribulations in her apostles and missionaries! And all this in order to bring to us the light of the gospel, to deliver us from the darkness of error and the shadows of death, and to bring us the knowledge of the true God and His Son Jesus Christ and of the high dignity of our souls redeemed by His blood; in a word, to deliver us from sin and slavery to Satan and to give us the life of

grace, making us sons of God and heirs of His eternal
kingdom.

From what has been said, we can easily deduce what are
our duties toward the Church. They can be summarized in
three basic duties: to love her, to obey her, and to cooperate
with her. Our love for the Church is manifested by the
intimate union of our life with hers. He who loves the
Church lives the life of the Church; he thinks with her
and has the same goals and interests, the same preoccupations and anxieties, the same fears and hopes. He suffers
when he sees the Church persecuted and humiliated and
he rejoices when he sees her defended and exalted, when
men honor and venerate her, when the faith is propagated
and good customs are introduced and preserved, when
virtue and sanctity flourish, when religious fervor reigns
in families and in society, and when the love of Christ
triumphs in hearts. He likewise rejoices when he sees that
her priests and religious are multiplied and adorned with
all the virtuous gifts and especially with the prudence,
wisdom, and zeal which their dignity and ministry require.
He who loves the Church lives the life of the Church,
uniting himself to her in order to love and glorify Christ
and attain his own sanctification. To this end he accompanies her in the rites and solemnities with which she celebrates the sacred liturgy, singing the divine praises and
invoking the graces of heaven on the world.

Because of his love for her, he feels an irresistible attraction for her temples and in them he finds all his delight.
There he forgets the world and is transported to heaven;
a sweet peace fills his soul and his heart throbs with the
most pure and holy emotions. There he is purified of his
sins and is reconciled to God, receiving an abundance of

graces and heavenly blessings. There, above all, he assists
at the great banquet of divine love wherein he receives the
Bread of Angels and drinks of that fountain of living water
that springs up into life everlasting. In a word, he experiences such great joy and consolation that he is forced to
exclaim with David:

How lovely are thy tabernacles, O Lord of hosts!
My soul longeth and fainteth for the courts of the Lord.
My heart and my flesh have rejoiced in the living God.
For the sparrow hath found herself a house, and the turtle a
    nest for herself, where she may lay her young ones:
Thy altars, O Lord of hosts, my king and my God.
Blessed are they that dwell in thy house, O Lord: they shall
    praise thee for ever and ever. . . .
For better is one day in thy courts above thousands.
I have chosen to be an abject in the house of my God, rather
    than to dwell in the tabernacles of sinners.
For God loveth mercy and truth: the Lord will give grace and
    glory.[2]

Lastly, he who loves the Church loves all her members as
his brothers and he performs for them the services which
love and Christian charity demand. He especially loves,
honors, and venerates her priests, and more so if they are
prelates or superiors. But the predominant mark and characteristic of every good Christian and son of the Church
is a profound love for the Pope as Vicar of Christ and
universal Father of all the faithful.

Our second duty toward the Church is to obey her. It is
not necessary to insist on this obligation, for it is evident
that one who disobeys the Church disobeys Christ, whom
she represents. But it is not sufficient to obey her only ma-

[2] Ps. 83.

terially by observing what she commands. We ought also to obey her lovingly, as a son obeys his mother, and all the more so because whatever our holy mother the Church commands redounds to our good and our eternal salvation. This obligation embraces not only the grave precepts of the Church concerning religion and morals, but also her directive and disciplinary ordinances. Moreover, it extends to all that is commanded by her ministers—superiors, prelates, pastors, bishops, and above all, the Pope—concerning those matters that fall within their respective authority and jurisdiction.

The third obligation of the faithful Christian consists in cooperating with the Church in the work of the redemption and salvation of the world. This obligation is perhaps the least known and most neglected by the generality of Christians. As a result, the majority of the faithful consider the problems and interests of the Church as the concern of only priests and religious, as if they were not also her children and her prosperity or adversity mattered not at all to them. They are heedless of the obligations contracted in baptism and confirmation which impose upon them the sacred duty of professing and defending their faith and religion as true soldiers of Christ. They are not aware that the Christian forms part of that kingly priesthood of which St. Peter speaks,[3] and that they should make the interests of religion and the Church their very own and endeavor to promote them within their sphere of action with the same ardor and zeal as do the priests themselves.

It matters not that within the Church there are priests and religious specially destined to exercise certain functions and ministries; the Church is an organic body com-

[3] Cf. I Peter 2:9.

posed of various members, each of which has its proper function and cannot do without the cooperation of the rest. As St. Paul says, the head cannot disregard the feet, nor the eyes the hands, but each should contribute in its own way to the final and harmonious functioning of the entire organism.[4] Every faithful Christian, then, is under a strict obligation to cooperate with the Church.

This is what Pius XI, of holy memory, so vigorously proclaimed and recommended when he organized Catholic Action as a medium through which all faithful Christians could fulfill their sacred obligation. There is no need to dwell here on the ways in which this obligation can be fulfilled, but to insist on the necessity of its fulfillment and on the culpability of those who do not observe it or who seek to prevent others from doing so; for example, by raising obstacles, creating difficulties, criticizing or murmuring against the zealous workers in Catholic Action. They are the worst enemies of Catholic Action and the constant blight of every noble and salutary enterprise. Instead of endeavoring to remedy the defects they criticize, by doing the work better, they make the situation worse and more difficult to remedy by sowing envy, jealousy, contention, discord, and by disparaging the workers and the work they do. This is one of the greatest evils confronting the Church, for the damage which these foolish people do is enormous. It is a principal cause of indifference and coldness in the faith and fervor of Christians and the reason why the Catholic religion progresses so slowly and with such difficulty in the conquest of the world. Such imprudent people should consider their responsibility before God and the Church and amend their ways while there is

[4] Cf. I Cor. 12:21-25.

yet time to repair the damage, for it cannot go without punishment from God.

It is impossible to explain and properly extol the spiritual fruits reported by souls who live in intimate union with the Church. Suffice it to say that, according to the masters of the spiritual life, one of the surest signs of a soul's progress in the way of sanctity is its increasingly fervent love for the Church. It is a well known fact that the greatest saints, such as St. Bernard, St. Dominic, St. Francis, St. Ignatius, St. Catherine, and St. Teresa, are also the ones who most loved the Church and sacrificed themselves for her. This fervent love of the Church is at once a cause and an effect of sanctity, for the more a soul unites itself to the life of the Church, the more it progresses in virtue and sanctity, and the greater its progress in these, the more does it love the Church. It is logical that this should be so because love for the Church, as we said above, tends to blot out our personal, niggardly interests and supplant them with the most exalted and noble interests of Christ Himself. Thus it detaches us from all egoism and from all that is material, temporal, and earthly and elevates us to the eternal, infinite, and celestial. It places us on a plane superior to the sensible, that is, on the supernatural plane, the only one on which the life of grace can be developed. How our heart and soul are ennobled by living in that atmosphere! How lowly and miserable do the goods of this world then appear! How vain and sterile all the labor and sacrifice which men expend in order to obtain worldly goods!

For those who live the life of the Church all human goods which have no relation to the divine have lost their value. On the other hand, divine values such as the glory of God, the salvation of souls, the extension of the reign of Christ, and the triumph of His love in all hearts inflame and consume them, allowing them no repose. Indeed, that divine restlessness makes them realize their union with Christ and their life in God. Their whole life becomes the pure practice of the love of God, for they no longer do anything except in Him, through Him, and for Him.

Moreover, since they are intimately united to the life of the Church, their own life is expanded and enriched with all the vital activity of the Church. Thus their charity finds a means of satiating its thirst for love and for the glory of God. They no longer love and glorify Him with their own heart alone, but with the hearts of all the elect and with the fire of all the heavenly spirits, for by virtue of the communion of the saints, they share in the goods and merits of all the elect and even of Jesus Christ Himself and of His most holy Mother. Moreover, their love of neighbor thereby attains its highest perfection, for they feel more profoundly their union with their neighbor in Jesus Christ in that great family which is the Church.

Finally, he who lives the life of the Church has opened wide the doors of his soul to all the torrents of its graces and benefits and has assured for himself the rewards and promises which Jesus Christ has pledged to His dearest friends. He who lives the life of the Church and joins with her in the toils and labors for Jesus Christ and in singing His praises and celebrating His mysteries, makes his own the life of the Church and all the glory and love which she gives to Christ. But souls who are self-centered and live like isolated beings, absorbed solely in their own security and salvation, will never acquire the increase and plenitude of the spiritual life of those who unite themselves to the

Church in order to live as members of the mystical body of our Lord Jesus Christ.

CHAPTER 56 🖎

The Conquest of Souls

THERE are two essential factors in the conquest of souls: the divine action of grace and the human activity of the apostle. In the supernatural order these two modes of action are parallel and simultaneous, but in the natural order the first presupposes the second, for grace adapts itself to nature's mode of operation. In this sense we can say that the first requisite for the conquest of souls is the conquest of hearts. Reason and experience verify this fact, and it is confirmed by the gospel. For if, as Jesus Christ tells us, from the heart proceeds all that is evil in man,[1] so also it is through the heart that goodness and holiness must enter. This is indeed the only entrance into the interior castle of a man's soul and if it is closed, there is no other way of gaining access to it and conquering it. If the heart is not properly disposed to give admittance to light and grace, neither science nor eloquence nor power nor skill of any kind will be capable of subjugating a soul so that it will embrace the truths of faith and submit to the precepts of religion.

Here we have the key and the secret of all apostolic science and technique. For even if we do not know how to

[1] Matt. 15:19.

conquer souls, we can readily learn how to conquer hearts.
We have only to study our own heart and see what it is that
attracts and enthralls it; what it is that compels us to exert
all the faculties and powers of the soul in the attempt to
possess that which the heart loves. We know well that this
is attained only through love and goodness, but since our
supreme object is God, this love and goodness must be
supernatural; it must be more divine than human; it must
be that highest possible perfection of charity which is called
zeal. Such has been the understanding and the practice of
all those truly apostolic souls who have dedicated themselves with true zeal to the sublime ministry of the conquest
of souls. That is why St. Dominic Guzman, a great apostle
and father of apostles, when asked where he had learned
the art of saving souls, answered that it was in the book
of charity.

Above all, this method of procedure was taught by our divine Savior Himself by word and example. As the gospel relates, He went about teaching and doing good.[2] By His good
works He attracted and conquered hearts. He lavished His
bounty upon all: He cured the sick, cast out devils, cleansed
the lepers; He gave sight to the blind, hearing to the deaf,
and to the paralytic the power to walk. He forgave sins,
defended the poor and humble, and ate and drank with
them. In a word, He treated all with such tenderness and
sweetness that He attracted the multitudes and conquered
their hearts.

However, before doing these things and as a preparation
for His public life, He first sanctified Himself, as He Himself tells us later.[3] To this He dedicated the first thirty years
of His life, hidden in the carpenter shop at Nazareth, living
a secluded life of obedience to His mother and foster father

[2] Acts 10:38; Luke 13:22.   [3] John 17:19.

and devoting Himself to prayer and labor. He did this, not because He Himself needed to become more holy, but in order to give us an example and to merit for us the graces of redemption.

Such is the example the divine Master gave us in the science of saving and sanctifying souls and He desired and commanded His disciples to follow this same example when He sent them forth to preach the kingdom of God. "When you come into the house, salute it, saying: Peace be to this house. Eat of such things as are set before you. Heal the sick, raise the dead, cleanse the lepers, cast out devils: freely you have received, freely give." [4] And when some desired that fire come down from heaven and consume ungrateful and rebellious souls, He answered, "You know not of what spirit you are." [5] It was as if He had said: "That is not the fire that I brought to earth and with which I desire to inflame the world, but the fire of divine charity; and the first who ought to be consumed with this fire are you, together with all who are to preach My gospel and propagate the kingdom of My Father."

Accordingly, the first task of those who dedicate themselves to the sublime ministry of saving souls is their own sanctification by means of a life of interior recollection, prayer, work, and the exercise of all the virtues. Thus, at the same time that they enrich their spirit and enkindle in their hearts the fire of that divine love with which they are afterwards to inflame the world, they are gradually transformed from earthly and simply human men into celestial and divine beings. They likewise become divinely lovable and this is the first requisite for the conquest of hearts. For if men are to love and venerate the apostle as

[4] Matt. 10:12; Luke 10:8; Matt. 10:8.
[5] Luke 9:55.

a representative of God, they must see in him something superhuman and divine, that is, a man totally dead to self and to all selfish interests, a man who seeks only the glory of God and the good of his fellow men and who for their sake is ready to sacrifice all, even his life. In a word, they must see in him a new Christ, possessing Christ's own thoughts, sentiments, heart, and works, and in such wise that through his words, his works, and his entire person, they may be able to see who it is that lives in him.

To think of becoming an apostle without first despoiling oneself of the old Adam, of the earthly man with his baseness, wretchedness, and disordered passions, without having uprooted all selfishness or being at least disposed to combat it resolutely and perseveringly, is a most rash presumption which brings in its wake the most deplorable consequences both for the apostle himself and for the work of the apostolate. This is the basic reason for all the falls and apostasies which history relates and the sterility of so many apparently fruitful apostolates. It is also the cause of the aversion and antipathy which many feel toward religion, for they unwittingly recriminate the Church with the transgressions of its representatives and preachers. Regeneration and transformation is therefore the first and indispensable requisite on the part of the envoy of Christ, be he preacher, director of souls, missionary, or simply a layapostle, so that his words may be well received and that his ministry may be fruitful.

The love and esteem of the faithful for the apostle must be such as to make them place him on a superior level, distinct from that of other men, even though the latter be naturally good. Likewise, this love and esteem for the representative of Christ should be such as to elevate the faithful to God and not attach them to the human person. Those who by reason of their ministry are obliged to deal frequently with subjects, such as superiors, missionaries, and spiritual directors, should be especially aware of this. Therein lies a great danger, and it is there that the devil more easily lays his traps and snares. For there is no very marked distinction between human and divine love whereby they can easily be distinguished at the beginning. Both reside in one and the same heart and they are not distinguished so much on the basis of sensible feeling as by reason of their elevation and the dissimilar effects they produce. Wherefore, in order to distinguish between these two kinds of love, it is necessary to exercise great vigilance and to examine profoundly all the movements of the heart to discover where they lead and the effects they produce. Here we can well apply the rule of our Savior: "By their fruits you shall know them." [6] It does not suffice that the object of the love be good and holy, for under the mantle of goodness and holiness Satan may very readily deceive the foolish and imprudent who rely solely on that.

Here, as in everything else, there is nothing better than to follow the example of the divine Master. He loved and allowed His disciples to love Him with all the intensity of the one, true love. For the love of His divine Person is the way that leads to the pure love of God. But because of the natural element and imperfections which even that love might contain, He proceeded to purify them of it and to detach them from whatever made His company delightful to them, by bringing before them the humiliations and torments of His passion, by announcing to them His departure from this world, and by telling them that it was expedient for them that He depart, for otherwise the Holy Spirit would not come to them.[7]

[6] Matt. 7:16. [7] John 16:7.

If Jesus Christ, who is God, did this, how much more should His representatives on earth do it. The latter, be they missionaries, teachers, or directors of souls, can and ought to take advantage of the esteem and affection which their subjects bear them in order to lead them ever more deeply into the interior life of renouncement, detachment, and the true love of God. In the beginning this is so necessary that it is hardly conceivable for a director to effect much good in souls if the latter do not have a great esteem and holy affection for him. But in the measure that it grows, this affection should become ever more purified until eventually it is free of every human element. When natural love has been purified and elevated, the soul no longer needs it for support in its spiritual life.

Hence the great error of those who think that the holier a soul is the more direction it needs. This may be true at times in order to arrive at holiness, but afterward, as a general rule, the more holy a soul is the less direction it needs. In exterior matters and as members of society in care of certain charges and offices, souls will always need the direction and counsel of their superiors or of those better informed than they about particular problems. But as regards interior matters, ordinarily, the holier souls need very little direction. However, this does not mean that there are not times and occasions when such souls need special attention or that they can do without direction altogether, for even in determining how much or how little direction a soul needs, a director is required: it is he who should decide or approve.

All that we have said with regard to the necessity of conquering hearts in order to take souls to Christ applies particularly to souls that are in the lowest degrees of the spiritual life, even more so when they are deficient in knowledge, as are many infidels and all savages. Especially in dealing with the latter it is absolutely necessary to win their hearts and this is the most difficult work of the missionary. For the faith and religion of the savage depend almost exclusively on the love and veneration he has for the missionary. The missionary must win him over at the cost of incredible labor and sacrifice and the exercise of the most heroic virtues.

The savage is a stranger to gratitude and he is destitute of many of the more noble human sentiments. It could be said that he has no heart and that one must be created within him and induced to express those noble sentiments of love and gratitude which are to take him to God through the instrumentality of the missionary. Ordinarily this goal is not reached until after many years and at the cost of a lifetime of limitless sacrifice and abnegation. The missionary should become all to all, as St. Paul says,[8] adapting himself as much as possible to the life and ways of his charges and being careful never to manifest any displeasure or opposition on account of the innumerable annoyances and difficulties they occasion by their unruly and barbarous nature. He therefore needs infinite patience and charity. As every missionary knows, this is the only way of conquering and saving their souls.

In this they have Jesus Christ as their divine model, observing the way in which He treated and formed His disciples. For although the latter were not savages, there was a greater distance between the divine life and infinite wisdom of Christ and the life and ignorance of His disciples than there is between the missionary and the savage. And yet, with what benignity, love, and tenderness did He treat them, never reproaching them for their uncouthness or

[8] Cf. I Cor. 9:22.

ignorance nor showing the slightest disdain for their pettiness and lowliness nor tiring of their annoyances and im-
pertinences. Little by little and in the measure that they
were disposed to accept the truth, He opened their eyes,
calmly and without precipitation, awaiting the hour of divine grace. This is what every apostle should do: prepare
the ground for the action of divine grace, for this is what
effects the conversion of sinners and the salvation and sanctification of souls.

As this noble work is absolutely divine, it belongs exclusively to grace; but the latter is also obtained by means
of the prayers and sacrifices of the apostle and of all those
who unite themselves to him in spirit for this intention.
This is perhaps the most difficult, but also the most efficacious task of the apostolate. All those who for want of
strength or by reason of their obligations or state of life cannot work in the mission-field or exercise any other apostolate should cooperate by offering up their prayers and sacrifices for this end. All contemplative souls living in the
cloister or confined in their homes, all who are hindered
by their obligations or by sickness could, by their prayers
and sacrifices, obtain from heaven the graces our earth so
sorely needs. This is not mere counsel, it is a most stringent
obligation of all Christians who realize the duties they contracted in baptism and confirmation. The hidden apostolate, in which we can all cooperate, has the added advantage
that it is not exposed to any spiritual danger, for it lacks the
applause of men and the satisfaction of seeing the fruits of
one's labors.

Lastly, everyone should follow his vocation and work
wherever divine providence calls him, realizing that it is
God's will that gives our works their value. Let us remember that the glory of God comes before all things, even

before those whereby we wish to glorify Him. If His will calls us to the active apostolate, in whatsoever field it may be, then let us remember that our own sanctification comes first and afterward, presupposing grace, the first thing required for the conquest of souls is the conquest of hearts.

CHAPTER 57 🖋

The Reign of the Sacred Heart

JESUS came to the world to establish His kingdom among men. But as He Himself said, His kingdom is not of this world. It does not consist in domination through force, in wealth, in exterior magnificence, nor in any outward display calculated to captivate the senses and dazzle the imagination. His kingdom is a kingdom of love; it is the reign of His divine Heart. To reign is not to dominate by power and force, but to subjugate sweetly by goodness and to bring hearts under the irresistible bondage of love.

When our Savior was about to ascend to heaven, His apostles, who were still somewhat imbued with the Jewish prejudices concerning the kingdom of the Messias, asked Him if He would then establish the kingdom of Israel. Jesus answered: "It is not for you to know the times or moments which the Father hath put in His own power. But you shall receive the power of the Holy Ghost coming upon you, and you shall be witnesses unto Me in Jerusalem and in all Judea and Samaria, and even to the uttermost part of the earth." [1] In other words, at the same time that Jesus

[1] Acts 1:7, 8.

rid the souls of His apostles of the desire for a temporal kingdom, He sent them throughout the world to establish His spiritual kingdom.

There are still many people who, like the apostles, would desire a temporal reign of Christ or at least seem to want to make His kingdom a temporal kingdom, one which would consist solely in exterior grandeur and magnificence and a ritual of worship and adoration that is also exterior. This would be commendable if it proceeded from an interior worship, but to make it principally or almost wholly exterior would be a very grave error.

If Jesus is to reign in the world, it must be primarily and principally through and in the hearts of men, for His kingdom is a kingdom of love, as He Himself so often explained. His kingdom is within us [2] and consists in our being one with Him, as He is one with the Father, in order that charity may prevail among us. The Heart of Christ is all of Christ, for it is the living incarnation of divine charity. The Heart of Christ is the spirit, the life, the sanctity, the goodness, the wisdom of Christ, and His kingdom in our hearts signifies intimate union with Him and possession of His spirit, His life, His sanctity, His goodness, His wisdom. It means that His sentiments and intentions are ours and that our hearts no longer dominate, but have been supplanted by that of Christ. This is the true kingdom of the Heart of Jesus.

He in whom this kingdom is fully established will not be exempt from feeling his many miseries and weaknesses, but neither misery nor sin will reign within him. These miseries remain in him precisely in order to give testimony to the fact that so great a good as the reign of Christ within him is not his own doing but God's; they remain, as it

[2] Luke 17:21.

were, as vassals to render tribute to the sovereign Lord or as trophies of His glorious triumph. Within him reign solely the spirit of Jesus, the love of Jesus, the Heart of Jesus. And because He alone reigns, the weaknesses of the old Adam have been rooted out and flung afar. Justice, peace, and joy in the Holy Spirit alone can abide there.

The kingdom of the Heart of Jesus, then, is the kingdom of divine charity, the kingdom of God, for "God is charity." [3] When the latter shall reign within us our spirit will be free and will rule our interior kingdom without opposition. We shall no longer follow the impulses of flesh and blood nor shall these rule our life. Neither ambition nor pride nor the desire for earthly goods will draw us earthward; on the contrary, all the aspirations and movements of our heart will be of the supernatural order. Our ambition will be to love God, our glory to glorify Him, our sole desire to be sanctified in the truth and that this truth may reign throughout the whole world. Then shall we, even as Jesus, call God by the sweet name of "Father" with all the fervor of our being, and like Jesus also, we shall be able to say truly that our meat is to do always the will of our Father. Having died to ourselves, the holy will of God will be accomplished within us without hindrance, for it is self-will that impedes its accomplishment. Then shall we also fulfill perfectly the precept of brotherly love, for the love with which we love God and our neighbor is one and the same!

All the evils of life, all hatred, envy, discord, and wars come from self-love, which demands all rights for itself and rejects whatever hinders self-satisfaction. Therefore, once this great enemy of charity is destroyed, the world will enjoy the most perfect peace and union. In order to estab-

[3] Cf. I John 4:16.

lish this kingdom in our hearts we must first destroy all other kingdoms and dominions within it, or rather, the sole kingdom of our ego, of our self-love, which is the origin, sum, and compendium of them all and which is diametrically opposed to the kingdom of Christ.

When the ego reigns supreme within a man, all his care and solicitude are spent in procuring for himself everything that he judges personally useful or advantageous. That is the law of self-love, the law of our ego. On the other hand, the law of divine love, the law of the kingdom of Jesus within us, consists in doing everything in God and for God. Man is oblivious to his own happiness and lives solely for God. He occupies himself solely with glorifying His Holy Name and leaves to Him the matter of his personal happiness. For it is self-seeking that radically opposes the kingdom of God; self-seeking in any and everything, be it temporal or spiritual, earthly or heavenly. Wherefore, in order to destroy this self-love, it is necessary to renounce all selfish interests, not only in goods of the natural order, but also in those of the supernatural order, unless the latter be the possession of God, which is attained by total death and renunciation. It is not by acquiring but by rejecting that one goes to God and gains possession of Him. Thus, all personal interests of whatever order are evil if they are not totally subordinated to the glory of God, for they tend to make us our own gods.

The matter of our perfection admits no half-measures; it is either all or nothing. From the moment we set limits or make exceptions in the total gift and renunciation of self, at least with regard to the disposition of our soul, we close the door to all perfection and even make ourselves liable to every imperfection. The connection of all the virtues and of all the faculties of the soul is such that what affects one affects all, and one defect is enough to tear down the entire interior edifice. We see this clearly enough in the practice of any virtue. For example, from the moment someone says he is disposed to suffer everything except this or that, we may be sure that he is disposed to suffer nothing at all. For suffering is one, although the things that cause it are many, and what irks us is not the things themselves, but the suffering they cause us.

Likewise, he who is disposed to renounce everything for the love of God except this or that thing, of whatever order it may be, is disposed to renounce nothing. An evil disposition of that type will vitiate every other act of renunciation he may make, when real renunciation is demanded of him. If we are to renounce ourselves, it should be precisely in those things which cost us the most, in those wherein we shall truly be practicing the virtue of renunciation. We must bear in mind that our self-love takes refuge and is exercised in the least trifle we refuse to renounce; there it revives and grows with all vigor. Wherefore we repeat: in the matter of our supernatural perfection there is but one motto: "All." For, as St. John of the Cross says:

> "In order to pass from the all to the All,
> Thou hast to deny thyself wholly in all." [4]

By "all" is meant, of course, whatever is opposed to the divine will or anything in which we wish to take pleasure outside of God. For we are not forbidden simply to desire, seek, and enjoy things; we are forbidden to desire, seek, and enjoy them outside of God. In God we may have everything; outside of God, nothing. However, in order to abide with Him, we must be detached from everything without

[4] *Ascent of Mount Carmel,* Bk. I, chap. 13.

exception. It is this disposition of total detachment that will enable us, pure and regenerated, always to do good with unbounded joy within the divine order. The Spirit of God will then reign supreme within us and the Heart of Jesus will have established His kingdom in our hearts!